'This is THE most wonderful, funny, clever, charming, evocative book'
India Knight

'Like a heated but enjoyable discussion with a best friend bookworm'
Jacqueline Wilson, *The Week*

'Beautiful and moving, it twirled me back in time to when books were my only friends and triggered all kinds of sweet memories of how books comforted me when nothing else could'
Marian Keyes

'To read Lucy Mangan's memoir of growing up bookish is to be taken back to a time in life when reading wasn't merely a gentle pleasure or mild obligation but an activity as essential as breathing'
Guardian

'Mangan has excellent taste. Those who share her passion for the books she adores (and it would be difficult not to find some common ground) will smile with recognition at her recollections'
The Times

'Anyone who has ever preferred books to life will recognise Lucy Mangan as a kindred spirit. Her moving, funny, honest and superbly written memoir about how childhood reading shapes our personalities, memories and chances could not be more timely or more needed in an age of library closures, embattled Humanities teaching and Philistinism'
Amanda Craig

'A charming love letter to childhood reading . . . Mangan's gratifyingly thorough research has unearthed a hoard of chewy ane lively account of t young reader'

'I felt like this was written just for me, and I think everyone will feel this way'
Jenny Colgan

'If you are a bookworm, any book that opens with the quote "People say that life's the thing, but I prefer reading" is going to press the right button.'
New Statesman

'A deliciously nostalgic treat that will make you want to pull out all those old favourites again'
Good Housekeeping

'Fiercely unsentimental and often funny, it's a memoir that will strike a ringing chord with anyone who spent most of their childhood glued to a book'
Irish Times

'A wonderful romp through the pages of childhood, illuminated by wisdom, humour and enthusiasm'
Bernard Cornwell

'Entertaining and hugely engaging . . . An entirely inspiring read'
Sunday Express

'Deft, warm and beautifully balanced. Made me smile. Made me glow. Made me think again and again'
Jason Hazeley, co-author of the adult Ladybird series

'In Lucy Mangan's *Bookworm* . . . childhood books are brought vividly to life, as are the remembered pleasures of first encountering them'
Times Literary Supplement

LUCY MANGAN

Lucy Mangan is the *Guardian* television critic, a columnist for *Stylist* magazine and a features writer for many other publications, including the *Daily Telegraph*. She broadcasts frequently on radio and occasionally on television, and is the author of *My Family and Other Disasters*, *The Reluctant Bride*, *Hopscotch & Handbags* and *Inside Charlie's Chocolate Factory*. She lives in London with a husband, a child, two cats and 10,000 books. She needs to move.

ALSO BY LUCY MANGAN

Hopscotch & Handbags: The Truth About Being a Girl

My Family and Other Disasters

The Reluctant Bride: One Woman's Journey (Kicking and Screaming) Down the Aisle

LUCY MANGAN

Bookworm

A Memoir of Childhood Reading

VINTAGE

2 4 6 8 10 9 7 5 3 1

Vintage
20 Vauxhall Bridge Road,
London SW1V 2SA

Vintage is part of the Penguin Random House group of companies whose addresses can be found at global.penguinrandomhouse.com.

Penguin Random House UK

First published by Square Peg in 2018

www.vintage-books.co.uk

A CIP catalogue record for this book is available from the British Library

ISBN 9781784709228

Printed and bound in Great Britain by Clays Ltd, Elcograf S.p.A.

For Alexander, whom I love more than books

Contents

Introduction

'People say that life is the thing but I prefer reading.' (American essayist and entirely correct person Logan Pearsall Smith.)

I still have all my childhood books. In fact, I have spent some of my happiest hours in recent months arranging them on the bespoke bookcases I had built under the sloping ceiling of my study for their ease and comfort. I may no longer imagine them, as I did thirty years ago, whispering companionably together at night when I have gone to bed, but I love them still. They made me who I am.

'Pallid,' says my sister, peering over my shoulder as I type this. 'Bespectacled. Friendless.' Which is also true. And yet, who needed flesh-and-blood friends when I had Jo March, Charlotte, Wilbur and everyone at Malory Towers at my beck and call?

Remember hiding a book on your lap to get yourself through breakfast? Remember getting hit on the head by footballs in the playground because a game had sprung up around you while you were off in Cair

Paravel? Remember taking yourself off to the furthest corner of the furthest sofa in the furthest room of the house with a stack of Enid Blytons and praying that everyone would forget about you till bedtime? Come bedtime, do you remember waiting four nanoseconds after the door closed before whipping out your torch and carrying on where parental stricture had required you leave off until tomorrow? Was your first crush on Dickon instead of Johnny Depp? Do you still get the urge to tap the back of a wardrobe if you find yourself alone in a strange bedroom, or keep half an ear out at midnight for the sound of Hatty in the garden?

If so, this is the book for you. But then, most books are. You are, like me, a bookworm. Little more needs to be said, apart from: I hope you enjoy this memoir of my own childhood reading and that it brings back happy memories of your own. It is a look back at the books I loved – needed, depended on – as a child. I've tried to contextualise them, give their backgrounds (why, for example, was *The Family from One End Street* considered shocking by some when it first appeared? Who was the first author to use a first-person narrative in a children's book?); potted biographies of their authors (which hugely successful female children's writer whose name was not J. K. Rowling began writing only because she was desperate for money? What did E. B. White's colleagues at the hallowed *New Yorker* think of him producing, of all things, a children's book about a spider and a pig?); and a sense of where they come in the history of children's literature. But this is a personal account of the classics and not-so-classics that shaped my world and thoughts, and so necessarily incomplete.

I read omnivorously but not well and certainly without a thought for posterity. I read because I loved it. I read wherever I could, whenever I could, for as long as I could. At birthday parties – not least my own – I would stealthily retreat as soon as the games began, to the most hidden corner of whatever house I was in, gathering any available volumes on the way and reading furiously through them until a hateful adult found me and demanded my return or, if I was lucky, told me it was home time. In the summer holidays, I could read literally from dawn till dusk, unaware of anything until forcibly recalled to real life.

Those were the days, my friends. Those were the days. Do we ever manage again to commit ourselves as wholeheartedly and unselfconsciously as we do to the books we read when young? I doubt it. I have great hopes for retirement but for the moment, as an adult of working age and a mother of a five-year-old, life is unfortunately too much with me to allow such gorgeous, uninterrupted stretches of immersion in a book.

But let us relive, for the next few chapters at least, a little of those glorious days when reading was the thing and life was only a minor inconvenience.

1

The Very Hungry Reader

I spent most of my early years – aged one to three, say – being trodden on.

'It was your own fault,' my mother explains. 'You were too quiet. You used to stand by my feet, not making a sound while I was washing up or doing the ironing, so I'd forget you were there. What toddler does that? So I'd step back – and step on you. And you still,' she adds accusingly, 'didn't make a sound.'

The same tone of mingled confusion and denunciation attends her telling of another story, of the day she put me in the baby bouncer she had bought (a sort of nappy-shaped harness attached to elastic cords that you hang from a door frame) 'and you just hung there. You didn't even TRY to bounce. Just hung there! What kind of baby does THAT?'

I think the explanation lies in the fact that I wasn't really a baby. I was a bookworm. For the true bookworm, life doesn't really begin until you get hold of your first book. Until then – well, you're just waiting, really. You don't even know for what, at that stage – if you did, you would be making more noise about it and be less covered in court-shoe-shaped bruises. But it's books.

My parents, I should say now, are northern. And Catholic. They came down south in the late 1960s to look for work. My dad, to the bafflement of his upper-working-class family, had wanted to work in the theatre since he were knee-high to the family whippet. Or ferret. I forget. Once the most pressing of his parents' many attendant anxieties upon this fact were relieved by his acquisition of a wife, they did all they could to help him realise his dream, eventually waving him, a bottle of dandelion and burdock and a bagful of clean underpants off at Preston station to start a new life as a stage manager at the newly formed National Theatre in That There London. Mum, a recently qualified doctor, went with him. Mainly to make sure he got off at the right stop.

My dad was – and is – a reader. Not great at school – I once unearthed in a boxful of photographs that passed to me as de facto keeper of the family archives (once you get a reputation as bookish, all sorts of admin falls to you) a school report of his full of barely average marks and which read, under his failing grade for Religious Instruction, 'Neglects to learn his catechism'. Father Paedophile's thunderous fury was still evident, sixty years later, in every thick black stroke of his pen. But he was a great reader. There wasn't much money in the family so there weren't many books in the house, apart from a few precious bound collections of *Boy's Own* comics given to Dad and his 800 siblings by a family friend after their own children grew out of them. Whoever had the most life-threatening lung disease at the time got to read them in bed until he or she got better or expired. However. In the centre of Preston sat the Harris Public Library (and museum and art gallery), the result of a £300,000 bequest from local lawyer and beneficiary of family railway investments Edmund Robert Harris in 1877. It's still there, performing all the functions its founder hoped for, a monument to civic-mindedness and one of the countless buildings and establishments across the country that make you shake your head and wonder how much worse a state we'd be in now if we hadn't had the Victorians. And it was to the Harris library that Dad took himself every week, working his way gradually through its offerings until he went to the local grammar school and transferred his allegiance to the panelled library room there, where he discovered Shakespeare, Marlowe and loads of other people who had written strangely formatted books called plays.

My mother was not a reader. She was – and is – a doer. For most of my life, until she retired a few years ago, she was a gynaecologist, specialising in gruesome anecdotes and family planning (my mother is the only Catholic in history to have thrown off her upbringing utterly and never looked back). She presided over a dozen different clinics a week, swiftly building a reputation as the fastest, most efficient doctor in south-east London. 'If they want to have their hands held and *chat*,' she used to snarl at anyone who occasionally wondered if she couldn't afford to take a little more time with patients, 'they can go somewhere else.'

At home she was an equally efficient plumber, electrician, cleaner, laundrywoman, gardener (actually more of an operator of a scorched-earth policy across the little patch of lawn and potentially herbaceous border behind our three-bed terrace, but no matter – neatness was the goal, not beauty), cook (burgers,

Findus Crispy Pancakes, whaddyawantchipsormash, and gravy) and chauffeur as needed, in ceaseless, indefatigable rotation, singing, talking to herself or shouting orders to others all the while. My sister in later years dubbed her the Noisemaker 2000. My own theory is that if she ever has an unexpressed thought, she'll die.

She was – and is – a marvel, not least because there was no martyrdom at all in any of this. Firstly, she did it because it suited her temperament, not because it fed some deep-seated complex. She is seventy-four at the time of writing and still cannot be quiet or sit still for more than twenty seconds unless she's eating her tea and *Coronation Street*'s on. Second, it was the only way she could get things done exactly to her specifications (in their utility room is a nine-volume laminated set of instructions solely about towel folding for Dad to follow if she ever goes away or he disobeys his own instructions and outlives her). And third, everyone else was required to pitch in as much as they could too. I put my toys away. And Dad . . . Dad just helped with everything. Buffered everything. Calmed everything. Mediated everything. Made sure Mum got a run out in the park every now and again to burn some energy off. Theirs was – and is – a marriage of true opposites. He will die if he ever has an expressed thought. It all works very well.

When I was tiny I didn't see him much because stage managing at the National Theatre takes you way past toddler bedtime. But at the weekends, once lesser activities such as eating, having baths and playing with visiting infants were out of the way, we would have a splendid time together. I am assured there was colouring, Play-Doh moulding and endless games of riding horses to Banbury Cross, but my first real memory is of Dad tucking me in beside him on the long, brown floral sofa that sat on a rug dyed three increasingly violent shades of orange that sat on top of an orange carpet (oh, the 1970s. May you never, never return) and opening a book almost as colourful as our sitting room. It was *The Very Hungry Caterpillar*, Eric Carle's paint 'n' tissue-paper collaged account of the larval lepidoptera's metamorphosis, fuelled by choice morsels of American culinary classics, into butterfly.

And yet although this is the first book I remember there must have been other books before it, because what entranced me, and millions of other readers since it was published in 1969, was the fact that it was so different from them. The caterpillar had eaten little holes through all the pages for a start. And the pages were all different sizes. Some were narrow enough to make turning them a fiddly business, some large enough to make them flappily unwieldy in tiny hands, and some were just right.

They had all been a fiddly business for the publisher. The Hungry Caterpillar's life began when Carle was using a hole punch on a stack of papers at his home. The little circles made him think of a bookworm and he created a story, using different-sized pages – a familiar device in Germany, where his family had moved when he was six – called *A Week with Willi the Worm*. His editor Ann Beneduce suggested that a caterpillar might be more likeable than a worm. Carle shouted 'Butterfly!' and got cracking on a rewrite that took narrative advantage of his new hero's transformative properties.

Beneduce then had to scour the globe searching for a printer that could cope with producing variously sized pages AND put holes in them without bankrupting themselves or her. She eventually found one in Japan, the book emerged and has been beating its wings all over the world ever since.

My father read it to me so many times that he swears when he dies we will find 'one slice of cake, etc., etc.' engraved on his heart. You will find it written all the way through mine, like a stick of rock. Not only did I absorb it when young, I have read it many times since – many, many, many times, enough times to begin to appreciate at last the fathomless depths of my father's patience – to my son.

With no conscious effort on my part, *The Very Hungry Caterpillar* was his first book too – at least if you discount the cloth and crackly things he gummed on as a baby. His *Caterpillar* was a fancy-dan edition, though. It had a finger puppet attached which can be pushed through the holes. I was not at all sure I approved of such interactive frivolity, but he was two, it was a christening present I'd put in the cupboard until he was older, and I was still too unsure of my authority as a parent to question anything too closely. It was fun, though. If you got your fingertip in there just right, you could make the puppet look almost as impudent as the real thing. I tucked my son in beside me on the sofa and we cocooned ourselves, the ghost of my toddler self and the spirit of my thirtysomething dad in a shared delight.

Another delight was shared even more literally. *Sugarpink Rose* was so large a hardback that it had to rest on both our laps at once. Its huge soft pink and soft grey pictures of girl elephants, boy elephants, anemones and peonies filled my entire field of vision. Written by Adela Turin and Nella Bosnia and published by a 1970s feminist collective, *Sugarpink Rose* told the story of a baby girl elephant called Annabelle who simply wouldn't turn pink like all the other baby girl elephants, no matter how many anemones and peonies she dutifully ate. (These, the reader was informed, tasted disgusting. I found this hard to fathom because both the words and the pictures were so beautiful.) And instead of being happy to be shut safely in a pen and wearing a pink bonnet and pink booties like all the other girl elephants, she would look longingly at the boy elephants, who were 'a lovely elephant grey' as they got to eat whatever they wanted, play wherever they wanted and to roll about in mud to their hearts' content. Annabelle tries her best to turn pink and not long for freedom, but eventually can stand it no more and bursts out of her pen, casting booties and bonnet to the wind, to join the boys. Gradually, the other girl elephants follow suit and soon everyone is covered in mud, their tummies are full of sweet green grass and they have turned the lovely grey elephant colour that nature intended.

Looking back, it's just possible someone was trying to make a point. Unfortunately, it was slightly lost on me because a) I wouldn't get allegory until many years later, when I read *The Last Battle* and suddenly realised that C. S. Lewis had been plotting Christian shenanigans all along, and b) though I shared her dislike of pink, I did not understand Annabelle's desire to leave the pen or to roll around in mud like her brothers. I liked things clean, and I liked things safe.

But I loved *Sugarpink Rose* even if the finer points of

the story eluded me and, four decades on, I love my dad for buying his three-year-old a feminist tract. He bought my mum *The Female Eunuch* at about the same time. I found it on a shelf many years later and took it to university with me. On the flyleaf he had written 'You can read this while I'm giving birth to the twins.' She never did, of course. Who has time or inclination to read about the theory of feminism when you're busy putting it into practice every day? You might as well hold someone's hand and *chat*.

A little later Dad brought me another classic – or at least a classic in embryo. Judith Kerr's *The Tiger Who Came to Tea* (1968) was probably only about ten or twelve years old by the time I got my hands on it – too young yet to qualify fully as canonical. It was Kerr's first book – she had trained as an artist and was then working as a television screenwriter – and a massive, instant success. It had begun life as a bedtime story invented for her two-year-old daughter Tacy. 'I told it to her again and again and again, and she used to say "Talk the tiger" ', Kerr remembers in her autobiography. She wrote it down and a friend recommended that she illustrate it in bright indelible inks rather than her customary water-colours. The tiger sprang vividly to life and rapidly into homes up and down the land.

I liked *Tiger* very much, but my enjoyment – as you might perhaps expect from a child who read *Sugarpink Rose* and basically thought 'Stay in the pen, little girl! Stay in the pen!' – was tinged with disquiet. A tiger who just turns up, without any explanation or invitation, and stays for tea? BOUNDARIES, PEOPLE. My sense of propriety was offended and the promise of domestic sanctity, upon which my childhood tranquillity largely depended had been breached. There are two types of people in this world – those who long for the arrival of a tiger at the door and those whose profoundest wish is that nothing so unexpected happens, ever. Ever, ever, ever. I have all my life been firmly in the latter. I blame temperament and my mother, who created such an overwhelmingly safe environment at home that the idea of venturing out even into normal life has ever seemed fraught with untenable amounts of risk.

Kerr herself, you sense from reading interviews with her, or her autobiographical novels or her account (mostly) of her career in a book published a few years ago to celebrate her ninetieth birthday, is one of the former. She is joyful, outward-looking, generous-spirited and optimistic, despite – or perhaps because of – a very unsafe childhood, spent in exile after her family fled Germany in 1933. Her father spoke out against the Nazi regime and was in imminent danger of being arrested and killed. The family received a tip-off that his passport was about to be seized and he escaped to Switzerland just in time. Judith and her mother and brother followed, catching the milk train to Zurich, on the eve of the election that brought Hitler to power. The nine-year-old Judith was only allowed to take one toy with her and had to decide between her pink rabbit comforter and a more recent acquisition, a woolly dog. She chose the dog. Her first book for older children was published in 1971, entitled *When Hitler Stole Pink Rabbit*. It was a remark from her second child, her son Matthew, that had prompted it. When he was eight he was watching *The Sound of Music* and said, 'Now we know what it was like when Mummy was a little girl.' Unwilling to let this misapprehension persist, she wrote the story of nine-year-old Anna and her family watching the rise of Nazism in 1930s Germany who has to choose between her toy dog and rabbit before they flee the country just in time. Though it doesn't gloss over the truth, it is infused with Kerr's innate optimism and by her own experience, shaped as it was by her truly heroic parents, who made the whole thing feel like such an adventure that she once exclaimed in excitement as they looked out over Paris from their tiny, squalid digs, 'Isn't it wonderful being a refugee!' It is this as much as the careful tempering of the subject matter for the audience that makes it palatable – is that the word? Accessible, maybe. Copeable with – for the young reader.

But to read it again as an adult – especially bombarded with today's headlines and proliferating horrors – is to be almost undone. You bring too much to it and long for a child's innocence to protect you once more.

Mog the Forgetful Cat, Kerr's second-most famous creation after the tea-guzzling tiger, was and remains a much simpler, safer proposition than the tiger or the pink rabbit. The first of what would become a long and lovely series of books based on the Kerrs' own cat was written with a simple vocabulary of about 250 words because as it was coming together, Matthew was learning to read from the *Janet and John* books and looked up at her one day and said, 'I'm sorry, Mummy, but these books are too boring. I'm not reading them any more.' So she adapted it for him. This is parenting of the highest order. I try not to feel bad.

I embraced Mog unreservedly when Dad added her to our repertoire. I *was* Mog. She liked to be at home, with her family, with her supper (despite being a picky eater) or curled up in bed. And in *Mog's Christmas*, she learned to love Christmas. It was like looking in a mirror.

By the time I had my child thirty years later, Kerr had very kindly written fifteen more sequels, including the distinctly hallucinatory *Mog in the Garden*, in which she falls asleep and ends up flying through the air on a mousedogbird, pursued by giant birds with teeth, which – aided by the repetitive yet elliptical text that uses just fifty words, to encourage children to read the book themselves – induces a feeling somewhere between 'Have I missed a memo?' and 'Have I accidentally smoked a spliff?' Quite nice at the end of a long day.

It is a measure of how deeply we revere our childhood books and the characters within them that when in 2002 Kerr published the final book, *Goodbye Mog*, in which Mog dies, there was a stricken outcry. And an only slightly tongue-in-cheek and really rather touching obituary in the *Guardian*. 'She was nice but not intelligent,' it read. 'A conservative of whom it was said "she didn't like things to be exciting. She liked them to be the same." '

I told you – like looking in a mirror.

I was three and life so far was excellent. Me, Mum, Dad and an ever-increasing number of books. This perfect harmony was violently disrupted when the powers that be decided that I had had literally got under her feet for long enough and that it was time for me to go to nursery school.

Nursery And Clinic

This was still the 1970s, so going to nursery simply meant being thrown into the local church hall for a three-hour stretch every morning to be semi-supervised by a handful of disaffected local women looking for somewhere to smoke in peace. It was miserable, but it could have been worse. At least children that age aren't keen on playing together and our overseers didn't care enough to try and make us, so I was left largely alone. I wandered around for a few days and eventually discovered nursery's one redeeming feature – the book bin, whose contents an adult could occasionally be prevailed upon to read. It contained about twenty dog-eared paperbacks, most of which have been lost to memory. But two remain vivid: Frank Muir's What-a-Mess books and Jean de Brunhoff's *Babar the Elephant*.

I didn't like either of them much.

The What-a-Mess series is about an Afghan puppy, Prince Amir of Kinjan, who is always on the brink of, or absolutely in the middle of, disaster. He tries to eat trees and dig holes in puddles and, unlike his endlessly elegant and self-possessed mother, is always covered in something sticky. People's first words to him have so often been 'What a mess!' that he thinks that is his name. I found the kinetic energy of his stories quite stressful.

With Babar, I had the opposite problem. He was

lumberingly dull. Jean de Brunhoff's pachyderm – an orphan elephant whose adventures were first invented by de Brunhoff's wife Cecile to keep their two little boys amused when they were ill – was first printed in 1933 in, relatively unusually for the time, bright flat colours and a child-friendly font that looked like handwriting. I loved that font. I hated Babar. I'd like to claim that my juvenile self took some kind of instinctive issue with the many arguments that have been made against him since the book was first published. The playwright Ariel Dorfman speaks for many critics ('official' and parental) when he claims that the Babar books are 'none other than the fulfilment of the dominant countries' colonial dream'. Babar escapes his native jungle and is generously embraced and civilised by the (rich, idle, if ya wanna see it) old lady in town. He becomes a product and ally of the very society that killed his mother in the opening pages. Green-suited and booted he returns to his home where, in recognition of his now greater sophistication than the rest, he is made king of the elephants and he begins to civilise them too. Houses, clothes, the accumulation of stuff, uncritical emulation of the old lady (and by extension – again, if ya wanna see it – the ruling class) are shown as the way to accomplish all of this. It's hard – very, very hard – not to become uncomfortable as you read it now. My son Alexander was given the collected Babar as a present. I read the opening one to him and then – especially after noting the 'savage cannibals' in the later *Babar's Travels* – quietly put it aside. The critic Adam Gopnik once argued in an essay that accompanied an exhibition of the Brunhoffs' artwork (Jean's son Laurent continued the saga after his father's early death in 1937) that Babar is not 'an unconscious instance of the French colonial imagination' but 'a self-conscious comedy about the French colonial imagination'. Which, I thought as I pushed it a little more firmly to the back of Alexander's bookcase, may be totally, objectively true. But not to a four-year-old.

As I say, I would like to claim that I instinctively grasped and recoiled from the whole 'four legs good; four legs clothed, driven everywhere and returning to the homeland in triumph better' vibe, but in truth it was just his dullness. If What-a-Mess was Too Much, Babar was Too Little. He is a very boring hero – patient, industrious and, for all his eventual willingness to hand off responsibility to Cornelius while he goes on balloon rides, basically an adult soul in a child-elephant's body. Honestly – whose first thought when they pitch up in an unimagined, unexplored city is to buy a suit of clothes? And events just happen, one after the other. Nobody explains anything, has feelings about or motives for anything. It is a book that depends on charm to sweep you along. I found it cold. And now that it's become colonially suspect for me too, I suspect the Gallic elephant and I will stay forever at a distance.

Why, then, do they stick in my mind? It is because they were the ones that revealed to me the bookworm's prime directive: any book is better than no book. Always. You don't necessarily have to enjoy the book – though obviously that's the ideal, and most books ARE enjoyable – as long as the space inside you that can only be filled by reading is receiving the steady stream of words for which it constantly hungers. So What-a-Mess, Babar and I were bound.

They and their companions in the book bins alleviated some of the drudgery of nursery school – I largely had them to myself and both staff and children happily left me to my own devices until my mother arrived at the end of the morning like a miniature tornado, to gather me up and sweep me off with her to her afternoon clinics.

Whichever one it was, the procedure was the same. I would sit in a corner behind the reception desk, trotting to and fro between my little chair and the books that had been provided by the council or donors in the futile hope of keeping children occupied while doctors took their mothers into their rooms to work out with them the best way of preventing more. As pills were issued, injections given and diaphragms checked for seaworthiness, I was benignly supervised by Joy or Gwen, who ran the place. (And by 'the place' I mean the clinic, the health centre it was in, the NHS and possibly most of south-east London.) Over the years they became firm family friends and from the earliest days they were my protectors. My mother would emerge from her room to call another patient in and roar at me – a three-year-old sitting so quietly in the corner that I should have been the occasion of medical concern rather than fury – to behave myself. Joy or Gwen would roar back that I was an angel, under their jurisdiction and she should get back in her room forthwith. It was most gratifying.

Even more gratifying were the books on offer. There were not many per clinic, but there were many clinics.

During those early tours of Lewisham and north Southwark's gynaecology and family-planning departments, I made many friends beside Joy, Gwen and assorted kindly nurses. Spot the Dog. Hairy Maclary. Elmer the elephant. And, above all, Miffy, who said the most by saying nothing. A design classic, 85 million copies of the thirty-odd books by Dick Bruna starring the world's most featureless yet boundlessly expressive rabbit have been sold since she first appeared in 1955. Forget yer Titians and yer Michaelangelos. To look into Miffy's face – two dots for eyes and a cross for a mouth comprising a face that somehow looked back at me with happiness, sadness, anticipation, bewilderment, surprise and all points in between even if I didn't have a name for them yet – is to appreciate the infinite power of art. I loved Miffy. I still love Miffy, even if these days she seems to gaze back at me with just one expression, which hovers somewhere between eternal reproach and sad resignation. But I think we're both hoping for better times to come.

Best of all were the clinics that had Shirley Hughes. I couldn't read the words to Lucy's and Tom's adventures yet, or Dogger's (or those of the many other books she illustrated but were written by someone else), but I didn't need to. I fell into her warm, untidy drawings wherever I found them with a sigh of satisfaction, responding instantly to the evocative gifts of a brilliant draughtswoman who, as she once said of her hero Edward Ardizzone, 'with just a few lines of pencil could open up this astonishing depth in illustration'. Hughes' pictures were a riot of autumnal colours rather than monochromatic like his*, but her books and her world was full to overflowing and endlessly appealing.

I got general delight from almost every book I came across, but hers were perhaps the first time I felt the sense of a specific need being met. I disliked, profoundly, being away from home. Nursery was the worst, of course, but even at the clinic, with Mum in her office and kindly protectors all round I was always unsettled and fretting inwardly until we were in the car going home. Then the small, gnawing worries, sometimes at the pit of my stomach, sometimes deep in my brain, sometimes both (at nursery they talked to each other up and down my oesophagus), as nameless as they were insistent, would start to lessen as the car ate up the miles between me and safety and finally cease completely once I set foot over my own threshold again.

But until that true safety could be gained, Hughes provided a fine proxy. I wanted to press my face on the pictures, but generally managed to refrain. Her interiors were Everyhome, not chaotic but comfortably messy, well appointed but not luxurious, recognisably contemporary but not aggressively modern. Hughes is a specialist in making the domestic and quotidian attractive. They contain something elemental – an intimation of what we all mean by 'home'. I could live here temporarily, without

* I warm also to the story of how she once spent hours entertaining children at a book fair in the north of England by drawing dozens and dozens of pictures for them in thick black felt tip. 'Now,' she said at the end of her Stakhanovite stint, 'any questions?' One little boy put up his hand. 'Yes, Miss,' he said. 'Where's tha' colours?'

too much fretting and anxiety. My mother would know where to find me. The notion that books could provide succour as well as entertainment was born. My adoration and my need for them grew accordingly.

I did eventually start to read as well as simply gaze adoringly at most of Hughes' stories a few years later but somehow I either overlooked *Dogger* or simply failed to appreciate then the masterpiece it is. The book won the 1977 Kate Greenaway Medal and made Hughes' name as an author–illustrator. I didn't remedy my lack until I bought it a couple of years ago for Alexander.

A word of warning: do not read *Dogger* as an adult unless you are in peak mental and physical condition. It will break you. The story of Dave and his lost toy dog, accidentally sold to another child at the school fair, turns on a selfless act of kindness by his big sister Bella. If you are a grown-up reading this for the first time you will be caught unawares and soon your bewildered three-year-old will have to let himself out of the bedroom and go looking for his father to 'come and help Mummy. She crying. Tears AND snot.'

It's a book you long to become your child's favourite so you can read it night after night, despite the pivotal scene in which Bella nobly trades the giant bear she has won in her three-legged race with the little girl who bought Dave's dog tearing a new layer off your heart every time, because you want him to absorb the lessons it offers – like all the best books, as adjunct and never as didactic driver of the plot – into the very marrow of his bones. Of course, my own child has never fulfilled this longing – he likes *Dogger* now and again, but it doesn't own him as I would like it to – but we have nevertheless read it many, many times over the last couple of years and it is still all I can do not to lie prostrate on the ground with grief, crying 'Look! Look what we are capable of if only we would try! Oh, the humanity! What is wrong with us? What is wrong with the world?'

Motherhood is very difficult.

Back in 1977, an indisputably Good Thing was at last about to emerge from the nursery situation. One lunchtime, the woman my mother occasionally asked to pick me up forgot to do so, so one of the supervisors walked me home. No-one, of course, was in. So, with the robust approach to child safety that characterised the era, she left me next door with a neighbour I had never met. Her name was Jenni and her house contained a lovely smell of baking – a large slice of cake with blue icing was soon pushed into my hand – and a tiny two-year-old child, also called Lucy. I loved her immediately and have not stopped yet. Jenni still lives next door to my parents and Lucy and I live ten minutes from each other and them.

We are very alike. We both like to stay in, wear three jumpers at all times, watch telly, not talk and sleep a lot. Our only real difference is that I also like to read and she prefers to put on a fourth jumper and another DVD instead.

At this point in history, however, Lucy's antipathy to reading was not yet apparent and so she had a bookshelf above her dresser that groaned with such delights as a full set of Jan Pienkowski's Meg and Mog books and Roger Hargreaves' Mr Men. Over the next few years it would become a rich resource for me. Lucy gave me free rein and I went round there a lot to borrow and exchange various volumes and take them home to Dad so we could marvel anew at the length of Mr Tickle's arms (he was the first in the series – Hargreaves made him up as a bedtime story for his son Adam and then thought – 'Hey – I might have something here'), the number of eggs Mr Strong could eat, and the heart-rending ceaseless clumsiness of Mr Bump.

Re-reading the Mr Men now with my son – and it was Lucy Donovan who bought him the full, boxed set for his third birthday – is a discombobulating experience. The stories that once wholly enraptured me stand revealed, usually, as miserably flawed, broken-backed things. Maybe one in five comprises something that actually qualifies as a plot. The rest leave you hanging in mid-air, wondering what kind of blackmail material Hargreaves had on his editors that they allowed this to pass muster.

At the same time, the drawings remain as thoroughly and elementally satisfying as ever. Hargreaves drew, as far as both my three- and forty-three-year-old selves are concerned, the Platonic ideals of fried eggs, of shoes, of houses, trees, washerwomen and wizards. And his colours are right. Of course uppitiness is plum-purple. Of course happiness is yellow. And of course, of course, of course ticklishness is orange. I just wonder, 612 rereads into fifty books, what colour Mr Satisfactory Narrative Resolution would have been.

The Birth of Illustrated Children's Books

Life, even including nursery school, had settled down nicely again. And then came *Der Struwwelpeter*, or *Shockheaded Peter*.

Dad just brought home this book full of bloody thumb-stumps, deaths by drowning and carbonised children who played with matches, all in saturated colour and heavy black ink one day as if it was *nothing*. When in fact Heinrich Hoffmann's 1845 creation, which he wrote for his three-year-old son one Christmas when he had not been able to find any book in the shops that he wanted to buy, was a hellscape from which parts of my wounded psyche are still struggling to emerge. The ear could no more refuse to hear the burrowing insistent rhymes (oh, the awful, insinuating cat chorus in 'The Dreadful Story of Harriet and the Matches'! '"Me-ow!" they said, "me-ow, me-o, / You'll burn to death, if you do so! Your parents have forbidden you, you know!"') than the eye could drag itself away from the jagged, evocative, full-colour illustrations accompanying Shockheaded Peter and his companions' travails. How Hoffmann's own tender toddler responded is not recorded. Maybe they breed them tougher in Germany. I hope so.

It came as no surprise to me to learn in later years that Hoffmann ran a lunatic asylum. At the time of my first exposure to this beast of a book, however, I had no recourse to facts that might validate my unease. I simply turned to the man who had brought it so carelessly into our lives and gazed at him with large, unblinking eyes, the better to let him read the horror now contained forever therein, until he closed the book and put it on a high shelf ('No – higher. Higher again') until I was much, much older.

*

Until Shock-Headed Peter arrived, the world of books my dad was reading to me had been divided neatly into two halves. One comprised the bright, simple books about cats, elephants, caterpillars and children dressed like me. And the other comprised books in more muted colours but full of much busier pictures. There was gilding. There were curlicues. There were more rhymes and less prose.

When I got a little older I would label them the 'Now' and the 'Then' books. 'Now' meant modern. 'Then' meant what I would only come much later to understand were the lush fruits of the great nineteenth century collaborations between Edmund Evans, Walter Crane, Randolph Caldecott and Kate Greenaway. Together, they invented children's picture books in the format we recognise today.

Of course, there had been picture books – or at least books with pictures – for children before Evans and his gang found each other. Even the earliest books for children, in the fifteenth and sixteenth centuries generally managed to squeeze a few crude woodcut illustrations onto the pages, and in 1658 John Amos Comenius stepped things up a bit by publishing the *Orbis Sensualium Pictus* – a sort of early encyclopaedia, which had a picture of an object at the top of each page and its name in Latin and English below.

But that was just the beginning of the good times.

A New Lottery Book of Birds and Beasts for children to learn their letters by was published in 1771, with the letters on the left-hand side of every spread and a pair of suitable pictures for each on the right. These were woodcuts but done by the absolute master of the art, Thomas Bewick.

His pictures bear as much relation to the massy, indistinct stuff children had been used to as Dr Scholl sandals do to Louboutins. When you look at them or the illustrations from his most famous book, *A History of British Birds* (intended for adults but doubtless pored over by children too) – the mind simply boggles to think that it is not done with pen, ink and hand but by drawing onto wood and carefully cutting away with infinitesimal care to different depths to leave the picture in relief and the block to take up (if, of course, the printer is as careful and as skilled at his craft as you are at yours) different amounts of ink in order to reproduce all the different gradations of blackness and bring all your precious details to life. As long as I don't think about it, I could look at them forever. If I do, I very soon have to go for a lie down. Still, I hope the children of the eighteenth century appreciated his efforts. The Brontës owned a copy of *A History of British Birds* and by all accounts cherished it. Then again, so would you if it was the only thing available to take your mind off the TB-ridden siblings dropping all around you like flies.

Then, in 1789, into this occasionally beautiful but defiantly monochrome world of woodcuts rode the poet and painter William Blake with nineteen poems collectively entitled *Songs of Innocence*, printed, elaborately illustrated and exuberantly hand-coloured by the author himself. It was perhaps the first book – if not for children, then still eagerly consumed by them – whose pictures did not simply reflect the words on the page but evoked and added to them. It is of course easier to do this in a book of poems about the innocence of childhood than it is in an ABC primer or natural history book. A 'D' is a 'D' and a duck is a duck. You would be looking at a mallard a long time before you were reminded of a numinous state of being. Nevertheless, Blake really went for it. Even coming from a Technicolor age as we do, the illustrations are still quite overwhelming, as perhaps befits a man who thought of the imagination as 'the body of God'.

I miss mad artists. There are times when Grayson Perry doesn't quite cut it, you know?

This new idea, of pictures enriching and adding to a story rather than straightforwardly depicting what was being said, wasn't followed up right away. In the Victorian era, toy books became popular – sixpence or a shilling got you half a dozen or a dozen five-by-six-inch pages whose colourful illustrations dominated, not to say simply overwhelmed, the text (which was usually a fairy story or condensed adult tale like Robinson Crusoe).

In 1865 the publishers Routledge & Warne hired Edmund Evans – a man whose talent and painstaking work in wood engraving and colour printing had made him a name to reckon with in the world of publishing – to make them some toy books. Little did they know they were inaugurating what would become known as the first golden age of children's book illustration.

Evans, a man with artistic vision as well as commercial nous, felt deeply that the still-crude pictures then being used to illustrate children's books could be improved upon without impoverishing everyone involved and bankrupting firms. You simply had to be able to justify a big enough print run to provide sufficient economy of scale. Which meant producing something beautiful enough that people would want to buy in droves. Which would be expensive, but practicable if you could do a big enough print run. Which you could because you were producing something beautiful enough that ... You get, I'm sure, the point.

To this beautiful and economically sound end he first commissioned Walter Crane, an artist he had worked with on adult 'yellow-backs' (inexpensive books with yellow covers, for adults and sold at railway stations – also known as 'penny dreadfuls' or 'mustard pla(i)sters', they were often re-covered editions of previously unsold books. Evans realised you could shift them if you commissioned good enough artists to repackage them irresistibly). Crane shared Evans' belief in the importance of giving children the best experience possible. 'We all remember the little cuts that coloured the books of our childhood. The ineffaceable quality of those early pictorial and literary impressions affords the strongest plea for good art in the nursery and the schoolroom.'

Between 1865 and 1886, they collaborated on around fifty books, starting with relatively simple affairs like the nursery rhymes 'This is the House that Jack Built' and 'Sing a Song of Sixpence' before moving onto richer, more fertile fare like the fairy tale *Beauty and the Beast*. The market exploded. Evans had been right. If you print it, they will come. Especially if 'they' are a population beginning to feel the mind- and literacy-expanding effects of recent educational reforms, living in an era of growing affluence and characterised by a rising middle class desperate to spend their new-found wealth on further self-improvement. The late 1800s were a perfect picture-book-producing storm.

By 1871 Crane had moved abroad, but he and Evans still managed to produce two or three books a year, exchanging illustrations, proofs and finished pictures by post, as if the process of transferring picture to wood block to page in full colour were not already laborious enough. Not for the first time you have to applaud the can-do, will-do, why-the-hell-would-we-not-do? spirit of the age.

And by the end of the decade, Crane and Evans were flying and confident enough to produce books so elaborate that they barely qualified as toy books at all. In 1878 they published *The Baby's Opera* ('a book of old rhymes with new dresses') made up of fifty-six pages (a nursery rhyme on each), a dozen of which are fully illustrated and all the rest of which have decorative borders round the rhymes and music.

My own childhood picture books have, alas, long since vanished; victims, I can only presume, of my mother's constant mission to maintain a house that shows no sign of human habitation. Even now, after 40 years in the same place, you would not be able to guess a single thing about the people who live there. Apart, possibly, from the fact that one at least must be a monomaniac who has forgotten more about decluttering than Marie Kondo will ever know.

But when I looked up *The Baby's Opera* online, its illustrations are so familiar that I think I must have owned a copy. Maybe as part of an anthology – I seem to feel a substantial weight in my hands as I scroll through them onscreen. Fruiting plants in delicate yellow, orange and green grow up the sides of 'Oranges and Lemons' while a row of children ring bells below. Children in clothes and a garden tinted an unmistakeable azure sit beneath 'Lavender's Blue'. A liberal scattering of cockle shells and smiling flowers answer the question of 'How Does My Garden Grow?' An intertwined gathering of crocodiles, puppy dogs and snails are similarly provided in response to 'What Are Little Boys Made Of?' It's completely beautiful. No wonder it sold 10,000 copies in a month. Both it and its companion two years later – *The Baby's Bouquet: A Fresh Bunch of Old Rhymes and Tunes* – look like miniature medieval illuminated manuscripts and went on to sell hundreds of thousands of copies.

Eventually, however, the prolific Crane needed a rest and Evans brought in an illustrator called Randolph Caldecott, whose work he had admired in magazines. With Caldecott, children's picture books took a giant leap forward.

Crane's drawings had been charming and immensely attractive, but as one contemporary put it, 'He knows too much, and has not enough inspiration.' There was a carefulness, a pedestrian quality to his pictures that you might not notice while you were being beguiled – until and unless, perhaps, they are set alongside Caldecott's. Suddenly, Crane is static where Caldecott is vibrant and fluid – you can better imagine life for his creations continuing while Crane's are consigned to oblivion once you've turned the page.

Here was the man who could pick up where Blake left off, adding another layer of complexity to texts and deepening the delights on offer. 'Caldecott's work heralds the beginning of the modern picture book,' wrote a man who should know – the writer and illustrator of his own and others' books for children, Maurice Sendak – many years later. 'Words are left out – but the picture says it. Pictures are left out – but the word says it.' Sendak also noted that his pictures conveyed a subtle darkness. 'You can't say it's a tragedy, but something hurts. Like a shadow passing quickly over. It is this which gives a Caldecott book – however frothy the verses and pictures – its unexpected depth.' There is an expression on the face of the wife of the hardworking linen draper in the poem 'The Diverting History of John Gilpin' that demonstrates this perfectly. The verse explains that she laments the fact that they have not been on holiday 'Though wedded we have been / These twice ten tedious years'. Her face is the face of benignly neglected and frustrated wives down the ages. Marriage, it says, is a long game, a mixed bag, an endurance test. More often than not, something hurts.

All of which goes some way to explaining why there is a Caldecott Medal – with a relief of the cover of 'The Diverting History of John Gilpin' on the front and of four and twenty blackbirds baked in a pie on the back, awarded every year by the Association for Library Service to Children to the illustrator of 'the most distinguished American picture book for children' – rather than a Crane medal. It commemorates the man who brought the genre to maturity.

Caldecott published two books a year with Evans for nearly a decade, including a set of twelve books of nursery rhymes that sold nearly a million copies and made him internationally famous by the time he died in 1886.

The third gilder of this golden age of illustration began her career as a poet. In the late 1870s, Kate Greenaway persuaded her father to show Evans her manuscript for a book of verse called *Under the Window*. 'I was at once fascinated by the originality of the drawings and the ideas of the verse, so I at once purchased them,' said Evans, and in 1879 persuaded Routledge to publish the book and engraved the necessary blocks himself. He then had 20,000 copies printed – an absurd number for an untried author/illustrator's first book, and he was roundly ridiculed for it. But – whaddya know? They sold out before he even had time to reprint. But reprint he did, and on and on they sold – 100,000 altogether, kicking off 'the Greenaway Vogue' as more and more children and, crucially, their parents, fell in love with her pastoral portraits of an idyllic, timeless English countryside populated by endlessly innocent children clothed in her own – cod, if you were feeling mean, and if you are I suggest you go away and look at some more Kate Greenaway pictures until the feeling in your savage breast subsides – versions of late eighteenth-century and Regency fashions. 'I do not know why I cared to draw children in old-fashioned dresses,' she once wrote to a fan who enquired, 'except that old-fashioned things were always very pleasing to me.'

They were evidently pleasing to many others too. Her style became part and parcel of the liberal, arts and crafts fashion of the time, chiming with the contemporary reverence for (and hankering after) past simplicities and kinder times. In the 1890s the department store Liberty (the retail mother ship of overeducated late-Victorian bohemians) produced their first ever line of childrenswear based on her pictorial costumes and a whole generation of a certain type of mother delightedly mobcapped, aproned, pinafore-smocked and bonneted their daughters. How their daughters felt about this is not recorded. Her popularity soared with every book she published. She did two or three every year for Evans, usually with print runs of 150,000, the most famous of which included *Mother Goose* and *The Pied Piper of Hamelin*.

Most critics then and since have agreed that as a poet Kate Greenaway was a very good artist. But her art too was not at the time, and certainly not since, universally adored. Caldecott, admittedly, she ain't. As Beatrix Potter put it – 'She can't draw.' Greenaway's entry in the *International Companion Encyclopaedia of Children's Literature* puts it slightly more kindly. 'Her figures', it notes, 'tend to have no bodies under their clothes.' The Kate Greenaway Medal for illustration was founded more in recognition of her popularity than her skill (though, I should point out, it's not and never has been awarded on that basis).

I see exactly what they mean and yet . . . And yet I know I would have been – I was, I am – a member of the masses who loved her unconditionally. I like to think I would have stopped short of forcibly mobcapping any offspring I had to hand but, oh! I want to live in her idealised, never-never world so much. If I had been a child immersed in their works during those golden years rather than just dipping into whatever anthologised bits and pieces I had that are now lost to memory I think I would have adored but eventually exhausted Crane and only confronted his successor whenever I was feeling particularly alert and energetic. I would have been glad and grateful to have effectively two Caldecott books – words and pictures – for the price of one, but they would have been right only for special times and places. Greenaway would have had my heart. It is telling that when I have the chance of buying copies or prints of the three for Alexander I have only ever opted for Greenaway. She seems to be the middle ground, and perhaps that was some of the secret of her success – she offers a more detailed, immersive world than Crane but without Caldecott's cleverness and shadows. She speaks to the escapist in all of us, who wants to be charmed not challenged. We're a lazy, mobcapped mob. But it is all so lovely there.

*

Once Evans and his trio had pointed the way, other artists followed in their talented droves and the genre flourished. Arthur Rackham, Edmund Dulac and Kay Nielsen dominated the early decades of the twentieth century and gave birth to the tradition of the lavishly illustrated gift book for children. My adult eye cannot discern much difference between them, unless I see them side by side, when it becomes apparent that Dulac and Nielsen prefer more subtle colours and have a slightly more exotic touch to them. But my heart can still pick out a Rackham image at forty paces. I first came across his eerie, twilight faerie world in the study of a family friend (I was four or five and I think I must have been put there while the adults were drinking. We are still in the late 1970s at this point). I, with difficulty, opened a gorgeous, massively heavy book that was on the floor by the desk and was confronted by all manner of sinuous, twisted horrors, made all the worse by the fact I had no names for them. Gothic trees and grotesque spirits intertwined. All the women had too much hair and too much gown flowing round them. How did they think they were going to escape when the next wizened dwarf or bony beast extracted itself from the fearsome forest and came after them? Especially with all those sinister pools everywhere, bathed in even more sinister light from suns set too low in the sky.

This kind of thing shouldn't happen to a Greenaway fan. I slammed the book shut and sat quietly, waiting for the 1970s to end so that my parents would stop abandoning me to terrors like this.

Rackham and I have managed a rapprochement since. But I keep my wits about me. When I am in the rambling Norfolk farmhouse of my dreams, with the freedom at last to shelve my entire book collection as it should be shelved, I will file a Greenaway volume somewhere nearby to counteract the horrors lurking within. Other people plan retirement cruises and look forward to dandling grandchildren on their knees. This is what I do.

The two world wars disrupted everything, of course, as wars do, and the accompanying shortages and austerity dampened publishing's lustre for a while. But when mental and practical resources began to return, a new generation of children's picture-book authors and illustrators began to make its presence felt.

One of its members was Maurice Sendak.

Sendak

I usually remember the first time and place I meet a book. Not with this one. I've no idea where or when I first met *Where the Wild Things Are*, except that I must have been very young and that there were other children somewhere, vaguely, in the distance carrying on with their normal lives as I held the book open at the double-page spread in the middle. The wild rumpus fills it from edge to edge as Max's imaginary world effaces reality, just as the book was effacing mine. The wild things' yellow eyes stared out at me, daring me to shut the book, daring me to keep reading.

It was the darkest book I had ever seen. Literally so because it was all heavy greens, cross-hatched browns and shadowy greys (which really make monstrous yellow eyes pop), and metaphorically because – well, because Sendak's motivating force had always been his 'great curiosity about childhood as a state of being and how all children manage to get through childhood from one day to the next, how they defeat boredom, fear, pain and anxiety, and find joy'. In *Wild Things* he went rootling round in his own and the collective subconscious for answers.

Max, in his wolf suit, begins the story – as some long-buried, possibly still bruised part of you probably knows – by 'making mischief of one kind and another' and is sent to bed without his supper and with the admonishment 'Wild thing!' Soon Max's room is transformed into a jungle and he sets sail 'in and out of weeks' to a land full of wild things, becomes their king and bids 'the wild rumpus start!' But unexpectedly soon he has had enough and sails back to where 'someone loved him best of all'. He is restored to his room and finds supper waiting for him – still, famously, hot.

It's a book about abandonment, about testing the

depth and strength of feelings and learning to control them. It's a book about love and hate and power and powerlessness and the wild things they make us do and the wild places they open up within us. It's about the power of dream worlds and the porousness of the boundary between them and reality for children. A drawing of a monster on Max's bedroom wall foreshadows the coming creatures. The same crescent moon hangs in the sky outside his room and over the land where the wild things are (at least until the wild rumpus starts, when it becomes – because it would, wouldn't it? – full). He remains in his wolf suit in both worlds, but the hood slips off as he returns home and his animal fury (and freedom?) abates.

Sendak drew his inspiration for the wild things themselves from the memory of his older Jewish relatives coming to visit. They couldn't speak English and 'they grabbed and twisted your face, and they thought that was an affectionate thing to do'. He and his siblings formulated the theory that, as their mother's cooking was so terrible, the relatives could well be planning to eat them instead. 'We couldn't taste any worse than what she was preparing.' There was also a dash of King Kong in there too. A friend of Sendak's once pointed out that the composition of one of the illustrations exactly matched a scene from the film Sendak saw as a child in the 1930s.

It was lauded by many – and won that year's Caldecott Medal – but was also accused of being too frightening for children; an inappropriate and unhelpful acknowledgement of unspoken fears. Other critics seemed simply to miss the point entirely. The reviewer in *Publishers Weekly* praised the illustrations but not the 'pointless and confusing story'. And some parents didn't seem to know what to think. One woman told Sendak she had read it to her daughter ten times and the girl had screamed every time. Why, Sendak wondered, had she kept on if her daughter had found it so distressing? 'It's a Caldecott book!' the woman replied. 'She's supposed to like it.'*

But there were, and have been ever since, enough fans like the eight-year-old boy who wrote to him soon after the book's publication to ask how much it cost to travel to the wild things. 'Because if it's not too expensive, my sister and I would like to go there for the summer.'

Sendak's favourite fan, though, was a little boy who sent him a card with a little drawing on it. Out of respect for a fellow artist, Sendak went to some trouble with his reply and included a little drawing of his own – of a wild thing – to the boy. He got a letter back from the boy's mother which said 'Jim loved your card so much he ate it.' Sendak considered it the highest compliment he had ever been paid. 'He didn't care that it was an original

* I feel for this woman. I can't tell you how long I tried to make Alexander enjoy Graham Oakley's *Church Mice* books. 'They're so dryly witty! Such deft characterisation! Who doesn't know an Arthur? And isn't there a little of Sampson the cat, his instinctive urges forever poised to undo all the good of his early training, in all of us? The whole series captures the gentle stoicism of the Anglican church like nothing else!' I used to cry, until the day I realised Alexander was a) two and b) asleep.

Maurice Sendak drawing or anything. He saw it, he loved it, he ate it.'

And I couldn't even bring myself to press my face against a Shirley Hughes picture. Go Jim. You go, son, for all of us.

Maurice Sendak. The author–illustrator nonpareil.

Where the Wild Things Are landed in my childhood with as little warning and as big an impact as it did in the world of children's books when it was first published in 1963.

Its creator had grown up as the sickly son of a tailor in Brooklyn who started drawing to pass the time (on the backs of the cardboard stiffeners his father packed each finished shirt around). He had come to prominence as an illustrator in the fifties with *A Hole Is To Dig* by Ruth Krauss, a collection of genuine definitions ('Toes are to wiggle', 'Hats are to wear on a train') she had gathered from real children and which were crying out for accompanying drawings that could do unsentimental justice to their straightforward innocence.

Four years later, Sendak had taken the leap into writing as well as illustrating, with *Kenny's Window, Very Far Away, The Sign on Rosie's Door* and the *Nutshell Library.* All of them have distinctively Sendakian heroes and heroines, who are by turns sulky, angry, passive, loveable and charming but always fully, uncompromisingly themselves. And they share that lovely, chunky look of all his child characters, which Sendak once described as 'look[ing] as if they've been hit on the head and hit so hard they weren't ever going to grow any more'. He attributed it to the slightly hunched look that he had seen in many of his childhood companions, developed in unconscious defence against the vicissitudes of immigrant life in 1930s Brooklyn. Whatever the inspiration, you can always tell a Sendak child from its low centre of gravity and the sense that it would take the application of severe physical force to deflect it from its goal. As a child who spent much of every morning being flung out of the way by children markedly younger than myself before I reached the succour of the book-bin corner, I admired them very much.

All his books had done well and Sendak was respected in his field. Then came the wild things that would make him a legend.

For a few years after *Where the Wild Things Are*, Sendak concentrated again on illustrating other people's work, including traditional nursery rhymes, a fairy tale by George Macdonald and stories by Isaac Bashevis Singer, and writing only one book of his own, *Higglety-Pigglety Pop*, an expansion of the Samuel Goodrich rhyme with his dog, Jennie, who had recently died, lovingly recreated in the starring role.

Then in 1970, he wrote and illustrated *In the Night Kitchen*.

From the moment Dad first put it into my hands I loved *In the Night Kitchen* without reservation. The story of Mickey's adventures as he falls out of bed, through the starry sky into the mad, nocturnal world of some friendly but committed bakers bent on making him into a Mickey cake until he escapes in a cake plane and goes for a swim in a massive bottle of milk before returning safely home to bed, fascinated me more deeply and in a different way from any book before, and quite possibly since. With its impressionistic style and dreamlike logic it was the first that spoke to my non-rational mind, and the nameless power it held over me almost frightened me. It was elusive, slippery – I knew the story didn't make 'proper' sense and yet, and yet, and yet . . . despite this (I thought then), and because of this (I think now), it was endlessly compelling.

Until *In the Night Kitchen* I had been a purely, almost pathologically rational child (and my mother was always vigilant for signs of whimsy amongst her young) but Mickey opened up another part of my mind, where things could make sense despite not depending on causes, resulting in foreseeable consequences or being wholly resolvable into words. I used to long to visit the night kitchen so much that I wondered whether the force of my desire might one day cause the comic-book-style panels to burst their bounds, swell up around me like the cake batter did around Mickey, and swallow me whole. The thought made me ecstatic and anxious. I wanted to go, but not to leave my family behind. Luckily it never happened. The panels held firm, time and space remained as they should, and I was never forced to make a difficult choice.

In the Night Kitchen was born out of the moment Sendak looked at the rhymes he had selected for a Mother Goose collection he wanted to illustrate and realised that they were all, one way or another, about food. Then he remembered an advertising slogan for the Sunshine Bakers that had annoyed him in childhood; 'We bake while you sleep!' it said. The young Sendak – who remained easily and richly infuriated all his life – thought this was 'the most sadistic thing in the world, because all I wanted to do was stay up and watch!' *In the Night Kitchen*, he once noted with satisfaction, 'was a sort of vendetta book'.

Not that there is any trace of hostility or mean-spiritedness in the book. It is a glorious experience, the book in which you can most feel the truth and effect of what Sendak called his 'dual apperception' – the way in which all his adult life events were often heightened by the fact that he experienced them simultaneously as the child he had been would too ('He still exists somewhere [in me] in the most graphic, plastic, physical way'). Into the kitchen are poured all Sendak's memories of the 1930s films that weren't *King Kong* (everything from Busby Berkeley extravaganzas to screwball comedies can be felt in the New York skyline composed of bags of flour, bottles, shakers, cartons of shortening and in the madcap joy that suffuses everything – plus, of course, there is that indefatigable trio of Laurel and Hardyesque cooks, who were animals until Sendak happened across a rerun of the duo's old films while he was working), of visiting the 1939 New York World's Fair (New York itself, he said, was always a magical land forever glittering on the far side of the bridge from his home in Brooklyn), his love of comic books (whose layout, flat colours and bold contrasts *Night Kitchen* mirrors) and the happier elements of his childhood. Instead of mutated relatives, there are authentic, homely period details like the Bakelite radio console (the 'Jennie' written on it is another memorial to his beloved late dog), the fringed curtains and the almost tangible warmth of the kitchen and weirdly cosy domesticity of that reimagined skyline.

Nothing perhaps illustrates the quintessence of

Sendak more than the fact that, although he loved it ('I'm mad for it,' he wrote in a letter to a friend, 'and *it's* mad'), he found the book that was most informed by happiness the most painful to produce. 'It comes from the direct middle of me,' he wrote in the same letter, 'and it hurt like hell extracting it . . . birth-delivery type pains.'

As with *Wild Things*, some critics poked their noses into the crib and recoiled at what they found there. One New York reviewer was perturbed by the sensuousness of Mickey's naked wallowing in dough and milk. 'Some', he said, 'might interpret [it] as a masturbatory fantasy.' Hmm. Okay. I guess . . . some might.

A German critic wondered whether the dough suit Mickey wears had connections, conscious or subconscious, to 'doughboys' – as US soldiers and Marines were commonly nicknamed during Sendak's youth, before 'GI' became the popular term during the Second World War – and whether the oven was a reference to concentration camps. Others were simply concerned that, as one put it, 'being baked in a cake is more disturbing than any wild creature', or with the mere fact of Mickey's nudity (which resulted in several librarians adding hand-drawn nappies to our hero in their institutions' copies). 'Yet parents take their children to museums where they see Roman statues with their dicks broken off,' Sendak once mused. 'You'd think that would frighten them more.'

Like a lot of criticism, this all tended to reveal more about the critic than the subject supposedly under scrutiny. And of course the book sloughed off detractors and has done pretty well in the half-century since. It has sold millions of copies and allowed who knows how many young readers access to a different part of their brains. It has sent them the message that their dream worlds count too and that not everything needs to make sense right now. What a tremendous gift to give a child.

My own child won't give it the time of day. But I read it to him every month or so regardless. Not only is it a Caldecott book, it's Mummy's favourite. He should like it. And by God, we will continue until he does.

Still, I'm giving it a few more years before I make him face *Outside Over There*. According to Sendak, this was the final panel in a triptych reflecting a child's developing psyche. *In the Night Kitchen* was a representation of the toddler mind, thoughts tumbling through space and time, unbounded by fear or rationality. *Where the Wild Things Are* gives us the four- or five-year-old who is just beginning to wake up to everything around him and wants to explore it, good and bad, for himself. The third book, Sendak promised a friend as he was writing it, would 'reverberate on triple levels'.

Outside Over There is a singularly terrifying story about a baby kidnapped by goblins and being rescued, eventually, by the sister on whose babysitting watch he was stolen – an intimation of that moment at the age of about ten or eleven when you begin to sense the horrors of adolescence starting to gather on the horizon.

I'm not quite ready to talk about *Outside Over There* yet. I've never been so frightened. It works on the same visceral, primeval level that all the most compelling and enduring fairy tales do. In *Wild Things*, Sendak is careful to walk the line between real fear and temporary insecurity. The wild things have scary yellow eyes, but soft cuddly bodies. They roar and make a fuss but Max tames them easily with a magic trick and quickly becomes their king. The rumpus is wild but ultimately under his control. In *Outside Over There*, that line is but a dot in the distance. The loss and guilt are real. The jeopardy is real. The malevolence is real. The baby is restored to his family, but everything has shifted. The outside has been inside and things can never be the same again. Maybe the family recovers someday. I hope so. This reader so far has not.

Speaking of babies . . . It was around this time that Mum and Dad disappeared for forty-eight hours, exhorting me to be a good girl for Grandma and promising to bring me back a present. I assumed they meant my own copy of *Spot the Dog*. In fact, it turned out they meant a baby sister. The disruption to my well-ordered routine caused by nursery school was about to fade into complete insignificance. Ah well. At least Grandma and I enjoyed our time together.

2

To The Library

Dr Seuss

Nowadays, children are prepared for this kind of upheaval with specially written books on the subject – John Burningham's *There's Going to Be a Baby*, perhaps, or Lauren Child's *The New Small Person* (to prepare the parents themselves, I recommend Kate Beaton's *King Baby*, as succinct yet comprehensive an explanation of the tyranny to which they are about to be subject as you could wish). I suspect, however, that even if they had been around In My Day,* my parents would not have bought any of them. They were, after all, still only recently down from the north. Native parsimony and a disinclination to indulge in any form of southern softness (that is, attempting to alleviate any of the difficulties, sorrows or infected sores that might be said to lie within life's natural exigencies with anything other

* At least one was, in fact – *Topsy and Tim's New Brother* came out in 1975. And in 1992 they had a New Baby. Their parents should be studied by science.

than a Hail Mary, salt or whisky) would have comfortably outweighed their respect for books and learning. A baby arriving and shattering everyone's peace, quiet and reading time was normal. Gerron wi' it.

So we did. But God, she was noisy. Relief came when Dad started taking me with him on his weekly trips to the local library, on Torridon Road. I had been there once before with nursery school, which was about fifty yards down the road, but it had been awful. Everyone (else) ran riot, and, reactionary little fart that I was, it used to make me hot with shame and fury. Looking back, I wish someone had had the wit to crush a little baby Valium into my milk every morning. Everything could have been so much nicer with just a bit of the edge taken off.

But the library with Dad – a man who spoke only when directly addressed and last initiated a conversation in nineteen sixty-NEVER and was unlikely to try and skid the length of the polished Victorian parquet floor – on a Saturday was wonderful. It had a beautiful dome – duck-egg blue on the inside – that I had no idea then was probably a homage to the British Library's famous reading room. Clustered in the sunlit area beneath it were a set of comfortable seats round a circular table covered in the day's newspapers where adults could sit and get abreast of the day's events. It was cool in summer and huge, curved iron radiators kept the place gorgeously warm in winter. The place wasn't silent – rather, it was full of what Jeanette Winterson recalling her childhood haunt, Accrington Public Library, called 'a sense of energetic quiet'. Dad and I would walk together through the heavy, brass-handled doors with stained glass windows, nod silently at each other and then peel off, him to the left and the grown-up books, me to the right and the children's.

This was divided into two sections. In the one for older children, whom I longed to join, there was a long oak table with matching long-backed chairs where they could sit and do homework – so industrious! So focussed! So meaningful! I *knew* all that stuff with Uniblox and pipecleaners was just pissing about! – or read for pleasure with their big books propped up. It was still mostly hardbacks then (and no soft chairs). By the time I was taking my GCSEs, late 1980s economics and the revolution in publishing for teenagers combined to fill the place with carousels full of paperbacks in thick plastic covers, but for now everything was designed to endure. It added to the sense of security, of calm certainty that seemed to pervade the building. Stop a while, the safe, solid brick walls seemed to say, like generations of a certain kind of seeker after a certain kind of pleasure have done before you. Take your time. The books are here. You've got them. They've got you. What is it you're looking for? An hour's escapism? A quick explanation of a DIY problem that's foxed you? A history lesson? A long investigation into some of the weightiest moral and philosophical issues that men have wrestled with down the ages? We've got 'em. And good radiators too.

In the younger children's section, I knew perfect contentment. Light streamed in through more stained-glass windows – bordered in amber, which for some reason used to fascinate me even more than the dome – and I would pick through the chunky wooden containers, appraising covers and titles, and putting aside possible candidates for taking home. When Dad had chosen his books, he would come and find me and we would sift through the shortlist – Another *Topsy and Tim*? Was I sure? Alright. And Usborne's *Understanding Dogs*? Did I understand that this still didn't mean I was getting a dog? Okay – and choose the final six. The Booker had nothing on us.

Library books have not, however, stuck in my mind. I think I – possibly unwittingly nudged by Dad – must have used them as 'filler'. The ones he bought me, the ones I was able to keep and read and reread (and reread and reread and reread and . . .) were the ones I loved. Partly, of course, this was because – well, they were the ones my dad had bought me and that I was able to keep and reread and reread and . . . Which is to say, I loved them as objects and the easy access led to familiarity and comfort and all the other things that make books important to children apart from content. And partly of course it was because, save the occasional *Struwwelpeter*-shaped misstep, everything he brought me was brilliant. And became more so every day because I was starting to be able to decode them myself. My father had availed himself of a box of flashcards and was teaching me, with his habitual patience, to read.

I remember the cards vividly – lovely rounded black letters on bright white backgrounds, out of a teal-blue box – but to my everlasting regret I don't remember any wondrous, epiphanic moment when I was transformed from Non-Reader into Reader. I know I could read before I went to school but I don't remember a particular point at which the random scatterings of straight and slanted lines, circles and curves on the card or page began to resolve themselves into recognisable patterns, predictable arrangements – to become letters, then words, then sentences, then stories. I wish I could. Who doesn't want to be there when a miracle takes place? When a finite number of marks on a page begin to yield an infinite number of meanings and carry you away to an infinite number of lands? But I have racked my brains, and my father's, and we cannot pinpoint anything. It must have been a gradual evolution, the end result of which has brought so much joy to me over the years that it would be churlish to lament how it unfolded. But I do wish I could remember the transition. I remember later breakthroughs and lights dawning. Wordy, in the BBC TV series *Look and Learn* that we watched once a week at school (while, I presume, the teachers took a twenty-minute break for fags and/or gin as preferred), thrilled me with the news that 'Magic E' at the end of words could transform them into entirely new words: 'hat' could become 'hate', 'cap' could become 'cape', 'tap' could become 'tape' . . . The elegance and efficiency of such a rule pleased me no end. But I liked the quirks too. I came across George Bernard Shaw's famous re-spelling of 'fish' as 'ghoti' in – of all places – *Jackie* magazine (it was in one of those kerrrazee 'Did You Know?' funky box-outs) and was entranced. It was a construction made to bolster the case for spelling reform, one of his pet causes. The 'gh' is the 'gh' from words like 'tough' and 'cough' and so functions as the initial 'f' sound. The 'o' is the 'o' from 'women', the 'ti' the 'sh' sound in words like 'nation' and so on. Also from *Jackie* I learned that you shouldn't sleep using more than one pillow if you don't want a saggy neck when you grow up. This has proved to be untrue. As indeed, I have just learned during fact-checking the ghoti derivation has the attribution of its invention to George Bernard Shaw. It looks like it was actually first invented by a man called William Ollier Jr, a year before GBS was even born. You live, wrinkle and learn, eh?

The silent 'k' at the beginnings of 'knife' and 'knee', and the 'g' in 'gnome', caught my attention one day at school. Why were they there? 'Nobody knows,' said the teacher. This again is not strictly true, as I would discover when I was doing my History of the English Language term at university (short version – they used to be pronounced. Over time, the pronunciations changed but the spellings did not, so you have little bits of linguistic history preserved in etymological aspic all over the place) but one of my great personality flaws has always been to accept without question whatever anyone in a position of authority tells me. This earned me a reputation as a model pupil when in fact I was nothing of the kind. I recognised myself perfectly years later, just after I finished my A levels, in a footnote in Garrison Keillor's *Lake Wobegon Days*. 'I learned that quietness could be used to personify not only goodness but also intelligence and sensitivity, and so I silently earned a small reputation as a [child] of superior intellect, a little scholar,' recalls one of the characters, 'while in fact I was smug and lethargic and dull as a mud turtle.' That's me, I thought, and hoped it would be enough to get me into university. And it was.

While Judith Kerr was writing *Tiger* and *Mog*, her son Matthew actually taught himself to read from Dr Seuss'

The Cat in the Hat. I am impressed not just with the talent and industry required by this feat but by the emotional robustness he must also have sported. I took *The Cat in the Hat* down from Lucy Donovan's bookcase and read – though the process at this point would probably be more accurately named 'slowly, laboriously but technically independently deciphered' – it. I thought I had hated Babar. No. It turned out I had merely disliked Babar. But *The Cat in the Hat*? That I hated. I hate it still. *Cat in the Hate* I call it. And a tip of the hat to you, Magic E.

Theodore Geisel – the real name of Dr Seuss – was approached by publisher William Spaulding who had read a famous book at the time called *Why Johnny Can't Read*, which criticised the 'look-say' method of teaching reading (what we would call 'whole-word recognition') and called for a return to the use of phonics and noted the growing wider dissatisfaction with the quality of reading material for young children, epitomised by the Dick and Jane books which, like the UK's later Peter and Jane books from Ladybird, dominated the market and were boring children to tears. As *A Game of Thrones* writer George R. R. Martin put it once in an interview, 'Dick and Jane and their little sister Sally and their dog Spot [were] the dullest family in the history of Earth . . . Oh boy they were boring. You know, the stories were stupid, even for a first- or second-grader . . . [T]hat couldn't convince me to keep reading.' So, legend has it, Spaulding challenged Geisel to 'Write me a story that first-graders can't put down', to produce the anti-Dick and Jane adventure but still using only words drawn from the list of a few hundred that children of that age were expected to know.

Geisel noticed that the first pair of words to rhyme in the list were 'cat' and 'hat'. Some weeks later he had the tale of two children alone and slightly bored at home being visited by the rule-breaking, chaos-loving, lanky feline in the stripy chapeau and all hell breaking loose.

The child who regarded a tiger who came to tea not as a glorious intimation of the wealth of possibilities offered by the world and the imagination but a threat to suburban propriety, and who exhorted freedom-seeking elephants to stay caged for their own safety, naturally rejected the hatted cat entirely.

He was malevolent. The anarchy was awful. The danger to life and limb was palpable. I was firmly on the side of the fish.

I came to assume over time, as my awareness of the critical and personal esteem in which Dr Seuss' most famous and enduring creation is held, that my feline animus must just have been childish prejudice, so I bought the damn thing a few years ago and sat down to read it with Alexander. But do you know what? I was right the first time. That cat is horrible, I would happily shoot Thing One and Thing Two, and the fish and I are more simpatico than ever. Alexander didn't like it either. Now, obviously I work on the principle of working towards the greatest happiness for the greatest number of people and I'm glad it freed a generation of children from the tyranny of traditional primers, but give me Dick/Peter and his concomitant Jane any day. The Cat in the Hat can take his anapaestic anarchy and bugger off.

That said, I bought *Did I Ever Tell You How Lucky You Are?* at the same time, which Geisel wrote in 1956 (it was published then in *Red Book* magazine and as a children's book in 1973), and fell immediately, wholly and irrevocably in love with the brilliantly sustained monologue by a wise old man sitting on top of a cactus and cheering up a child with a riotous procession of examples of how much worse off he could be. He could be a Hawtch-Hawtcher bee-watcher watcher, or poor Herbie Hart who has made the mistake of taking his Thromdibulator apart, or Mr Potter, the t-crosser and i-dotter at an 'i and t' factory out in Van Nuys (although, truth be told, I would quite like to have Mr Potter's job). It's a bravura display of wild and wonderful invention and the only book I actively enjoy reading aloud. In it I find all the joy and generosity that other people seem to find in *The Cat in the Hat*. I allow it as a bedtime book even though it goes on forever because it is such an unassailable treat. How lucky am I!

Blake – Burningham – Scarry – Briggs

I was now coming up for five and my sister was nearly two and much improved. I liked her fluffy hair, enormous eyes (so sweetly babyish until you looked closer and saw the fierce roving intelligence that would in a few years' time settle on the BBC Micro computer Dad brought home from his office and be channelled into building Catford's answer to Skynet) and, above all, the fact that she now stopped screaming for whole minutes at a time. You could also push her sideways on the sofa and she would slowly topple over without changing position, like Del Boy falling through the bar.

Look, even bookworms occasionally had to make their own entertainment, okay?

Mum had gone back to work within ten minutes of giving birth ('Stitch me up! Let's get on!') and Dad had just started a new job, teaching at a drama school in Sidcup.

One day he brought home a book by an author and illustrator he had never heard of but who was on sale everywhere near the school because it was the creation of someone who had grown up nearby. His name was Quentin Blake.

Today, of course, Sir Quentin – as he is now – is virtually synonymous with Roald Dahl and has been since they first united in perfect harmony on *The Enormous Crocodile* in 1978, but for me he was the man who created *Patrick* (a book about a man whose violin music floods everything with colour. It was born at the end of the 1960s out of Blake's frustration with the fact that he was at that point seen as a black-and-white illustrator. So he wrote a story that would give himself free, polychromatic rein at last) and – above all – the stories of Lester, and his boon companions Otto, Flap-eared Lorna (always on roller skates), and a variety of other idiosyncratic and captivating characters who live in a land where everything you need – including general hardware – grows on trees. Who else but Blake would conjure up The String Thing (what does it look like? It looks like a string thing. Brown potato-y blob – not to be confused with the potato animal, you understand, whose low singing is often the only way you can distinguish it from a non-animal potato – with a thin black line running out of it) and make you love it?

Blake drew his first cartoons on the backs of his school exercise books and was selling them to *Punch* before he had left sixth form. After university and national service he was soon producing covers for the *Spectator* but realised that what he really wanted to be was an illustrator of children's books. So he asked a friend of his, John Yeoman, if he would write a book that Blake could illustrate. Yeoman could and did – it was called *A Drink of Water*, and they have collaborated many times since. *Mouse Trouble*, about mice that save a cat brought in by the owner of the mill in which they live from being drowned because he has pleasingly little interest in catching any of them, is this household's current favourite, though the household has had to reach an understanding that it is a little too long to qualify as a bedtime book. Downstairs only. Mummy would like to get to her dinner before midnight.

Blake's spiky, kinetic line is always unmistakeable. It united disparate books wherever you came across them as easily as Shirley Hughes' did. His drawings' sense of movement, the energy alone, makes them compelling. Many illustrators draw parallels between their work and theatre or film but most of them liken it to set design or, at the outside, direction. It is telling, perhaps, that when he was interviewed by the principal of Rose Bruford College of Speech and Drama in his native Sidcup at an event celebrating his status as a local lad made good, Blake likened his work more to the most dynamic element – acting. And like an actor, he thinks himself into the part of the child reader. 'I never think of myself as an adult and ask "What do they want?" ' he says. 'It's more a feeling of being a child with them.'

His actors, conveying as much in two dimensions as their fleshly counterparts do in three, are probably the dominant images of any young modern reader's childhood. As well as being hugely attractive in their own right – so colourful and full of life, fun and happiness – they look completely spontaneous and chime with a child's sense of immediacy. 'I like to work in a lot of rapid bursts, with much sitting about in between!' he says. The results are exactly the drawings you want when you live, as children do, in an eternal present. He retains all his original instincts and early experience as a cartoonist who had deadlines to meet and topical events to distil but which have become married to a talent for narrative exploration. He still distils characters – the Twits' supreme awfulness conveyed as much by the exact degree of their squints and pop-eyedness as by Dahl's words or the close-up view of the rotting food bits in Mr T's beard – but everywhere else he adds detail that expands the text and leaves books pulsing with vitality. And so his work propels you helter-skelter through the book, 'the focal point frequently a little ahead of the drawing' as Douglas Martin puts it in his essay on Blake in *The Telling Line*, until you fall exhausted and exhilarated across the finishing tape.

I have often wondered whether he must be a pathological optimist to produce such endlessly witty, cheerful, energetic drawings. I was almost relieved when I read an interview with him in which he said 'I can draw much more cheerfully than I feel.'

My other great love brought home by Dad was John Burningham. He had become famous with his first book, *Borka: The Adventures of a Goose with No Feathers*, which won the 1963 Kate Greenaway Medal, but it was the two Shirley books that captivated me.

In *Come Away From the Water, Shirley*, her parents unfold their deckchairs and drab lives in equally drab line and wash on the left-hand side of each spread while our heroine stands at the shoreline and lets her imagination carry her off into colourful adventures on the right. In *Time to Get Out of the Bath, Shirley* she goes on medieval quests within the confines of the tub. Both books juxtapose imagination and reality without comment. The contradiction stands like a riddle, waiting for the moment the child reader is ready to solve it.

Elaine Moss once carried out an experiment with *Come Away From the Water, Shirley*, reading it to different groups of children between the ages of five and eleven. She found that roughly the same proportion of listeners in each age group realised (or didn't realise) that Shirley was off in her imagination while her parents remained obliviously rooted in reality on the beach. I don't remember my own eureka moment, only the delight of being in on the joke, but one librarian remembers being there at the moment light dawned for one little boy. 'Her think,' he suddenly exclaimed, 'is on THAT side!'

But at whatever age that realisation dawns, when it does it is like being let in on one of the great secrets of the universe – which, I suppose, you are. A door of perception opens. Dude, a door of perception opens *into your own perceptions*. You see that your mind can respond to reality, or it can escape from it. Engage or ignore.

Your thoughts can bear no relation to what other people are thinking about or to what other people think you are thinking about. You contain multitudes. And so – bizarrely, bogglingly, terrifyingly and yet thrillingly – does everyone around you. Except those silly, prosaic parents of yours and Shirley's, obviously. Imagine!

In similar fashion, Burningham also opened up the eternal horrors and pleasures of the thought experiment to me, via his *Would You Rather* . . . The book's premise is simple – make a choice. Would you rather . . . be crushed by a snake, swallowed by a fish, eaten by a crocodile or sat on by a rhinoceros? (Fish.) Would you rather . . . jump in the nettles for £5, swallow a dead frog for £20 or stay all night in a creepy house for £50? (Nettles.) But why? And why not? And why does the person reading it to or with you disagree? Why do they fear the fish but you fear the snake? Why do they envisage one set of consequences and you see entirely another? Oh, it is a book of fathomless depth and endless wonders, to be debated long into the night with your ever-patient father. It was one of the few books I kept begging Dad to read to me again long after I could read it for myself, and the only one he, my sister (in a few years' time) and I would ever read together. It was so good that even Mum got involved occasionally, though to be honest she never got wholly into the swing of teasing apart intricate philosophical conundra; 'Easy!' she'd exclaim. 'You'd stay in the creepy house of course. Anyone would. There's no such thing as ghosts'.

For light relief there was Richard Scarry, with his riotous, action- and character-packed tales of life in industrious small American towns who manage to stay pleasingly old-fashioned and homely despite their plethora of power plants, logging activities, paper mills, road-building, train stations, multiple car pile-ups, renegade gorillas and much, much more. Scarry's books last you, as a reader, a pleasingly long time. In your earliest days, the pictures are more than enough. There are hundreds to pore over in his crammed pages, thousands of details to absorb. Finding Goldbug somewhere within every spread of Richard Scarry's *Cars and Trucks and Things That Go* is, I assure you, a full afternoon's work alone. Later, you can begin to puzzle out the words – the labels first, maybe, then the speech, then eventually the longer captions carrying the story itself underneath. If you are wired like me you will stop there. If you are wired like my sister, you will move on to understanding the diagrams showing how electricity and so on is made, graduate immediately to David McCaulay's *How Things Work* and be able to rebuild society in the event of an apocalyptic crisis by the time you start school.

Later on, of course, if you have your own kids, you start breaking the books down into their component parts once more so you can build the stories anew with them. Look, *there's* Goldbug.

Scarry's books depict a very 1950s world so he has tweaked them over the years and revised them relatively extensively in the early 1990s to bring them up to date and address evolving concerns about gender roles and so on. Now father rabbits as well as mothers cook for their families, lady bears drive steamrollers and the cat labelled 'beautiful screaming lady' being rescued by a 'brave hero' in one of Busytown's many conflagrations is the more prosaic but accurate 'cat in danger' being saved by a 'firefighter'. I regret the loss of whimsy, but times change and what we lose in gently wry humour we gain in the next generation growing up to be not quite so rigidly sociosexually codified and casually racist as the one before, I guess. Good work, Lowly Worm and pals. Now if you could just take out that equally 1950s sense of optimism and can-do that also infuses Scarry's anthropomorphic world and replace it with a more cautious, fearful sense that everything is about to fall apart, you will have a true reflection of the modern age and our children need not be perplexed or unsettled by the cheery faces on every page.

Or, of course, they can simply turn to Raymond Briggs, the man that gave the world Fungus, conscientious but dispirited bogeyman, a snowman that comes thrillingly alive but eventually melts away despite the magic and a grumpy Father Christmas. They all made a terrible kind of sense. Who said bogeymen had to be happy in their work? Snowmen melt. That is their nature, alive or not. And why on earth, when you thought about it, wouldn't Father Christmas be grumpy? All that work, crammed into such an absurdly short space of time. The loneliness of the rest of the year, never able to share your secret or talk about your work with others. And the awful expectation of cheerfulness. Briggs' sensibility was once described as Philip Larkin meets Hogarth, and it was one I warmed to immediately. It didn't exactly introduce me to the concept of misanthropy but it gave form to the inchoate stirring in my own breast, an embryonic feeling that Other People were not a welcome addition to life but an energy-sapping intrusion into it.

I count myself very lucky to have got Raymond Briggs under my belt so young. I was about to start school. This is not a good time for a misanthropic, introvert bookworm. To deal with it I would need all the help from similarly tortured souls I could get.

School

My mother took me down to the big Victorian building, ten minutes' walk from home, 200 or so away from the library (and built the year after it, finishing off the estate nicely), on my first day. Thirty-three of us were decanted into a single, separate classroom in the playground. It was a perfectly square, squat building with sides made almost entirely of huge glass windows which had then been spread with a thin layer of concrete to well over head height – an early health and safety measure, I presume. I like to imagine a world-weary teacher coming down with a mug of tea from the staffroom just as the architect finished his proud first circuit round the completed cube and saying to him: 'Floor-to-ceiling plate glass housing three dozen mixed infants? Nice going, you modernist tit.'

I waved my mother off in relatively sanguine mood. I could read. I was keen to learn to write, and willing to have a crack at sums if need be. What else was there?

At half-three Mum picked me up. I staggered brokenly down the steps. What, she asked, with interest if not concern, was the matter? It was hard to put into words, but the writer Florence King managed it in her (scabrous, hilarious) autobiography *Confessions of a Failed Southern Lady*. 'Until I began school,' she wrote, 'I hadn't realised I was a child. I thought I was just short.'

It was as new and terrible a revelation to me as it had been to her. My parents treated me and my sister as miniature adults – which is to say, they let us be ourselves. Not in a hippy way (I think my mother once bought some cheesecloth but in all other respects the Age of Aquarius passed my parents by) but in the old-fashioned way, born more of polite intergenerational disinterest than anything else. As a family we practised a sort of non-rugged individualism. We were thoroughly schooled in manners, ignored if we cried (absent free-flowing wounds or splintered bones), intimidated into a healthy respect for our elders, and if you wanted to 'express yourself' via any medium other than grammatically sound conversation held at a reasonable volume you were best advised to try it elsewhere.

They didn't see it as their job to intrude much on our actual selves or require us to pretend to be anything we were not. My sister is energetic, practical, gregarious, a born manager of others and as a child – at least before the computer arrived – most liked to spend her time building Lego behind the sofa, bringing in friends for company/quasi-military campaigns to annex the rest of the sitting room, or whenever there was a tricky engineering problem with the scale model of Porton Down she was building that she couldn't solve alone. She was left, largely, to get on with that. I was bookish, inert, unsociable and could generally be found wherever you'd seen me eight hours ago. And I was left, largely, to get on with that. Sure, people wanted you to be tidier, not drop crumbs, be more sensible about where you plonked yourself to read for eight hours and would occasionally push you outside for some sunshine before your bones started to soften and that sort of thing, but these were just superficial adjustments to extrinsic house rules. You were not being asked for radical personality change. You could be yourself.

At school and out in the wider world things were different. Over the next six months in that cuboid, concreted pressure cooker I would discover that much, in fact, was expected of little girls. They should be polite, charming and lively, interested in everyone and everything and not afraid to show it. And, from a grotesquely early age, coquettish. If you were naturally bookish and showing early signs of being good at exams, you had to compensate for that by aping all the feminine graces you could even more intensely. As the novelist Henry Adams told his studious wife Marian, whom he felt didn't own enough gowns – 'Those who study Greek must take care of their dress.' At five I was largely studying the difference between upper- and lower-case letters, but in my spare moments I was already having to contemplate tearing down my entire personality and starting again from scratch.

It seemed like a lot of work and I am absolutely sure that Raymond Briggs' *Father Christmas* and *Fungus the Bogeyman* both aided me in my deliberations in the weeks, months and years to come. The outcome of which was that I decided I wouldn't fucking bother. Passive resistance became my watchword. I would nod and say yes I had seen a TV programme, liked someone's shoes, was looking forward to the infant school disco, fancied the fanciable boy but saw what others saw in the less fanciable one and then discreetly withdraw from the conversation before anyone could press me for details. I would memorise phrases people used about sports or personalities or pop songs I knew nothing about so that I could drop them in at apposite moments to maintain a protective veneer of common knowledge. It was tiring, but not as tiring as either actively resisting everyone's urgings to giggle and skip and run about and grow my hair and tilt my head and laugh and all the endless rest of it, and not nearly as tiring as giving in and actually doing it.

This is an important step in the evolution of the bookworm. Until then, you've just been a soft, larval mass of love for books and reading. Now, through repeated exposure to Other People you begin to acquire a carapace that will both protect and alienate you from them. I don't say a cocoon or chrysalis. That would – as you know already from your Eric Carle – imply that there's going to be a process of magnificent transformation. There isn't. There's just going to be more of the same. It's bookworm, not bookbutterfly. This is your life now. It's just your good or bad luck that this is the only way you're ever going to be happy.

You will know the true bookworm, by the way, by its response to another of Raymond Briggs' most famous books, *When the Wind Blows*, the story of retired Hilda and Jim Bloggs living through a nuclear attack on Britain and gradually succumbing to radiation sickness afterwards.

The greater part of the bookworm's young mind will, of course, be consumed by the horrors therein and need to talk it through many times with whichever parent is best suited to the task. I knew where I should head. My dad was good for good things. But nuclear war? That was Mum's department. I expressed concern that a door propped up against a wall might not be adequate protection against radioactive fallout. 'If I put it up,' she replied, 'it will be.' I was wholly reassured.

But part of the bookworm's brain – the same part that will read *Papillon* twenty years later and not really get it, because it doesn't immediately understand that solitary confinement is meant to be a punishment – will quietly consider that, given enough time to make proper arrangements for her own survival, a world suddenly purged via one sky-melting blast of the scourge of humanity has much to recommend it, and face the likelihood of nuclear holocaust within its lifetime with no little interest and almost perfect equanimity. As long as there are enough books in the bunker,* how bad can it really be?

* I could have lined a small shelter with mine already. I had just been given my very own bookcase to house them all. I have it still. It's in my study – white, about four feet tall by three and a half feet wide with four shelves of increasing depth as you go down; fortifying in every sense.

3

Now I am Six

Plop

I have envied my sister many things over the years. At this point, it was her cuteness, so much greater than my own. Partly, I knew, this was simply because she was younger, and that much I was willing to resign myself to. I must have had my moment in the sun at the same age, I figured, even if it was one too early to remember. But she also had a lovely, open face and fizzing energy that I lacked – and knew I would always lack – that drew people, already smiling, towards her. This I found harder to reconcile myself to.

I found a certain solace in the My Naughty Little Sister books by Dorothy Edwards.

These are written (for readers of about six or seven, just about the time younger siblings are really starting to encroach on your citadel) from the point of view of a responsible, long-suffering but essentially kind and generous-spirited older sister who recounts the crimes and misdemeanours of her – yes, you've guessed it – naughty but equally good-hearted little sister and her occasional accomplice Bad Harry, a child with a capacity for consuming stolen trifle that almost equals the little sister's own.

The stories' settings are quaintly endearing now. Written more than fifty years ago, they are set in a world of taffy pulling, Bonfire puddings, doctors with Gladstone bags, party frocks that must be kept too clean for fun, and red ink bottles (for faking chickenpox spots), all illustrated by the ever-wonderful Shirley Hughes' warm, untidy drawings. But the themes are timeless – the charms and frustrations of having a younger child whose imagination periodically runs away with her and must be explained to the neighbours (yes, she picked your flowers but only because tulips make such very good pretend cups for pretend tea when you are a pretend lady out shopping in the lane), the fascination with a being who does not yet comprehend consequences, and the love for the incorrigible little bugger that infuses all.

My own sister wasn't naughty – though, dear God, she liked her own way – but Edwards' tales showed me that you simply couldn't fight nature. Older and quieter was always going to lose to younger and livelier, even when the latter was bent on destruction. The older sister was telling the story and even then the younger was the star of the show. Such was the natural order of things. It helped – in an odd and roundabout way, but it helped.

Still, sibling rivalry can come rushing back to you at odd, unguarded moments.

A few years ago I mentioned to my sister that I was planning to visit Penshurst Place in Kent for the first time. 'Oh yes,' she said. 'Dad and I went there once, when I was little.'

'Without me?!' I said, ever alert to potential acts of favouritism and not about to let an intervening three decades dampen my outrage.

'Yes, of course,' she said, looking baffled. 'We used to go every weekend.'

'To Penshurst Place?' I said, equally baffled in my turn. My sister is not known for a love of either Philip Sidney, Renaissance poetry or Elizabethan architecture. She likes computers, dogs and *Mythbusters* on the Discovery channel.

'No, turd,' she said – she has never quite shown me the full measure of respect I feel is due to elder sisters – 'different places, on the Mangan Magical Mystery Tour.'

It transpired that she and Dad used to set off in the car every Saturday and take it in turns to choose whether to go left or right at each junction and see where they ended up.

'And where was I?' I asked.

'Where do you think you were?' she said. 'You were at home. Reading. We told you we were going every time and you never broke eye contact with your stupid books. Sometimes you'd wave goodbye as you turned a page.'

I have wracked my brains, but I truly do not remember them going. I would question her veracity but a) I'm scared of her, and b) there's no point. They surely went and I as surely didn't notice. Such was the hold of a book back then. The intensity of childhood reading, the instant and complete absorption in a book – a good book, a bad book, in any kind of book – is something I would give much to recapture.

And it all began with Plop. He was the hero of the very first book I remember being wrenched out of my hands by a bellowing mother as she marched me towards a plate of burnt fish fingers and chips – *The Owl Who Was Afraid of the Dark* by Jill Tomlinson. It had been published only about ten years earlier, in 1968, but it hasn't been out of print since and is now (God, I am so old) an acknowledged classic for young readers. Modern folk can get it in heavily illustrated picture book, audio and abridged board book form as well as the original paperback that was my delight.

Tomlinson's book is the story of a baby barn owl called Plop (and have you ever come across a more perfectly appropriate name for a character? What else could a fat and fluffy baby owl with 'a beautiful heart-shaped ruff . . . enormous, round eyes . . . and very knackety knees' possibly be called?) who suffers from the eponymous affliction. In vain does his mother explain to him that he is a night bird. 'Nocturnal,' said Dad, who though no longer storyteller-in-chief maintained his vital role of explicator and synonym supplier. He would be constructively dismissed the day I found out what a thesaurus was. I still feel bad about that.

Anyway. Plop wants to be a day bird. 'You are what you are,' says Mrs Barn Owl firmly. 'Yes, I know,' agrees Plop. 'And what I are is afraid of the dark.' I read this now to my son and it makes me howl with laughter, though I don't remember laughing then. Perhaps reading was too serious a business still, or perhaps I just didn't know enough about grammar to appreciate the joke. But I loved it all, nevertheless. In the course of seven beguiling chapters, including 'Dark is Exciting' (in which Plop sees fireworks for the first time), 'Dark is Necessary' (where he meets a little girl who explains to him about Father Christmas) and 'Dark is Wonderful' (when he meets an astronomer who identifies the stars for him), Plop gradually loses his fear and eventually comes to feel that Dark is Super.

I was careful of my books – I was careful of everything; mud turtles are like that – but that late-1970s copy of Plop's adventures is undeniably battered. It became a fiercely private possession and reading – and re-reading and re-reading and re-reading – an intensely personal experience.

It was with *The Owl Who Was Afraid of the Dark* that I truly fell in love with the act of reading itself. I had adored being read to, enjoyed the stories, but the ability to take down a book off a shelf, open it up and translate it into words and sounds and pictures in my head, to start that film rolling all by myself and keep it going as long as I pleased (or at least until the next meal, bedtime or other idiotically unavoidable marker of time's relentless passage in the real world was announced) – well, that was happiness of a different order. When I was reading, the outside world fell away completely and it required the application of physical force to break my concentration. Though my mother, as one for whom fiction could never assume any kind of reality, never believed me (any more than she would believe in the years to come that her children were hungry, thirsty or tired outside the appointed hours) I never deliberately ignored her calls to come to lunch or dinner or to start cleaning my teeth and get ready for bed. Like every bookworm before and since, I simply and genuinely didn't hear them. Wherever I was with a book – on the sofa, on my bed, on the loo, in the back seat of the car – I was always utterly elsewhere.

Adults tend to forget – or perhaps never appreciated in the first place if lifelong non-readers themselves – what a vital part of the process rereading is for children. As adults, rereading seems like backtracking at best, self-indulgence at worst. Free time is such a scarce resource that we feel we should be using it only on new things.

But for children, rereading is absolutely necessary. The act of reading is itself still new. A lot of energy is still going into (not so) simple decoding of words and the assimilation of meaning. Only then do you get to enjoy the plot – to begin to get lost in the story. And only after you are familiar with the plot are you free to enjoy, mull over, break down and digest all the rest. The beauty of a book is that it remains the same for as long as you need it. It's like being able to ask a teacher or parent to repeat again and again some piece of information or point of fact you haven't understood with the absolute security of knowing that he/she will do so infinitely. You can't wear out a book's patience.

And for a child there is so much information in a book, so much work to be done within and without. You can identify with the main or peripheral character (or parts of them all). You can enjoy the vicarious satisfaction of their adventures and rewards. You also have a role to play as interested onlooker, able to observe and evaluate participants' reactions to events and to each other with a greater detachment, and consequent clarity sometimes, than they can. You are learning about people, about relationships, about the variety of responses available to them and in many more situations and circumstances (and at a much faster clip) than one single real life permits. Each book is a world entire. You're going to have to take more than one pass at it.

What you lose in suspense and excitement on rereading is counterbalanced by a greater depth of knowledge and an almost tangibly increasing mastery over the world. I was not frightened of the dark like Plop. But now I knew that some people could be. This was useful. I could be more sympathetic to people who suffered from the same affliction in the real world, and I could also dimly and in a more complicated way understand why some people might find it difficult to understand fears I had that they did not share. The philosopher and psychologist Riccardo Manzotti describes the process of reading and rereading as creating both locks and the keys with which to open them; it shows you an area of life you didn't even know was there and, almost simultaneously, starts to give you the tools with which to decipher it.

'There is hope for a man who has never read Malory or Boswell or *Tristram Shandy* or Shakespeare's Sonnets,' C. S. Lewis once wrote. 'But what can you do with a man who says he "has read" them, meaning he has read them once and thinks that this settles the matter?' Exactly. The more you read, the more locks and keys you have. Rereading keeps you oiled and working smoothly, the better to let you access yourself and others for the rest of your life.

I don't mean to place too much of a burden on Plop's tiny feathered shoulders, but if we were able some day to trace back a person's development of kindness, toleration or compassion, or their willingness to entertain an alternative point of view, or lifestyle or decision – how much of it all wouldn't come back to a myriad such tiny moments as learning that others can be afraid of the dark? In 1932, the French scholar and admirable optimist Paul Hazard wrote a book called *Les Livres, Les Enfants et Les Hommes* in which he reckoned children would learn about each other through books and that eventually this would end conflict. So far at least it hasn't quite worked out like that, but the point he was making – that as soon as you begin to read, you begin to cultivate empathy, if only at first in the very smallest of ways – stands.

This is why it slightly frustrates me that my son has never really had a favourite book. Even when he was very young and we were reading picture books to him, he never demanded the same one night after night, and he hasn't become impassioned about any others since. I imagine his mind littered with half-formed locks, and bent, useless keys. There is hope for a boy who has never read *The Gruffalo* or *Come Away From the Water, Shirley* – but what can you do with one who has listened to them a handful of times and then buggered off to his Tonka trucks and thinks that settles the matter? Ah well. We watch, keep trying new books, and wait.

Teddy Robinson and Mildred Hubble

My dad was still working long hours during the week, and in recompense had started coming home with a new book for five-year-old me every Friday. I'm sure he brought Emily something too. A ratchet spanner set or a carburettor, perhaps, or maybe a jar of depleted uranium depending on the project she was working on behind the sofa at the time. I don't know. I was reading. Bliss it was to be alive every Saturday morning, when I would come down and find a shiny, pristine paperback on the breakfast table by my cereal bowl. Thus was Plop joined on his shelf by several biographical volumes about the life of 'a nice, big, comfortable teddy bear with light brown fur and kind brown eyes', owned by a little girl called Deborah and named Teddy Robinson.

When I picked them up again a year ago to read to Alexander, I remembered them simply as delightfully domestic micro-adventures about a bear who accompanies his owner on a bus, goes with her to hospital or accidentally stays out all night in the garden that managed both to thrill and soothe me. But it turns out that in later life, like Plop, Teddy R is hilarious too. In one story he performs magic for an audience that includes a noisy toy spotted dog who has seen it all before. '"The marble's gone under the other bowl, the white one. That's not a new trick!"' I recounted to Alexander one evening. 'Teddy Robinson waited, looking mysterious and important. Deborah lifted up the white bowl. There was nothing there. Then she lifted up the red bowl. There was the marble! "You see," said Teddy Robinson, "it IS a new trick."' I paused. 'It's the lack of exclamation point at the end there that gives it its true genius,' I explained. 'Stop talking, more story,' Alexander instructed succinctly. 'Fair enough,' I said, turning to

Teddy Robinson Goes to the Fair. 'But thirty years from now, this stuff is going to slay you.'*

More Fridays passed and more delights accumulated on my top shelf. Amongst them was a purple-covered volume with a black silhouette of a girl with a broomstick, pointy hat and cauldron on the front. She was *The Worst Witch*.

Long before J. K. Rowling, Harry Potter and Hogwarts, there was Jill Murphy, Mildred Hubble and Miss Cackle's Academy. Murphy was fifteen when she first sketched the gangling girl whose adventures she would still be writing half a century later. She wrote the first story to accompany her drawings three years after that, employing her experiences of attending an Ursuline convent, whose fearsome teacher-nuns no more enjoyed or embraced their artistic, scatty pupil than Miss Hardbroom does scatty Mildred, and it was published in 1974 by a new publishing company Allison & Busby. Several older outfits had rejected it on the grounds that children would be frightened by the idea of a school for witches. Its first print run sold out within two months and it has been a bestseller ever since.

I had many favourite moments in this consistently

* I don't wish to brag, but I have met Teddy Robinson. Yeah, the real one. And Deborah. She is now in her mid-sixties and living in the same house in Hampstead as she did as a child and in which her mother set the books. She showed me the original drawings for the books and some of the unused ones. I actually held unseen bits of Teddy Robinson's life in my hands. I lifted his purple dress too, out of his little suitcase, and then I had to excuse myself and nip to the loo for a small cry. Yes I are a fool.

charming book. Mildred breaking her broomstick two days into her first term and having to fly it thereafter with a giant bundle of sticky tape in the middle. Mildred accidentally turning spiteful teacher's pet Ethel into a small pink and grey pig. Mildred being given a tabby who hates flying on the broomstick even before it gets broken and simply clings on for dear life underneath the twiggy end. (The endearing illustrations of this by the author have, incidentally, left me with a lifelong yearning for a tabby kitten of my own, which, I note ruefully, has still yet to be fulfilled even though I am now 802 years old.) And of course the climactic, triumphant enchanting by Mildred of Miss Cackle's evil sister and her coven, who are all turned into snails after she uncovers their plot to take over the school. The whole thing fizzed with energy and invention and held me spellbound.

The book's deeper attractions emerged over time. In the patient loyalty of Maud, the slightly older reader can see her ideal best friend. Mildred's combination of incompetence, resilience and unapologetic eccentricity resonates and inspires. I have pretended to buy the umpteen sequels for nieces, nephews, godchildren and now my own child over the years but somehow they have all ended up in permanent residence on my shelves. The enchantment endures.

Mildred was soon followed by a host of other companions. *Ginnie* by Ted Greenwood (who took a dislike to her frizzy hair and cut it off in handfuls. I thrilled to the courageous depravity of such an action. I could never be so brave. But then I did have a mother who would have cut my own hands off if I'd tried, so maybe it was all for the best). Catherine Storr's *Lucy* and *Lucy Runs Away* (which sparked a lifelong commitment to always having a running-away fund and a running-away bag. My first was a matter of 5p pieces in a china toadstool and Victoria Plum satchel filled with Panda Pops stashed under the bed. Now it is three ISAs and an Asos rucksack filled with cash, and I advise all women to keep a similar set of provisions handy). And then, head and shoulders above them all – yes, even those that doubled as survival manuals – there was *Tottie: The Story of a Doll's House*, the first book to break my heart.

Tottie And Milly

It's a masterpiece. First published in 1947 as simply *The Doll's House*, Rumer Godden's story concerns a family of dolls and their owners, Emily and Charlotte, who are bequeathed their great-aunt's magnificent Victorian doll's house after she dies. Tottie is the little 'farthing doll' made of wood, as old as the house itself and who used to live there years ago but who now takes care of Mr Plantagenet (a nervous doll, after years spent with other, far more careless, owners), Birdie, a flighty celluloid doll upon whose noble sacrifice the book ultimately turns, chubby boy-doll Apple, and Darner the dog, in the two-shoebox house Emily and Charlotte have made.

Within a story as beautifully and finely worked as the little tapestry chairs the dolls sit on in their lovely new home, acts of loyalty, betrayal, courage, vanity and folly play out somehow on a grand scale in their tiny rooms.

The dolls' happiness is shattered by the arrival of one of the house's original residents. Unlike Tottie, however, she is a very grand doll, made of kid and china and clothed in lace. 'Marchpane is a heavy, sweet, sticky stuff like almond icing,' explains Tottie to Apple who, like me, didn't understand the word. 'You very quickly have enough of it. It was a good name for her.'

A new lock. A new key. Like the doors of a doll's house swinging open to reveal all the hidden rooms inside, this sentence opened up a new space in my mind. The cleverness of this sentence, the allusiveness, the indirection – not that I knew those words either at the time – took my breath away. I read on even more furiously than before, eager for the first time not just to find out What Happened Next but to discover more of these brilliant, brilliant things that words and writers could do.

Marchpane drives a wedge between Emily, who wants to turn the whole house over to the beautiful doll and make the others her servants, and the younger Charlotte, who struggles to articulate her sense of injustice until – spoiler alert – the tragedy of Birdie's death towards the end of the story reveals the truth. So you see, it's not about dolls at all – it's as neat a portrait of humanity as you could ever wish.

Soon after Tottie came another small figure, flesh and blood this time instead of wood but with almost as unvarying a wardrobe – Milly-Molly-Mandy.

Oh, Milly-Molly-Mandy. Until she came along, I didn't know that either the countryside or the past even existed. But by the end of the first story in Joyce Lankester Brisley's collection of tales (published in 1928) about the little girl in the nice white cottage with the thatched roof I was wholly possessed by the desire to live in both. So great was my need for fuel for this fantasy that, for the first time ever, Dad bought me the rest of the series – five whole books! Count them! Five! Whole! Books! – at once. We were on holiday, which was already happiness enough, comprising as it always did two weeks with our beloved grandma in her flat in Preston (or 'home' as my mother, now fifty years a resident of the capital, still calls it) eating chip butties under lowering skies and drinking deeply of the philosophy that has sustained Mangans for generations: 'If we had some ham we could have ham and eggs, but we've no eggs.' It wasn't exactly restorative but it was fortifying. Then suddenly, in flagrant contravention of all family tradition, there they were – Milly-Molly-Mandy books in lavish excess, waiting for me in a pile on the sideboard when I woke up in the morning. I am forty-three years old as I write this, and still waiting for a moment of greater joy.

Every Milly-Molly-Mandy story is a miniature masterpiece, as clear, warm and precise as the illustrations by the author that accompanied them. They are crafted by a mind that understood the importance and the comfort of detail to young readers without ever letting it overwhelm the story. Maybe the creation of this calm, neat, ordered world was a comfort to the author too. In 1912 when Brisley was sixteen her parents had – very unusually for the time – divorced and she had been helping to support the family ever since, by illustrating Christmas cards, postcards and children's annuals. Those illustrations were, she once said, 'bread and margarine for a good many years'.

Milly-Molly-Mandy began life as part of a doodle of a family group done on the back of an envelope – yes, really – as Brisley was, in a struggle familiar to many writers and artists, trying to come up with 'a speciality' that would 'earn something or other'. She then wrote a story to go with it. It was published in the *Christian Science Monitor* in 1925, followed by others, and young readers from around the world (the *Christian Science Monitor* was an American magazine with a wide readership) started to write in asking for more.

Milly-Molly-Mandy leads a delightful existence in a pink-and-white striped dress (red serge in winter, but the books are set in an eternal summer). Her time is largely taken up with buying eggs for Muvver and Farver (these spellings are the closest Milly-Molly-Mandy comes to subversion), stripping village-fete stalls of home-made cakes, courtesy of sixpences bestowed by munificent grandpas, fishing for minnows in the stream and having picnics in hollow tree trunks with Little Friend Susan and Billy Blunt. You could ask for literally nothing more out of life, except, possibly, another dress. She never seemed to do anything on laundry day and I suspected she had to sit naked on an upturned bucket until her single frock was dry again, which seemed a waste of a day's gentle village adventuring. Who bought Grandma's skeins of wool then?

Ah – 'skein'. This was my first meeting with the word. It looked strange then and it looks strange now. But I stomped off to ask Dad what it meant and so bent it to my will. It has not come in particularly useful since, but if you make usefulness your metric for life it will not be much of a life. I know this because in all fields other than words it is my metric, and I have had no life at all.

But words I seized on, always, gloating over new acquisitions like Silas Marner over his chestful of gold coins. I remember so many of our first meetings.

I learned 'Lumme!' from *The Wombles*, upon which there has been even less call in the subsequent 30 years than there has been on 'skein'.

Knowing what 'blueing' was came from doing laundry with a well-intentioned Ramona in one of Beverly Cleary's ebullient books. Again, this has not been too useful in real – pah! – life but proved an invaluable little nugget of knowledge when my passion for historical fiction and autobiographies of people who had lived in the ancient days of the 30s and 40s hit a few years later.

The Phantom Tollbooth – well, where to begin? Amongst a billion other gifts it gave me 'dodecahedron', 'din' (via the Awful Dynne, Dr Kakophonus A Dischord's genie assistant, whose grandfather the Terrible Raouw died in the Silence Epidemic). 'Humbug' as something other than a sweet (which I'd learned about in Enid Blyton). The hitherto unknown 'piccolo' and the 'crooking' of a finger arrived in the very same sentence. As you might expect from a book set largely in a city called Dictionopolis, it was a treasure trove.

'Peculiar' in the sense of 'particular' – that one came from *Little Women* (as would the discovery of 'Atalanta' a few chapters on). Jo had a peculiar sense of something that didn't seem at all strange to me, so I applied again to Dad for further elucidation and he explained that words can change their meanings over time. Well! Who knew? [Many years later this single tiny instant gave me a small but appreciable and much appreciated headstart in understanding at least the part about semantic shift when it came to studying for my linguistics paper at university.] It also caused Dad to lead me for the first time to the dictionary, where I found that some kind person had charted its evolution in minute detail for my delectation. I would discover similar kindness in the 'Ms' for marchpane.

Later he showed me that the family dictionary could also teach me the correct pronunciation of 'skein' and 'lumme' and – a moment's further investigation soon revealed, ALL OTHER WORDS TOO. It could even unpack the likes of 'dodecahedron' for you. 'Dodeca' – twelve, because 'do' and 'deca' mean two and ten – 'hedron' giving it faces. I don't think I'll ever get over the amazement of realising that a word could contain such multitudes and explain its own meaning to you as it went about its daily business.

If memory serves, I think the only time the dictionary failed me was with 'Atalanta' (oh, and on the occasion of William Brown's swaggering in to the local sweetshop with a whole shilling to spend and 'the air of a Rothschild'), causing me to realise that proper nouns are, of course, the mighty tome's Achilles' heel. But it turned out that there were variants on the form. Classical dictionaries – Atalanta was a runner, apparently – yielded endless delights (though alas, no Rothschilds. I had to return to Dad for that) including a very useful story about Achilles and his heel.

These, then, are the moments I adduce as evidence of the value and wonder of reading, when people ask me (as they often used to when I was younger, and still, though less frequently now that time and inclination have enabled me to surround myself with more likeminded souls, do) why I spent – and spend – so long curled up with a book. It's not the whole story, of course, but it's a usefully tangible part if you're preaching to the unconverted.

Reading Milly-Molly-Mandy was a joy that transformed into an exquisite torture when I realised that although The Countryside did still exist (somewhere – I didn't find out where until I was in my twenties and got a boyfriend who came from Kent. Apparently it was thirty minutes south of Catford the whole time. Who knew?*), the world in which these tiny, domestic non-adventures were set had already vanished. I would never live there, never buy that skein of wool for Grandma or wait for potatoes to bake in the village bonfire on Guy Fawkes Night. It all seemed deeply unfair. It was the first time a reading experience became infused with yearning – a lost art that makes most things sweeter. Milly-Molly-Mandy is proof that dictionary definitions lie. You can be nostalgic for a time you never knew.

But maybe I was lucky. At least it was a way of life still culturally comprehensible to me. I'm about to start

* Oh. My sister did. 'We went there on a number of Mangan Magical Mystery Tours,' she says. It was a mistake, overall, to let her read this before publication. She is upsetting me.

reading them to my son and there is every chance that he will turn a bewildered gaze upon me, mutely mystified by references to village post offices, cottages unsold to developers, and hollow tree trunks that haven't been turned into branches of Tesco Express. He may, in an age that measures attention spans in nanoseconds, start writhing in frustration before we are even halfway through the chapter devoted to spending a penny on mustard and cress seeds or making a miniature garden in a china bowl.

I think there's reason to hope not. I think the power of Milly-Molly-Mandy to comfort and compel will endure. The stories are simple, not stupid. They provide succour, not sentimentality. And if they spark a flicker of yearning within a child for a lost world, you can always point out that they only have to turn back to the first page for it to live again. That is what books are for.

It was maybe what the country as a whole was using Milly-Molly-Mandy for at the time. What better or more vital balm could there be for a wounded and shell-shocked nation? Like her post-World War One contemporaries Winnie the Pooh and Doctor Dolittle (the latter was based on illustrated letters the author Hugh Lofting sent to his sons from the trenches of the Great War imagining that the horses there could talk when, he said later, the truth was either too awful or too dull for them to bear), the little girl in the striped dress offered sanctuary, a quiet, idealised rural retreat from horror. It is almost a defining feature of children's books, of course (especially for younger readers and especially before very recent years), that they offer a vision of perfect childhood that rarely exists in real life. But in times of need they are perhaps taken more fully into our collective hearts. Maybe this is why Milly-Molly-Mandy has survived so well while Joyce Lankester Brisley's other creations have fallen by the wayside. Bunchy and Marigold, created in the 1930s, are not a million miles from Millicent Margaret Amanda as characters but their adventures have magical elements (Marigold's godmother warns her not to go beyond the gate, where her enchantments will not work), while *Adventures of Purl and Plain* concerned dolls. None offers quite the solace or redemption of Milly-Molly-Mandy in her perfected but real-world idyll. Readers dearly wanted and needed an enchantment that didn't end at the gate.

I feel now that I should not have clung with such fierce insistence to books that recreated – with minor variations in time and form – the predictable, familiar and safe world I knew. I had undergone not a whit of upheaval in my own life, and I should have had plenty of capacity to cope with adventures and upheaval in imagined lands. I was the luckiest child I knew. We had a nice house (three bedrooms, terraced, in Catford. When I went to sixth form in the moneyed neighbouring borough of Bromley people would look at me as if I'd made it out of 1970s Detroit, but really, it was fine), enough money and my parents were still together. At school, we had some foster children – who seemed to arrive each day already running on empty but still expected to put in a full day's civilised behaviour and absorb six hours of teaching – and people's parents had begun to divorce. These days, I hope, things are handled better but back then the protocol seemed to be that parents (drawn, angry-looking fathers and tear-stained mothers) would come into the classroom, mutter a few words to the teacher – who would nod and make a note in the register – and then, walking stiffly and without touching each other, leave. The teacher would treat the quietly devastated child with brisk sympathy for the rest of the day and resume normal service thereafter.

There is nothing stranger than the recent past.

It's possible that this awareness that my lovely life was the exception rather than the rule prompted me to try and shore it up with lovely safe stories about lovely safe families doing lovely safe things. More likely, I think, it was simply that the reactionary force, which is present in every child for sound evolutionary reasons (when you are the weakest, most vulnerable member of your tribe, any change to a currently survivable status quo is always a threat), was simply strong in me.

'It's because you were a midget,' says my sister, when I make the mistake of musing upon this out loud in her hearing. So there's that possibility too.

I was able to remain comfortable and unchallenged because my tastes were so well served. In the late 1970s and early 1980s, publishers had not yet fully embraced the notion of looking outside or representing anything other than traditional (white, Christian, able-bodied, straight and so on) middle-class children. Children's literature emerged originally in response to the rise of the new, and newly affluent, Victorian bourgeoisie, who were eager to spend the money the Industrial Revolution was making for them on improving and entertaining books for their children and it was shaped by their tastes from the beginning. Efforts were starting to be made to break this historical stranglehold with books for older children, and I would reap some of the fruits of these by the time I was ready for them, but nothing much had yet filtered through to the younger market. I carried on buffing my mud-turtle shell to a high shine. Mostly in the school library.

The School Carousel

A year or so on from my pedagogic/social baptism of fire, school was proving to have some redeeming features. It was still full of children but it also had old *Beano* annuals in a box in the assembly hall. Look and Learn and Wordy were introducing me to various orthographical delights. I had a special card that had my name on it in big black letters with little red arrows showing me which way the pen should go so I would never forget again. And there was, in half a classroom set aside for the purpose, a library. There, on the carpeted area reserved for the very youngest infants, I found a lot of books about caterpillars that weren't a patch on Eric Carle's, a lot of books about elephants that weren't a patch on *Sugarpink Rose*, and a lot of books about dogs that weren't a patch on Frank Muir's What-a-Mess. Still, they were all better than going out into the playground and playing and so I stayed there as much as I could. Some of the dinner ladies let me (thanks, Mrs Hill) and some didn't (thanks, Mrs Bananaface. You had a face like a banana, I hope you know).

As you got older and more sophisticated – and I was thinking about turning six by this stage – you were allowed to move beyond the carpeted area, towards the shelves where the proper books were kept. That was where I found Allen and Janet Ahlberg's perennially charming Happy Families series and worked my way happily through the stories of *Master Bun the Bakers' Boy, Mrs Wobble the Waitress, Mr Tick the Teacher, Mr Cosmo the Conjuror* et al., and longed to visit them in their cartoonish yet cosy little houses in their cosy little town where everything was suffused with the Ahlbergs' trademark warmth. Then there was a run of Antelope books, a series of small hardbacks aimed at readers just about happy to be left alone with a chapter book. They were short enough that you could finish them but long enough that you still felt a sense of achievement when you did, and my favourite was *Adventuring with Brindle.* It was a riveting story about a boy who runs away from home with his Great Dane Brindle, when he fears she is about to be sent away. I took it out so many times I was eventually forbidden to have it any more. I wept. In the early 2000s I found a second-hand edition on the Internet and bought it – my own copy at last! It was stupidly expensive, but you can't put a price on justice.

Finally, there was *Maggie Gumption* by Margaret Barry. It was another book about dolls in a doll's house, but an altogether simpler, more rambunctious affair than Godden's tour de force. Maggie was a periodically furious plain wooden doll who stomped about her untidy house eating sago pudding and hoping that her mimsy, snobby neighbour Pinky Dars (which may be the best name in all of literature, incidentally), or indeed anyone else, wouldn't come round. I liked her very much.

The paperback carousels in the school library also

yielded such delights as *Flat Stanley* by Jeff Brown, and *Henry and Ribsy* by Beverly Cleary – both American authors, which makes me hope that the books turned up in a care package from some former pupil who'd made it big in the States, along with nylons for the teachers and cigarettes for the headmaster ('Who knew we'd ever hear from little Kevin Glaxosmithkline again!') but which I sadly suspect is no more than coincidence.

Flat Stanley is the tale of Stanley Lambchop whose giant bedroom pinboard falls on him during the night, rendering him completely – you may be ahead of me here – flat. It is, like a secret garden, or a magical chocolate factory, or a race of tiny people living under the floorboards, the kind of perfect, simple, fertile conceit that every author longs to come up with and which delights every reader. And, once again, in later years it turns out to be hilarious. 'How do you feel?' Doctor Dan asks the newly squashed Stanley. 'Sort of tickly for a while after I got up,' says the patient. 'But fine now.' 'Well, that's mostly how it is with these cases,' replies the doctor.

Henry and Ribsy is a collection of stories about a boy called Henry Huggins and his dog Ribsy, a stray whom he acquires in the first chapter. This was my introduction to Beverly Cleary's books – appropriately enough, since writing it had been her introduction to authorship too. She wrote it in 1949, with the boys she had met ten years ago as a children's librarian in mind. They had been deposited with her by their school and told to find books they liked in order to write a report on them later. It couldn't be done. There were simply no books catering to that market. She empathised particularly with them because she too had been a reluctant reader as a child. At first this had been because of a heavy-handed approach to its teaching at home and school. 'I wept at home while my puzzled mother tried to drill me on the dreaded word charts,' she remembers in her autobiography *A Girl from Yamhill*. 'By second grade I was able to plod through my reader a step or two ahead of disgrace'. Then, once the ability kicked in and she started ploughing her way through the children's side of her branch library, her reluctance grew again because she became bored and critical of the books on offer. 'Why couldn't authors write about the sort of boys and girls who lived on my block? Plain, ordinary boys and girls I called them when I was a child. Why couldn't authors skip all that tiresome description and write books in which something happened on every page? Why couldn't they make their stories funny?'

The childhood thought was father to all Cleary's books. They all centre round ordinary children – Henry, his friend Beezus and her younger sister Ramona, a peripheral character in the early books but soon to star in a series of her own – having small, realistic adventures in the suburban streets of Portland, Oregon, where Cleary herself had grown up after leaving the farm in Yamhill at the age of six. Cleary's ear for naturalistic dialogue and succinct and heartfelt evocations of childhood frustrations, passions and arguments made every page so clear and fresh and lively that there were times when I honestly believed I was living on Klickitat Street.

When news of my latest discovery reached Dad's

ears, he started furnishing me with something even better – that Ramona series. She is four when we first meet her, in *Beezus and Ramona*, wiping her paint-smeared hands on the neighbour's cat in Klickitat Street, slowly learning to negotiate the monkey bars in the park and the maddening world of school and grown-ups, and she is ten (or 'zeroteenth' as she dubs it in order to secure the respect she feels moving into double figures demands) by the time we leave her – monkey bars mastered, wider world semi-conquered – in *Ramona's World*.

The eponymous heroine has 'brown eyes, brown hair and no cavities'. Cleary did indeed skip all tiresome description, leaving only good stuff behind. A chapter in *Ramona and Her Mother* contains the most glorious account of what it feels like to squeeze an entire (large economy-size) tube of toothpaste into the sink. 'How fat and smooth it felt in her hand . . . She squeezed the tube the way she had been told she must never squeeze it, right in the middle. White paste shot out faster than she had expected.' It continues for another whole page as Ramona fully relieves her frustrations at not being able to sew slacks ('American for trousers,' explained Dad, and into my mental file it went) for her favourite soft toy. I don't think I read anything quite as satisfying again until I was twenty and Dr Iannis works that pea out of the old man's ear in *Captain Correlli's Mandolin*.

One typically compact descriptive line in another story captivated me for hours – 'Ramona chewed a nail as painful as her thoughts.' I still don't quite know what this technically is – it seems to hover at the border between simile and zeugma – but I loved this yoking together of words to make something entertainingly more than the sum of their parts. It was of the same order of linguistic magic as Marchpane and her metaphorical powers and dazzled me accordingly.

But if I loved the writing, I loved Ramona more. I loved her stubbornness, her inexhaustible curiosity, the noise she made, the exuberant fun she had and the space she unapologetically took up. I knew I would never be able to emulate it, but reading about her was like running through a strong, fresh breeze. She was also an antidote to the girls at school who were changing all around me and making me more and more uncomfortable. They had started wearing strappy sandals instead of solid school shoes. Looking out from under lowered lashes instead of directly into boys' faces. No longer throwing their hands up in class. Pretending they couldn't do sums. Unwritten rules were changing fast, and from what little I could gather as they flashed past me, they were an exercise in humiliation. I was confused, yet fascinated and in some strange way envious, although I didn't yet know what I was envying. It turned out to be embryonic arts that would one day make those who had mastered them sexually attractive. Ah well. Ramona's spirit ran counter to it all. She hadn't got the memo either, and still preferred to wear trousers, still threw herself at the monkey bars and still sported the resulting scabs on her knees with pride.

But the greatest thing about Ramona was that unlike Milly-Molly-Mandy – though I mean this as no criticism of my cotton-frocked beloved – she had an inner life. Between Milly-Molly-Mandy's 1920s origin and

Ramona's birth in 1955 psychology had been invented and Cleary's great talent was to make Ramona not just lively, but recognisably alive. She came from a happy family but still burned with a need for as much love and attention as they could possibly spare. She was boisterous but never meant to be naughty – her thoughts and motivations simply worked to a purer logic than those outside could be counted on to understand. Thus on her first day of kindergarten she produces a delicate snore at resting time – not to be a pest, as the teacher assumes, but to try and prove what a good rester she is. And she was, as every child is, frequently the victim of simple misunderstanding. The injustice of the telling-off she gets when she refuses to move from her seat (because Miss Binney does not realise that she told Ramona to sit there 'for the present' and Ramona doesn't want to lose her chance of a gift), is a moment that will resonate with children forever. It was good to know that there was no such thing as perfect understanding in the world for anyone. You hear a lot about books expanding the mind – less gets said about its occasional usefulness in battering your expectations of life down to manageable proportions. But it really ought to be credited with both. High hopes are the thief of time, and contentment.

Ladybirds

There was one other very important carousel in the school library. It was full of hardbacks, yet they were the size of paperbacks and even slimmer. I had a couple at home but they were learning-to-read books about

Peter and Jane that were now in use with my sister. These were different. They seemed to be about everything. There was one about computers. One about a man called John Wesley. One about knitting. These I did not go a bundle on. The one about John Wesley in particular haunted me. It seemed to have more words per page than was physically possible. And although I could literally read them all – 'Me-th-od-is-m' – I could not make sense of them. I could not hold the sentences in my mind. By the time I got to the end of one, the beginning had vanished like one of those tracing games where you press down with a stylus and then lift the top sheet to erase everything and start again. Or like shaking an Etch A Sketch, if you come from a home slightly better stocked with basic contemporary entertainments.

Better – much better, put-in-a-request-to-the-parents better – were the ones full of princes (in funny trousers), princesses (in lovely gowns), flaxen/ebony-haired children, brave hens, foolish chickens, lively gingerbread men and talking pancakes, who variously became embroiled with wicked witches, evil stepmothers bearing poisoned apples, furious goblins, menacing bears, hungry villages, wily foxes, murderous wolves and enchanted spinning wheels against a backdrop of dark woods, shining castles, thickets of thorns and doorless towers.

They were of course Ladybirds, the little books that emerged over seventy years ago at Wills & Hepworth, a small printing firm in Loughborough, and swiftly achieved iconic status. To keep their presses rolling during the war, the firm devised a storybook for children that could be printed on just one sheet of paper. When one of their employees, Douglas Keen – a committed educationalist and believer in self-improvement – came back from the war he saw the format's potential, sat down at his kitchen table and laid out the first factual Ladybird, about birds. It was the beginning of the longest series – Nature – Ladybird would run, and the genesis of the brand as we know it.

The measure of the love and esteem in which the multiple series that eventually made up Ladybird's output were held can be seen in the number of letters that appeared in various newspapers after Douglas Keen's death in 2008. One correspondent remembered checking out the Ladybird *Napoleon Bonaparte* from the library to get him through his history A level. A minister wrote to the *Guardian* to say he still dishes out copies of – ahem – the Ladybird *John Wesley* as the perfect primer for anyone interested in Methodism. To which I can only say, God be with you. I tried again recently and still couldn't get through it. Though this time possibly because my brain shut down as a protective measure after reading that he was one of nineteen children. Imagine giving birth nineteen times. Hundreds of years before epidurals, pethidine or anything other than a 'Just say another prayer, Susanna, if it's starting to sting!' That's one of the few things more exhausting and painful than ploughing through a primer on Methodism.

Another person wrote in to say that the Ladybird *Book of Printing Processes* had been required reading on his design course, and the one about English spelling and grammar went on at least one university lecturer's reading list for freshers. And the rumour persists that the Ministry of Defence put in a covert order for copies of *The Computer: How it Works* – to be delivered in special plain covers – when it came out in the 1970s.

The application to my parents for more of these delicious, tiny books that felt so right in childish hands yielded over subsequent weeks and months the publishers' gracefully filleted versions of Bible stories, Aesop's Fables and, a touch more fancifully, the adventures of the Garden Gang, a series of short stories (really short – two per Ladybird) about Percival Pea, Bertie Brussel Sprout, Colin Cucumber and assorted other produce invented and illustrated by a twelve-year-old girl called Jayne Fisher. They, and the age of their author, transfixed me. I held the gang's efforts to supply Polly Pomegranate with the ballet clothes she needed and solve Oliver Onion's lachrymose problems in exactly the same esteem as Aesop's finest and ancient Greece's best efforts to limn the human condition. A good story is a good story is a good story. They were followed by *Gulliver's Travels*, *The Swiss Family Robinson* and a number of other literary and folkloric – *Stone Soup*! – classics distilled into fifty-six pages a time.

I ploughed my way through as many of the classical titles on my reading list as I could at university, but still all I will ever reliably know of Hercules and his labours, Andromeda and her rock, Perseus and his Gorgon comes from the 102 small pages comprising the two Ladybird volumes of classical myth and legends – thrilling text about minotaurs, moving cliffs, men holding up the earth, golden fleeces and goldener apples on the left, on the right pictures destined to live for ever in the mind's eye. Baby Hercules strangling a snake in each hand, people. Each hand. Snake. Strangled. I note that these days, ladybird.co.uk offers you the chance to narrow your book choices by age range. Ignore it. How safe do your children really have to feel?

While I was accumulating fairy tales and other filleted fiction, a boy 200 miles away unknown to me but whom I would one day, slightly against my better judgement, marry was industriously amassing with the zeal of a born fact-seeker and completist a complementary collection of the History and How To series. Looking at his collection now gives me a new and even deeper respect for the mighty minds behind the books. There is almost literally nothing of even the most fleeting interest to a child that they did not cover. There is the Story of the Cowboy, of Oil, of Houses and Homes, of Ships of Clothes and Costumes and everything in between. Want to learn about the history of the British Isles in 102 titchy pages? Ladies and gentlemen, I give you a brace of volumes called *Our Land in the Making*. They aren't books, they are nuggets of pure knowledge that still glitter in the man's mind thirty years on. It is my hope that our son will read our amalgamated collection and become the world's first fully rounded person. My other hope – that Ladybird would revive the non-fiction series in order to fill the ever-growing gaps in my knowledge of the contemporary world – was fulfilled in 2017, with the publication of the first books in a new Ladybird Expert series, including volumes on climate change, quantum mechanics, evolution, the Battle of Britain and Ernest Shackleton. This is a good start, but

I need much more. I need ones on Syria, Brexit and Putin's Russia, along with new additions to the old How It Works series; Mortgages and Pensions, Antidepressants, Maintaining Your Sanity on Mumsnet Given the Impossibility of Staying Away from Mumsnet.* Could someone see to it, please? Ta.

Dahl

Eventually, and in the safety of my own home, I broke – after a fashion – the tyranny of the 'safe' story. I discovered Roald Dahl. Dad had brought home *The Magic Finger*, which – looking back – was an odd one for him to choose. It's not one of the famous ones, perhaps because it's not 'pure' Dahl. It's the story of an unnamed eight-year-old girl who is deeply angered by her neighbours, the Greggs, who hunt animals for pleasure (Dahl was an ardent anti-bloodsporter all his life). She possesses a magical power to transmogrify people, so she changes the Greggs into ducks. They find themselves threatened with their own guns by the birds whose children they killed on their last hunt. It was written in

* Meanwhile, I am greatly enjoying the pastiche series. The page in *The Ladybird Book of The Hipster* – 'Hipsters think plates are very old-fashioned. They prefer to eat from planks, tiles and first-generation iPads. This tofu self-identifying cross-species is being served on a spring-loaded folder that contains the script of a short film about a skateboarding shoelace designer', alongside the picture from *The Gingerbread Man* of him on a baking tray – is the only thing that can still make me laugh sober.

1962 as one of a series of books that the publisher had planned for beginner readers, using words only from approved vocabulary lists, which were very much in educational vogue at the time. So although many Dahl touches are there (there's a twist at the end as befits the writer of the dark adult short stories he was then most famous for, and the vengeance theme is treated as robustly as it is in all his other children's books), it was at least in part an exercise for him rather than the usual explosion of anarchic brilliance touched off by a moment of natural, inner inspiration. No matter. I liked it, I looked out for the writer's name and I soon found it – on *Fantastic Mr Fox* and *James and the Giant Peach* from Lucy Donovan's bookshelf, *George's Marvellous Medicine* from Dad and on *The Twits*, which our teacher read to us at school.

I enjoyed them all, with reservations. *The Twits* and *Fantastic Mr Fox* gave me no one to root for (the Twits were irredeemably vile and all the other characters were simply ciphers; Mr Fox's stealing was bad and the fact that Boggis, Bunce and Bean were worse didn't really pull the universe into alignment for me). *James and the Giant Peach* fell foul of my talking animals rule (also, rereading it now with Alexander it does – by Dahl's standards especially – take an AGE to get going) and I adored my own grandmothers so unconditionally that *George's Marvellous Medicine* simply made no sense to me.

But then came *Charlie and the Chocolate Factory*. *Charlie and the Chocolate Factory* had everything. *Charlie and the Chocolate Factory* WAS everything.

Perhaps it most spoke to me at the time because, like

its hero, I wasn't getting enough chocolate either. Or sweets. Not because we were poor, like Charlie, and not because my parents – and I need to be very clear about this again, because they will sue – were hippy, anti-sugar, pro-wholegrain types, but because in their minds rationing still hadn't ended. In our house, butter was only for grown-ups. Children got margarine. We weren't allowed a drink with soup, because my mother insisted that soup was a drink AND a meal. And so on. So chocolate, sweets, biscuits and so on were rarely seen, especially in comparison to the abundance in which they existed in my schoolmates' houses. I was allowed to take a decorous few (OR a fairy cake) at parties, or a chocolate digestive after lunch on a Saturday and Sunday, and my beloved grandmas each gave me a Cadbury's Buttons egg every Easter. Outside that, it was lean pickings. I knew intimately Charlie's experience of watching children wolfing down seemingly illimitable quantities of chocolate, and yes indeed, it was pure torture; I could only imagine how much more intense the longing to have your mouth filled with that rich, creamy sweetness would be for someone on a pure cabbage diet.

But *Charlie* transported me with other delights, too. First published in 1964 it remains, I think, Dahl's masterpiece. The conceit is simplicity itself; a poor but deserving child wins a golden ticket to a semi-magical chocolate factory run by a mesmerisingly maverick inventor, Willy Wonka. His fellow winners are uniformly awful and (this being a traditional fairy tale with modern trimmings) justly punished for the various sins they embody. And Charlie inherits the factory.

Narratively, it is all as richly and deliciously satisfying as a bar of Whipplescrumptious Fudgemallow Delight. I also remember vividly that unexpected and at the time unprecedented breaking of the fourth wall at the beginning of the book: 'This is Charlie. How d'you do? He is pleased to meet you.' That sense of a supportive hand reaching out from the book to take yours is very comforting to a young reader.

But it was the energy and invention underpinning it that kept me going back and back for more. The chocolate river, mixed by waterfall. The edible meadow (mint grass! Of course). A boat made out of a boiled sweet. The idea of the gum alone I could sit and contemplate for hours. A tiny stick of gum! That held a three-course meal! Imagine! The amount of detail in the drawing on the front cover, by Faith Jaques, of the machine that produced it suggested that even if it wasn't quite a possibility yet, it soon would be. Clearly someone only had to retro-engineer her design.* These inventions

* Just as everyone has 'their' James Bond or Doctor Who, so everyone has 'their' edition of favourite childhood books. For anyone who like me came of Dahl-reading age in the mid-1970s to late 1980s, Jaques is the illustrator of 'our' Charlie. She always grounded her drawings in reality and amassed (for this was before the Internetz, children) a collection of 15,000 pictures of clothes, food, faces, architecture, plants, animals, games and everything in between to help her research. That's why her squirrels looks so squirrelly, Charlie looks so starving and the gum machine – monochrome inside the book, but with glorious green metalwork and multicoloured pipes on the cover – really looks like it might work. AND she was a compulsive reader who loved to be alone and kept cats because they were the only pets that allowed her to be both. I could not love her more. She

were all perfect examples of Dahl's unerring ability to craft ideas that slotted perfectly into the waiting imaginations of childish minds.

And then of course there's Willy Wonka. He's an avatar of Dahl himself – maverick, unpredictable (it is his irresponsible-adult reactions to his child visitors and their fates that gives the story its torque), teetering on the brink of arrogance, but always so charismatic that you forgive him everything and follow him anywhere. And of course, they were both devoted lovers of chocolate. To the end of his life, Dahl kept a red plastic box of all the chocolate bars he considered the best (mostly the ones that were invented during chocolate's heyday in the 1930s, when the Quaker families of Rowntree, Cadbury and Fry were pouring all the innovation their religion forbade them applying to the alcohol or caffeinated beverage industry into sweet production and coming up with the likes of Dairy Milk, KitKat, Maltesers and all the delicious rest) that would be pulled out at the end of however posh a meal and however grand the guests who had enjoyed it, as a final course.

Dahl's ego being what it was (healthy – as an adored eldest son and a boy of genuine charisma and sporting talent Dahl always had a fair degree of self-confidence and his subsequent life as a wartime fighter ace, spy, famous author and husband of the film star Patricia Neal did nothing to dent it), he is probably his own

---

also illustrated possibly my favourite children's book of all time, *Private – Keep Out*, and its two sequels. BUT WE'LL GET TO THAT.

inspiration for the father in the next Dahl book I read: *Danny the Champion of the World*. This is one of Dahl's quieter affairs, but still with another wonderful conceit at its heart: a carefully planned and brilliantly executed mass sedation – via sleeping-pill-stuffed raisins – and evacuation of a horrible local landowner's stock of pheasants before his annual shoot, and a truly touching evocation of the loving relationship between a boy and a father who at first seems blandly competent but is revealed to be a fascinating well of hidden passions, quirks and recondite knowledge who is willing to induct his son into a life of glorious adventure.

I remember being surprised that my very staid, reliable teacher Mrs Robson read *The Twits* to us. But now it makes more sense to me. For all their inventiveness and surface anarchy, Dahl's stories are, at bottom, quite safe. The good are rewarded, the bad are punished. *Charlie*, *The Twits*, *The Witches* et al. are all ancient fables in modern dress, innovative in content, not form. They were all fun and bracing reads that occasionally butted up my conservative, Tiger-wary boundaries, but they never breached them.

Strangely, I cannot say quite the same today. Reading Dahl to Alexander as I am just starting to do, I find myself not exactly in sympathy with (all) the critics he has had over the years, but certainly less than as wholly sanguine about him as I was. I don't mind the frequent swiftness and brutality of his narrative justice, unmuddied by any modern nonsense about moral relativism (Dahl's was very much a pre-1960s sensibility), unconcerned about the possible bruising of young readers' tender psyches. This is an intrinsic part of fairy tale and fable, and children are well able to understand it as a literary convention, not instruction or benediction.

But there IS something quite aggressive about his treatment of George's grandma that goes beyond childish exaggeration or burlesque. To call it misogyny, a charge that has been levelled several times at Dahl over the years, particularly after the publication of *The Witches*, I would still say is going too far. If you're going to call Dahl a misogynist, you have to ignore the heroic grandmother in *The Witches* itself, Matilda, Miss Honey, and a number of other matters – including the fact that those who damn him for the awfulness of James' aunts must also be required to damn everyone from Richmal Crompton to P. G. Wodehouse for their similar dependence on ill-favoured kinswomen. But. But. There IS a touch of sadism about some of the punishments doled out, and it IS disproportionately often that fat people and vulgar people are their recipients. I see now, for the first time, why he has always made some adults feel uncomfortable – and indeed some children. The writer, and editor of the *Author* magazine, James McConnachie remembers reading Dahl as a six- and seven-year-old and feeling uncomfortable and 'dirty' afterwards. He was unquestionably a preternaturally mature and sensitive reader, as befits a man who would grow up to be a writer and the editor of the *Author* magazine, but still – it gives another pause for thought.

All that said – I must discount here, as I must discount in many areas of life, the oversensitivities brought on by motherhood. I am these days basically someone who would crawl into a lead-lined bunker with my child for the rest of my and his days, because my being is secretly strung to the single desire to keep him safe rather than allow him any quality of life at all. Once that underlying pulse of madness is controlled, I can see that Dahl is still, surely, a force for good. With my rational side to the fore, I cannot honestly feel that Alexander is likely to be damaged by even repeated exposure to Charlie et al., even if I am nevertheless quietly glad that he currently prefers Dahl's later books – *The BFG* and *Matilda* – by which time Dahl had mellowed, just slightly, with age and started to let some kindness in.

*

But all these critical complexities lay far in my future. For now, all was mindless, glorious consumption. Dahl, Ladybirds, Ramona, Flat Stanley, Happy Families and myriad Antelopes – all in all, I was evolving a diverse and flourishing mental landscape. In between all the books I remember in detail at this distance were dozens more about which I retain only hazy – though equally happy – memories. The slim paperback biography of Louis Braille, housed in the classroom bookcase, which told how as he was punching through leather with an awl one day as a child it slipped and stabbed him through the eye. It became infected and the infection soon spread to the other eye too, leaving him blind. By the age of fifteen he had developed a tactile alphabet using six raised dots arranged in different patterns, and opened up a way to transform millions upon millions of lives. (And, incidentally, to give bookworms something to cling to on the nights when they wake up gibbering in fear at the thought of losing their sight and not being able to read again.) *The Bears' Bazaar* (bears, making things for a bazaar). A *Giant Book of Fantastic Facts.* Joke books. Pop-up books (including Jan Pienowski's magisterial Haunted House). A tiny little book about the origins of sayings and proverbs. *It's Not the End of the World, Danny* about a boy with epilepsy and a teacher who was frightened of him. A proto-survival manual in the children's section of Torridon Library that taught you how to live off the land (or, in my case, taught you that it all sounded like very hard, time-consuming work and that if there ever was a global disaster you would, all things considered, probably just prefer to read until all the food in the kitchen was gone and you quietly starved to death). There was also a story about a girl's family moving house (which I read and reread trying to understand why she wasn't having a nervous breakdown at the prospect), one about the exciting parts of history that had an eye-opening chapter on dungeons, thumbscrews and iron maidens, and after that, dozens of others which have vanished from conscious memory altogether, though I like to think somewhere in my deep unconscious they all did their bit, tilling the soil, fertilising it, making it ready for other books, words and ideas to take root in time.

This was all about to end. A species of invasive megafauna was about to arrive and colonise my mind. Enter Enid.

4

The Blyton Interregnum

I can barely bring myself to talk about my Enid Blyton years. Who wants to let daylight in upon magic? Like generations of children before me (Blyton published her first book – of poems for young readers – in 1922 and her first full-length book for them in 1937) and like generations since (she still sells over 8 million copies a year around the world) I fell head over heels in love. No, not love – it was an obsession, an addiction. It was wonderful.

It was an older girl that got me into the stuff. Becky-next-door lent me her copy of something called *Five on a Secret Trail*. It was a floppy, late 1970s Knight Books edition with, I believe, the original 1950s illustrations inside. I read it. It was good. Very good. I enjoyed it. I enjoyed it very much. I asked Becky if she had any more. She did. It was called *Five Run Away Together.* I read it. It was good. Very good. Possibly even better than *Five on a Secret Trail*. I enjoyed it. I enjoyed it very much. I noticed it had a number '3' on the spine. *Five on a Secret Trail* had a '15'. What did that mean? I decided to look for clues. Even without a loyal canine companion to help me, it didn't take long. The endpapers carried a list. Apparently Enid Blyton had written twenty-one books! What excellent news! What riches! What vital, absolutely essential riches!

I took the news and the list to my parents. 'I'm going to need all of these,' I said, gently.

And so it began.

Looking back, Blyton's blissful reign over my life seems to have lasted both forever and no time at all. In fact it was about two years. Because of course the former schoolteacher-turned-publishing phenomenon hadn't just written twenty-one books. She had written around 760 in the course of her fifty-year career. It was so hard to keep up with her (and publishers weren't as punctilious about record-keeping then as now) that it is impossible to say exactly. At her peak she was writing 10,000 words a day – on a typewriter perched on her knee – and had thirty-seven books published in a single year.

She once explained in correspondence with a psychologist who was researching writers' creative processes how it was that she could produce such astonishing amounts of material. She described having her characters always walking and talking in her head, and needing only to look in on their dialogue and actions for her next story. It was, she said, 'simply a matter of opening the sluice gates and out it all pours with no effort or labour of my own. This is why I can write so much and so quickly – it's all I can do to keep up with it, even typing at top speed.'

All of which meant that I had the fruits of half a century's diligent dictation-taking at my disposal. Even allowing for my disdain for the series for very young readers (I had my six- to eight-year-old pride), involving

Amelia Jane, Wishing Chairs, Faraway Trees and something called Noddy, there was still enough to let me gorge unceasingly. She wasn't my sole sustenance (though when not with her I was still more likely to be found rereading old favourites like *Lucy Runs Away* and *The Worst Witch* than trying new things) but she was unquestionably my staple diet. I was in thrall to alpha-male Julian, dickless Dick, poor Anne, proto-feminist/Sapphic role model George and her loyal, rabbit-loving dog Timmy, a character only marginally simpler than the rest. And then to the Secret Seven, the girls of Malory Towers and St Clare's, the Five Find-Outers and Dog, and the children (and parrot Kiki) in the Island/Castle/Valley/Sea/Any Other Concrete Noun adventure series. They went down whole and never touched the sides. I snacked on stand-alones (or near stand-alones) like *Come to the Circus!*, *Six Cousins at Mistletoe Farm*, *Children of Willow Farm* and the Adventurous Four in between. I read and reread the captivating stories that I didn't know had long ago become cultural clichés. I thrilled wholeheartedly to the thought of finding smugglers in coves, camping on moors, stuffing my face with the home-grown produce that was apparently handed out gladly and for free by apple-cheeked farmers' wives, and asked for nothing more out of life than that one day I, too, would get to sleep on a bracken bed under a starlit sky, next to the picturesque ruins of a castle on an island owned by a gender-busting friend of mine as unswervingly loyal and good-hearted as her dog. The Owl Who Was Afraid of the Dark, Milly-Molly-Mandy, *The Worst Witch*, Teddy Robinson, Maggie Gumption, Ramona and Beezus – they had been good. Blyton was better.

Love, of course, blinds us to all faults. While child readers had been consuming her unstoppably and en masse since she started writing in the 1920s, and her popularity amongst them had only grown as the decades wore on, there had always been adult critics on hand to adumbrate and condemn her limitations. In the 1930s the BBC effectively banned her from the airwaves because they deemed her output to be of an insufficiently high literary quality. In the mid-1950s, the stricture was only reluctantly lifted. The head of the BBC's schools broadcasting department at the time, Jean Sutcliffe, explained the lifting (and possibly, inadvertently, much else about the BBC at the time) thus: 'No writer of real merit could possibly go on believing that this mediocre material is of the highest quality and turn it out in such incredible quantities. Her capacity to do so amounts to genius and it is here that she has beaten everyone to a standstill. Anyone else would have died of boredom long ago.' Several libraries still refused to stock her, again on the grounds of (lack of) merit. The pioneering librarian Eileen Colwell (who was a gifted storyteller in her own right and possibly a little frustrated by Blyton's output, whose sheer volume did tend to crowd other writers out of the marketplace) summed up the literary world and many 'smart' parents' feelings about Blyton's relentlessly formulaic resolutions of fantastical plots when she mockingly reviewed *The Sea of Adventure* in 1948. 'But what hope', she asked rhetorically, 'has a band of desperate men against four children?'

It pains me more than I can say to admit the truth of such criticisms, but I must. It ranks as one of the greatest disappointments of my adult life to discover on returning to the serried ranks of Blytonian tomes that line the far wall of my study that they have become in the cruelly intervening years, unreadable.

That I never even contemplated such a possibility, even though a moment's reflection on her work-rate alone should have told me it was not one that lent itself to the refining of prosaic ore into literary gold, is a testament to the strength of her hold over me during those obsessive years. But of course it is true. She was a one-woman mass production line, turning out workmanlike units that perfectly serve a particular need at a particular time in a child's life, not finely wrought pieces of art destined to have their secrets delicately unpicked over the years by a gradually maturing sensibility. That cinemascopic mind was of course a unique gift in itself, but not one of the same order as the subtle, layered genius of Rumer Godden, the light, delicate evocations and humour of Teddy R's creator Joan G. Robinson, or the darkly flashing visions of Maurice Sendak, all of whose works – along with those of a million other children's authors I was yet to meet – would turn out to provide countless rewarding rereads at any age.

So what was her secret? What did she do for me and innumerable thousands of other children to cause us to count her amongst our greatest loves and most important formative reading experiences?

Blyton gained her greatest popularity during the Second World War and its aftermath, when readily identifiable villains and the neat resolution of tangible, finite problems doubtless fed a heightened need in children for reassurance that justice can, will and should prevail. She was national comfort reading at a time when mental and emotional resources were too depleted to deal with anything more complex. The need for books that functioned amongst anxious, insecure and often fatherless (temporarily, as men were called up, permanently if the worst happened) children as a refuge was wider and deeper than it had ever been.

Now, her success still depends on such feelings, but on a smaller, more individual scale. When you're young, even if you like it and are good at it, reading is hard. It is important to have somewhere you can go and know that your efforts are guaranteed to be rewarded. You need a satisfying story and an unbroken contract of delivery from your author. And you know – you know as surely as there are Findus Crispy Pancakes for tea and *Wonder Woman* on at seven – Enid Blyton will provide. It is exactly the same instinct that will, when you are an adult and knackered, lead you to Lee Child and reruns of *Law & Order: SVU* instead of Trollope and the BBC2 documentary about Ugandan politics. Like a good thriller or police procedural she is a great de-baffler and balm to the soul. Her characters, male or female (or canine or psittacine) have, like Jack Reacher or Eliot Stabler, only the barest, simplest of psychologies. With Julian, the O'Sullivan twins, Fatty, Peter or any of the rest, to think is to act. To feel is to express, in thunderously straightforward manner. 'I say Gwen/Peter/Margery – you are the most tremendous sneak/ass/rescuer of Erica from the burning sanatorium! Jolly bad/good show!' No misdirection, no circuitous calculations, no contrary thoughts held in the same head, no messy, true humanity of any kind. Restful. Sometimes you've just gotta take a break from it all, y'know?

More positively, Blyton lays down a great base for future reading. Her formulaic stories build an unyielding confidence within the young consumer. One expert in children's literature, Victor Watson, called Blyton 'the great nanny-narrator'. She leads her charges slowly and carefully by the hand through plots that may make the *Beano* look like Tolstoy – and in prose that definitely makes the *Beano* look like Tolstoy – but nannies are there to keep you safe, to make you feel secure. Real ones do it by not letting you roam too far in the park and not leaving you alone in the bath. Writerly ones do it by keeping their descriptions simple (Blyton uses only a handful of adjectives, the main two of which – 'queer!' and 'rather queer!' – weren't even as interesting then as they are now) and their characters simpler still as they march them towards their neat conclusions and happy endings. All is literal. Nothing is evoked. All is illuminated. No dark shadows lurk. She sweeps and tidies as she goes. The band of desperate men have no hope against four children.

So. Blyton is not demanding. She is not an expander of minds like any one of the imaginatively and linguistically gifted authors already mentioned or still to be discussed. Her great gift lies in proving beyond doubt to children that reading can be fun, and reliably so. That the marks on the page will translate into life and colour and movement with ease. This is a thing you can master, a foundation upon which you can build, and also a retreat into which you can escape. She makes it all possible, time and time again. It was for this reason that Roald Dahl – whose own professed primary aim in writing for children was always to entertain them and thus induct them into the world of books – went to bat for her when he was on the 1988 Committee on English in the National Curriculum. He fell out with the rest of the board on the issue of whether her books should be welcomed in schools. Despite being no fan of either the work or the woman (he played bridge with her once and said afterwards that she had the mind of a child) he thought they should be embraced because they got children reading. The rest of the board disagreed and Dahl resigned his place.

Books were already my delight but I came to believe in both their power and in myself as a reader through Blyton. For others – later starters than me, perhaps, off making friends and developing early social skills instead of communing with baby owls and noting down old words for marzipan, or for children with less support at home or school – the Blyton effect was more dramatic. If you don't have a father on hand to walk you through, supplying you with synonyms and explaining turns of phrase, or able to delve deeper with you into quirks of human nature you've found on the page but not yet experienced in real life, then a nanny-narrator is a very good substitute. Blyton becomes the wedge that first cracks open the pleasure-filled world of reading; Kirrin Island the promontory from which you catch your first glimpse of the promised land.

Beyond what she offers children as readers lies what she offers to them as negotiators of the real world. If she does not explain it, she at least offers refuge from its growing emotional complexities. Blytonmania tends to hit just as the halcyon days of early childhood are beginning to retreat. Life was beginning to tell on me a bit.

As well as the growing cliquery of school, where the girls had taken to forming and reforming into tiny splinter groups in accordance with a logic as convoluted as it was unspoken, work was becoming harder. Maths, for example, had stopped being about adding up tens or taking away units and become about dividing and multiplying and occasionally even about drawing graphs. Worst of all, a teacher had introduced the concept of nuclear war in some lesson or other, which dreadful information burrowed deeply into my brain and festered there for months. I felt doomed mathematically, actually and socially. When the mental ulcer caused by my nuclear-war worries finally burst (the promise of post-apocalyptic solitude could not salve it forever), I spent nights convulsed with fear and hacking sobs under the bedclothes until my mother heard me, held me and once again placed unbreachable maternal barriers between me and my demons. She promised, above all, that the four-minute warning would never go off while I was at school. 'There'll be a lot of fuss before then,' she promised. 'So we'll know if it's likely and we'll keep you and your sister off school and all die together.' This, I thought, would be fine.

What people forget about pessimists is that although we're often anxious, we're also very easily pleased.

*

Concerns about quality and literary merit, however, gave way in the 1960s and 70s to more troubling questions about prejudice in Blyton. She and her books were a product of their time (and again, that work rate and that temperament did not lend themselves to a detached consideration or critical analysis of her books' contents or possible effects) and the unholy trinity of sexism, class snobbery and racism could all be found therein. She was removed from many libraries (slightly bowdlerised editions started returning in the 1980s, but I don't remember any at all in my local or school library) and – if your parents had any pretentions to liberalism or to what was not yet called political correctness but which amounted to the same thing – from homes.

At the time, of course, I noticed none of this. I noticed that Anne was always the one set to work making bracken beds and cooking meals for five on a tiny oil stove, but I thought this was because she was a drip rather than because she was a girl.

But perhaps she was (too) a drip into the ocean of assumptions about what boys were and did and what girls were and did, in which I swam unknowing, as we all do. I can't deny the possibility – even the likelihood – that she was, with every fresh-laid egg she boiled for Dick and Ju, undoing the good Annabelle in *Sugarpink Rose* had wrought and crippling what would otherwise have been my flourishing sense of the unfettered possibilities of womanhood. At least, not without effectively claiming that I alone amongst humanity am impervious to all external influences. This seems a bit of a reach.

Class snobbery, I must confess, I missed altogether. If my fellow or today's readers recognise(d) the Secret Seven's cheery politeness to coalmen and groundskeepers as condescension to the working classes, they are better social historians than I ever was. And if readers of her own time recognised it, then they should have become Marxist revolutionaries and overthrown the whole system by the time I got there forty years later. I would still have enjoyed the stories but cursed the dialectic, comrade.

But again, you don't have to notice these things to be affected by them. In fact, it's probably better for an ideology's propagation if you don't, which is why the question of her attitude to race is a particularly difficult one for a fan (or erstwhile fan) to face. As I learned the word 'swarthy' for the first time, it's hard not to suspect that I was – less directly, more insidiously – also learning that it was shorthand for 'foreigner', 'gypsy' and 'criminal', and that the three were virtually interchangeable. I had more overt rebuttals of these messages, at home and at school – especially the latter, where in a 1980s multi-ethnic institution the need was rightly felt to be increasingly pressing – than I did of the notion that girls were generally more useless than boys at anything but domestic tasks. But if I was internalising the latter to any degree, I must also have been doing so with other, even less savoury messages.

For young readers today, I wonder whether the protections have reversed. As the fine spray of fourth-wave feminism begins to permeate everything around her, I can imagine eight-year-old Jemima iPad being puzzled or infuriated by Anne's role – or perhaps simply pitying it – but Blyton's distaste for anyone not dazzlingly white can more easily be imagined as playing into the prejudices that are an ever more live issue today.

Many of Blyton's most egregious examples of racism have been quietly removed. *The Little Black Doll* (an Enid

Blyton Sunshine Picture Book, first published in 1965), about a gollywog who had his blackness gloriously washed away by 'magic rain' by a helpful pixie ('No wonder he's happy – little pink Sambo'), was – surprisingly – reprinted in 1976 but has not been seen since. This, and the expunging of troubling adjectives, is a level of censorship I can accept. To leave them in, in order to maintain a sense of period or cleave to the author's vision, risks too much harm – especially in view of this author's vision being more akin to dictation – for too little good. What you find, at best, amongst supporters of leaving things unaltered is a presupposition that all children have on hand a watchful adult who can inoculate them against any unbeneficial effects via lively, contextualising lit-crit debate whenever a 'dirty caravanner' pops up. And this is, of course, not so.

In more recent years, the debate has been over how much to update the rest of Blyton's language. A few years ago the Famous Five were brought out in new editions, to be sold alongside the previous ones, that had had their vocabularies 'subtly' updated by the publisher so that they did not alienate readers – as, in the publisher's view they were now at risk of doing. 'Mother and father' became 'Mum and Dad', 'school tunic' became 'school uniform', 'She must be jolly lonely all by herself' was changed to 'She must get lonely all by herself' and so on.

The cost/benefit analysis of this works out very differently from that of excising racist terms and attitudes. The benefits amount to a short-term gain in immediate comprehensibility but amongst the costs we can count the fact that a constant updating of books decreases the opportunities for making those little intellectual leaps that make reading both fun and valuable. If 'straw boaters' had been replaced by 'hats' or excised entirely in Dorita Fairlie Bruce's Dimsie adventures, I probably still wouldn't know what they were. A few years later I would feel the rush of triumph when I worked out what 'colours' were in Antonia Forest's *Autumn Term*, although it took me most of the book and the end-of-term prize-giving scene to be sure that they were indeed a kind of sporting award. Children can and should be left with these little leaps to make. No harm will come to them. If a child reader cannot discern the meaning of 'school tunic' from its context, said child reader shouldn't be left unsupervised on the sofa with a book anyway, lest they accidentally suffocate themselves in the cushions or blind themselves with their own thumbs.

In addition, such changes collapse time and remove all sense of history. But placement in time is important. As a child you naturally believe that the world around you is immutable. A gradual realisation that people once spoke, dressed and even thought differently from the way we do is a profound pleasure. 'Queer' once primarily meant 'odd'. How weird. A tunic and a boater comprised a uniform. One day, of course, our children will be asking, 'What's a uniform?' and we will have to revise again. 'The honour of the school' was once a real and motivating force. I remember asking a teacher about the last one. She gazed at me with such sadness that I wished I had one of those handkerchief things I'd also read about. It struck me they would have been as good for mopping tears as they were for binding gorse-wrenched ankles during cliff-top rescues.

Without a sense of time, the integrity of the book begins to break down. More changes will soon be needed to make sense of 'mums and dads' who let their children roam free on Kirrin Island. Of girls who 'get lonely' because they are forced to stay behind and make bracken beds and tea for the boys. Root out 'jolly' and you have to root out all these oddities – and the gorse bushes, too. How likely is it, after all, that our increasingly urbanised young population has ever seen one of them? And then you'll be left with an awfully queer set of books indeed.

It was with a great sense of satisfaction, therefore, that I greeted the recent announcement that the updated books are to be discontinued. Parents, who still buy the bulk of books for children of Blyton-reading age, were apparently staying away in droves. I suspect this was for nostalgic reasons rather than philosophical principle, but hey – whatever works, right?

Perhaps years and years and years from now, Blyton's 1950s idioms will be truly impenetrable and change will be genuinely necessary if she is to continue to be fit for her particular purpose, which is to serve perfectly the purely narrative appetite of a child that precedes more sophisticated tastes – and which must be stimulated and satisfied if those tastes are ever to develop. If the gap between her written and their modern language becomes wide enough to deny children this inestimable good and this incalculable pleasure, then by all means let us throw our handkerchiefs, uniforms, mothers and fathers to the wind. But we are not there yet.

*

All that said, when I look ahead to my son's Enid Blyton years* I am divided. On the one hand, I long simply for him to be reading independently (and not just because it will leave me with much more time to read myself, though this is a large part of it and also a large part of what makes me a terrible mother) and to find as much happiness there as I did. On the other – if he finds his reading feet amongst more modern fare, less riven with outmoded attitudes and almost certainly better written (as virtually all contemporary writing for children is, the market and level of competition having changed beyond all recognition since Blyton's day), there would be relief in that.

But imagine having a child who had never raced around Kirrin Island with the Five, or crammed into the meeting shed with the Secret Seven, or teased the village policeman with Fatty ('What's a village policeman, Mummy? And couldn't even Enid have come up with a less profoundly literal, deadeningly prosaic title for a series than "the Five Find-Outers and Dog?"'), or swum in the rock pools of Malory Towers with Darrell and the gang. Bone of my bone, flesh of my flesh he may be, but could we ever really be close without that?

My parents did their duty unquestioningly and

* They may not come, of course. Some children pick her up, do not like her and put her down again. These are generally clever, sensitive children who are more or less born ready for literature and for whom an absence of psychological realism and complexity is both baffling and frustrating rather than soothing or relaxing. I think my son – who is currently trying to burst a balloon with his teeth – will have his Enid Blyton years.

unhesitatingly, simply shovelling the necessary volumes at their grateful (albeit wordlessly – sorry about that) offspring for the two years or so the enchantment held and trusting that something would eventually come along to break the spell. I can hardly do less for my own.

I won't even have to spend the money that they did. All my paperbacks are here waiting for him. They are mostly horrible Knight editions – not like Becky's – with stills from various television series* on the covers instead of proper illustrations, a practice I abhorred then and abhor now because there are some prejudices we should never give up. The remainder have awful 1980s drawings of schoolgirls in modern uniforms and clutching modern pencil cases, but they are mine. I may now read 'em and weep with boredom, but it was not ever thus. Every volume is a slice of my heart. How can my son, who is all the other bits of my heart, not take them down from the shelf and complete the circle? What else do we have kids – or keep our horrible Knight editions – for?

I wish I could say that a particular book came along and broke the spell. It would be much more dramatically

* Which I did not see. I was four in 1978 when the Famous Five adaptation began, and in those days, children, if you missed something on TV even by a day, an hour or a minute, let alone five or six years, that was it. No iPlayer, no YouTube, no Netflix, no second chances, that was it. You were done. Oh, the past was cruel. But – fun fact for you! – the actor who played Dick in the Famous Five series also played Lord Edward Dark in the Dark Towers serial which was part of the BBC's Look and Read series that had Wordy teaching us all about Magic E! Pleasing, no?

pleasing if I suddenly happened across a set of Dickens or something – calfskin-bound in a dusty attic I was exploring one Sunday at a friend's house, why not? Or on the book stall at the school fete – whose fragile, ancient pages revealed to me a whole new world, a transformative understanding of what life and literature could be. But I didn't. Wrong kind of friends (none), wrong kind of houses (modern, non-rambling) and wrong kind of school.

Instead, I came out of my Blyton phase slowly, as one emerges from a fog, until I stood blinking dazedly in the sunlight, ready for something new. My eight-year-old mind wanted something more. It didn't know precisely what. But something.

While I'd been away, several new additions had been made to my bookcase by my dad and occasional visiting relatives. They had been bought as tokens of faith in a non-Blyted reading future, looked for a long time like hostages to fortune but now they took on the sheen of sound investment as I turned my avid, covetous gaze upon them. What was there? A golden age.

5

Through a Wardrobe

The first book I picked out of the waiting row was pale pink and earned my respect immediately because, like Milly-Molly-Mandy's adventures, it had been both written and illustrated by one person – in this case, a former art student called Eve Garnett. She had been commissioned in 1927 to illustrate a book called *The London Child* by the suffragette and social reformer Evelyn Sharp about working-class conditions in the capital. The book I was holding in my hands fifty years on had grown out of the research Garnett did for that commission. It was called *The Family from One End Street* and told the story of the Ruggles family – two parents (dad a dustman, mum a laundrywoman) and seven children, Lily-Rose, Kate, Jim, John, Jo, Peggy and William – who lived at number 1, One End Street in a small town called Otwell-on-the-Ouse. I was captivated by it from the start, including and especially the drawings – as sweet, strong and deceptively simple as the book itself – because I knew, as I had known with Milly-Molly-Mandy, that they depicted the 'real' thing, straight from their creator's pen. (I was, I see now, bound to end up the person I have indeed become – one who screams herself hoarse before the television screen and seeks to bring down the blackest curses upon any casting director who has deviated from the on-page description of anyone in a book's adaptation).

Unlike Blyton, *The Family from One End Street* was episodically structured – each chapter is a little self-contained adventure had by one of the children – and all the characters were all rendered equally lively and interesting but all utterly different from each other and all utterly real. It was the first book I had loved for a long time for its characters rather than its plot.

It was also the first book – not only for me, but for all of its readers when it was first published in 1937 – to make urban, working-class children its heroes. It was almost universally lauded for this upon publication. Some critics later came to discern a patronising tone from Garnett towards her characters, but others praised her for avoiding both sentimentality and condescension and replacing them with what one called 'a careful truthfulness' instead.

Not that I knew or cared about any of this at the time, of course. I just knew it was a strange relief to spend time with book-children who, like me (whatever the technical differences in our respective classes were), had more experience of a world bounded by building sites, patches of grubby parkland and knackered working parents than they did of one strewn with rolling moors, private islands and spies.

The Family from One End Street won the Carnegie Medal in 1937/8. It beat – and this gladdens my heart more than it should, for reasons we'll come to soon – *The Hobbit*. Eve Garnett should, as far as I was concerned, have had at least another two medals under her belt. Because even better than her first book, I soon discovered, was the sequel – *Further Adventures of the Family from One End Street* – in which Peg, Jo and Kate go to recuperate from measles in The Countryside, the place I longed to be and which I was still unaware lay barely a dozen miles south of Catford. The rest of the family remain in Otwell having almost equal fun raising a pig on the allotment. Even better than that was *its* sequel, when Kate gets to return sans siblings to the picture-perfect village of Upper Cassington and stay for the whole summer with the Wildgooses, owners of the local hostelry, in *Holiday at the Dew Drop Inn*. This seamless progression gave me a wholly misguided sense of life as a process of cumulative improvement, which would take several painful years of experience to dispel, but on the plus side, *Holiday at the Dew Drop Inn* trod the pleasures of reading even deeper into my soul than Enid had.

It was as if, with the story of Kate Ruggles' summer-long stay and enthusiastic embrace of village life in Upper Cassington, Eve Garnett had peered into my mind and written down exactly what she knew would delight me most. It was Milly-Molly-Mandy writ longer and with a character I could feel in my very bones. Kate, you see, was bookish. She was the reader in the family and had her heart set on a scholarship to the local grammar school. And she longed to live in the country, not the town. I didn't know exactly what a scholarship or grammar school was, but I knew that they were things from The Past and that I too would have wanted both if I had not had the towering misfortune to have been born in The Now. She was me and I was her and when, in the midst of my devotion, the Mangan family rented a cottage in Cornwall for our fortnight's summer holiday for the first time instead of staying with Grandma in her Preston flat for a fortnight, it was as if the already porous boundary between books and reality had finally done the decent thing and collapsed completely. I looked up from Kate's collection of wild flowers and water lilies for the village fete and saw them as well. She wandered in awe along overgrown lanes and I totally would have too if I hadn't been so busy reading. But I could see them. My sister went down them and reported back ('Yeah – plants. Fields, both sides. Brown things in one of them. I wanna say – horses?'). By the end of the holiday I knew what Kate meant by cow parsley, stiles and haystacks. I'd seen a thatched roof. It was more than enough.

I identified less thoroughly with the heroine of the next book Dad brought home, but I loved her nevertheless. It was a book by Mary Norton who once described herself as 'a fits and starts writer . . . I love just living – unless some wonderful idea suddenly appears.'

Here in my hand, thirty years after it was first published in 1952, was her most wonderful idea: *The Borrowers* – the story of Arrietty and her parents Homily and Pod Clock, who belong to the race of tiny people who live secretly in the houses of 'human beans', under the floorboards (in the Clocks' case), above the overmantel or behind the pictures on the wall. They use drawing pins as candleholders, stamps as pictures on their own walls, small coins as plates and cotton reels as stools – oh, the joy the skewed perspective conveyed by these repurposed objects gave me! – and that is why you can never lay hands on any of these vital items, no matter how many you know you bought.

Shut up underground, with only a grating to give a glimpse of garden and sky, Arrietty (for years I thought it was a misheard 'borrowing' of 'Harriet', but a musical friend of mine thinks it's meant to recall 'arietta' – a little aria) longs to be taught to 'borrow' and to be allowed outside, despite her people's fear of being seen by their giant, unwitting hosts. This is why our protagonist/reader identification broke down. I could think of nothing worse. Being outside, being actively engaged in honest and/or physical toil does not a happy bookworm make. To this day I cannot relax unless I am wholly enclosed by four sturdy walls and a proper roof, where the wind will stop messing with my clothes and blowing my hair across my face so I can't see the page, and the sun will not cause me to be distracted from full reading-immersion by worrying about skin cancer. My husband puts the fact that I won't even have a window open, even at the height of summer, down to my Irish peasant ancestry. 'It's always raining in your DNA,' he explains. Which may also be true.

But Arrietty is made of braver and livelier stuff and eventually convinces her parents to relent on the borrowing front. She is soon spotted by the lonely boy who has come to stay in the house. They become friends, but when the rest of the household discovers his secret, the Borrowers are no longer safe and and the little family must flee.

The perfectly realised miniature world is, naturally, people's strongest memory of the book. Norton was very short-sighted her whole life and the Borrowers' environment, whether under the floorboards, out and about in the house's drawing room and nursery or in the fields and furrows across which they travel in the sequels, always has an absolute authenticity about it – the textural truth of someone who has spent her life with her nose squashed up close to things. 'Where others saw the far hills, the distant woods, the soaring pheasant,' she once wrote in an essay, 'I, as a child would turn sideways to the close bank, the tree-roots, and the tangled grasses. Moss, fern-stalks, sorrel stems, created the *mise en scène* for a jungle drama . . . One invented the characters – small, fearful people picking their way through miniature undergrowth; one saw smooth places where they might sit and rest; branched stems which might invite them to climb; sandy holes in which they might creep for shelter.'

And of course that kind of detail, with which *The Borrowers* is strewn, is both memorable and delightful. But I suspect that it is often cited simply because it is also the easiest element to put into words. Because if you first read it as a child, you cannot put a name to the uneasy feeling within you that the book evokes, and so perhaps as the years pass, the memory falls away. I had forgotten it myself until I reread the book a few years ago. Beneath the melody of Arrietty's story – the fun and adventures swinging across curtains with your hatpin, meeting the Boy and evading capture by exterminators – there is a haunting strain of melancholy compounded of her hunger for freedom, the fragility of their essentially parasitical lives (part of Arrietty's journey to maturity involves her facing up to what the Boy sees as a self-evident truth – that the Borrowers are dying out) and the ceaseless circumscription of their activities by the need for secrecy and the concentration of generations of fear under the floorboards.

Looking back, I can see that this dark undertow, tugging me in a different direction from where I thought the book should be taking me, was a milestone in what I suppose we should call, though it feels unsuitably clinical, my reading development. Even if I didn't understand fully at the time what was going on, it prepared me at some level for the fact that good fiction – future fiction – might not be just about the story, but that it could and would give a voice and a shape to larger, wider truths. That it could, in short, be greater than the sum of its tiny, perfectly proportioned parts. Now that was indeed a wonderful idea.

The Borrowers was my first foray into fantasy. Technically – and appropriately enough for a beginner who was also temperamentally very much inclined against abrupt change and preferred gradual introductions to new things, if new things had to be introduced at all – it was what is called 'low fantasy'. In other words, very little magic is used – and sometimes, as in *The Borrowers*, none at all. A thing that could not actually occur in reality – like little people living under the floorboards – is simply presupposed to exist and normal life goes on around it. High fantasy is stuff set in alternative 'secondary' worlds, which will have their own internal rules and logic but differ vastly from the real 'primary' world. *Lord of the Rings* is generally held up here as the *ne plus ultra* and possibly the *sine qua non* of the genre and we'll come back to that, even though I get tired just thinking about Tolkien.

Thus I was primed by the little people to take the next step, a little further up, a little further in – to Narnia. I went through the back of a wardrobe, of course.

Narnia

'Here,' said Dad awkwardly, when he handed me a paperback showing a lion and two girls capering on the greensward with a garland of flowers, 'I think you'll like this.' I knew what this kind of impassioned speech signalled. This was not just a book my dad thought I would enjoy. It was a book he had enjoyed as a child. I said thank you and added a nod to show that I had understood. He nodded equally eloquently back. My watching mother rolled her eyes and poured a gin.

The book was called *The Lion, the Witch and the Wardrobe*. 'The *Lion* all began with a picture of a Faun carrying an umbrella and parcels in a snowy wood,' its author C. S. Lewis once wrote. 'This picture had been in my mind since I was about sixteen. Then one day, when I was about forty, I said to myself: "Let's try to make a story about it."'

The heroine was called Lucy. Not enough books, to my mind, had heroines called Lucy. Since reading Catherine Storr's *Lucy* and *Lucy Runs Away*, I had not really seen that there was any argument for calling any heroine anything else. Now, at last, here was another one, and I couldn't have asked anything more of her.

She was brave yet sensible – pushing through those fur coats yet being careful not to close the wardrobe door behind her in case she got trapped – and I knew I shared at least one of these characteristics with her. She was a beleaguered underdog – who isn't? – who nevertheless endures and emerges triumphant, just as I planned to do one day when I was really old, probably about twenty.

Her siblings Peter, Susan and Edmund all eventually follow her through the wardrobe and into the snowy lands of Narnia where it is always winter and yet never Christmas, thanks to the evil spell cast over all by the White Witch. But Edmund has been enchanted by her too, thanks to his greedy acceptance of her proffered Turkish delight (never take sweets from strangers and/or majestic allegorical satanic figures on a sled, kids!) and harbours treacherous intent in his bosom.

On her first visit, Lucy meets a talking lion called Aslan who fills her heart with love and she promises that she will return to help him. But her brothers and sister do not believe her (though Edmund is lying – oh, Edmund! The hate I felt for you then may never fully leave me) and she almost has to go on without them. At the last minute, Aslan becomes visible to them – he exists! In your FACES, arrogant older siblings! – and the stage is set fair for an epic battle between good and evil, sacrifice and selfishness, courage and cowardice played out amongst an array of characters – including Mr Tumnus the faun, Mr and Mrs Beaver, a wish-granting white stag and other talking beasts, unicorns, dryads, dwarves, naiads and centaurs – as the children and Aslan fight to end the reign of the White Witch and restore Narnia to its people. Who will then be ruled over by the four children who will sit as kings and queens at the castle of Cair Paravel, but a benevolent monarchy still beats monstrous dictatorship, so all is well. Their adventures play out against backdrops drawn from the medieval poetry, fairy tale, folk tale, Celtic, Norse and classical myths, legend and scholarship that Lewis loved and had immersed himself in all his life.

Interwoven with these, and providing the overall spine for all seven of the chronicles, is a version of the Christian story, and this aspect has caused some controversy over the years, best summarised by an exchange I had a few years ago with the friend of a friend. I was flicking through the bumper Christmas *Radio Times* at a party, like the vibrant social butterfly I am, when the hostess looked over my shoulder and told me (I don't know why; I hadn't asked her. But that's people for you, always yapping) that she would let her children watch *The Lion, the Witch and the Wardrobe* film that was being advertised as that year's big festive centrepiece but would never buy them the books 'because of the Christianity in them'. She also objected to their snobbery and misogyny – I should have left a set of Enid Blyton behind and listened to the screams all the way home – but apparently trusted the celluloid version to have been run through more modern moral filters and be less injurious to infant psychic health.

I'll be honest with you. I do have one friend who got about halfway through her first perusal, at the age of nine or ten, of *The Lion, the Witch and the Wardrobe*, turned to her mother and said: 'This is about Jesus, isn't it?' But she was the offspring of two vicars (long story) and I suspect at that time was probably seeing Jesus in her cornflakes.

Me? I was about fourteen and ploughing through the very last pages of the final volume in the Narnia series, *The Last Battle*, when the Pevensies return to stay for ever in the magical land after they are killed in a train crash. It was only then – after the biblio-equivalent of being hit over the head with a claw hammer – that I began to feel the semblance of a shadow of an inkling that something funny was going on.

Lewis was an atheist who became a devout and publicly proselytising Christian. By the time *The Lion, the Witch and the Wardrobe* was published he was already famous for his faith and for his accessible prose and radio broadcasts about aspects of his belief, which gave succour and strength to a nation during and after the Second World War. Even as a child there had been times when a profound sense of the ineffable had moved through him. In his autobiography, *Surprised by Joy*, he tells the story of how as a boy his older brother Warnie once constructed a miniature twig-and-moss forest for him on a biscuit-tin lid, and the young Jack (as Clive Staples Lewis was always known by friends and family) was overcome by a mixture of longing and elation: 'an unsatisfied desire that is itself more desirable than any other satisfaction'. That was before his mother died in 1907 when Jack was nine. 'With my mother's death,' he says, 'all settled happiness . . . disappeared from my life. There was to be much fun, many pleasures, many stabs of joy; but no more of the old security. It was sea and islands now; the great continent had sunk like Atlantis.'

Almost immediately afterwards he was sent, by his loving but grieving and misguided father, to a boarding school in England that was run along strange and – even for a child who hadn't just been bereaved and, in effect, abandoned – unsettling lines by a headmaster who was later declared insane. Jack retreated into the Norse myths and legends whose 'pure Northernness' – bleak, wild, cruelly magnificent – was both purgative and balm for a boy in mourning. Out of that came a career at Oxford and then Cambridge, as an English and medieval scholar. He was involved for thirty years from the age of twenty with a woman called Mrs Moore, the mother of his friend Paddy. The young men had met during officer training and had promised to take care of the other's single remaining parent should one of them die in the war they were about to go off and fight. Paddy was killed in action in 1918. Lewis lived with and loved Mrs Moore – certainly as a second mother, probably as a lover – until she died in 1948.

Maybe without that great motherless void to fill he would have been satisfied with myths, legends, an 'ordinary' wife and an ordinary academic life giving us another scholarly tome or two to add to the Bodleian shelves. As it was, he found God, Mrs Moore and writing for children, and gave us Narnia instead.

At the time, however, I did not know all this heartbreaking stuff and I was simply furious at the deception. Sneaking this God stuff in without telling me! Turns out Aslan, with his rightful-kingness and his infinite-wisdom-and-forgiveness schtick and willingness to sacrifice himself for sinful Edmund was Jesus! The Pevensies are his disciples, Edmund a bit of a Judas, and the White Witch the Devil! Narnia's heaven! Gerroutofit!

But eventually my rage subsided. It was still a very, very good story after all. As were all the others. *The*

Magician's Nephew (the one with the magic rings and the hero Digory's dying mother, miraculously restored to health – as building your own fantasy world allows – by Narnian fruit), was written after *The Lion, the Witch and the Wardrobe* but forms a prequel to it. *Prince Caspian* is the *Lion*'s sequel, written by Lewis while the *Lion* was going through the process of acceptance and publication in 1949/50 and, according to a letter from Lewis to an American reader, is about 'the restoration of the true religion after a corruption'. For oblivious me, it was simply an even more potent rendering of and deeper immersion in the Narnian landscape. The Pevensies return to the magical kingdom to find that hundreds of years have passed, civil war is dividing the kingdom and the Old Narnians (many dwarves, centaurs, talking animals, the dryads and hamadryads that once animated the trees, and other creatures) are in hiding. The children must lead the rebels against their Telmarine conquerors. The warp and weft of Narnian life is seen up close, in even more gorgeously imagined detail than the previous books. Lucy, awake one night in the thick forest that has grown up since she was last in Narnia, feels that the trees are almost awake and that if she just knew the right thing to say they would come to Narnian life once more. It mirrored exactly how I felt about reading, and about reading Lewis in particular. I was so close . . . if I could just read the words on the page one more time, bring one more ounce of love to the story they told, I could animate them too. The flimsy barriers of time, space and immateriality would finally fall and Narnia would spring up all around me and I would be there, at last.

Alas, it never quite happened. Nevertheless, despite this betrayal, *Prince Caspian* remains my favourite of the Narnia stories. Although if you ever confront me I will deny it to the ends of the earth because my first loyalty must always be to my dad and the piece of his heart he handed to me with *The Lion, the Witch and the Wardrobe*.

The Voyage of the Dawn Treader (the third to be published, in 1952) finishes Prince Caspian's story with his quest to find the seven lords who were banished from Narnia when Miraz took the throne. It's too good. In fact, on the days when *Prince Caspian* isn't my favourite, this is. Unless it's *The Lion, the Witch and the Wardrobe*. Which, let's face it, it always is. Even when it's *Prince Caspian*. Yes.

The Silver Chair is great but it has none of the Pevensie quartet in it, so must regretfully be relegated to the second tier of favourites, wherein also languish *The Horse and His Boy* (fifth to be published – in 1954 – but third in reading, which is to say Narnian chronological order) because it has no children or animals from the real world at all and goes far too nearly the full Tolkien for my comfort and, of course, *The Last Battle*.

For anyone worried, like mine hostess, about their children being secretly indoctrinated into Christianity, let me just say this: no child ever has or will be converted to Christianity through reading about Cair Paravel, Aslan, naiads, dryads, hamadryads, fauns and all the rest. If they notice it at all, they are far more likely to be narked than anything else. And they probably won't notice it at all. They are relatively literal creatures. At most, they will spend a few days tapping the backs of wardrobes hopefully (yes, I did – well, only the old wooden one in the spare room. All the others in the house were white melamine-covered chipboard, which was inimical to mood), but they are unlikely to go up to the nearest cleric and say: 'I'm looking for a saviour analogous to a fierce but benevolent lion who died on a stone table to free his people from tyranny – do you have anyone who might do?'

The tale of Lucy Pevensie discovering the secret world beyond the wardrobe door is a story about courage, loyalty, generosity, sacrifice and nobility versus greed, conceit, arrogance and betrayal. You can call the former Christian virtues, or you can just call them virtues, let the kids concentrate on the self-renewing Turkish delight, magically unerring bows and hybrid man-beasts and relax.

I should have told my interlocutor over the *Radio Times* that she could probably relax about the 'snobbery' too. Just because Lewis refers to 'whatever grapes your people may have' doesn't mean the modern child feels crushed beneath the weight of interwar class distinctions. They haven't even noticed – there's a bacchanalian rite going on at the time, for a start. Sanitised for juvenile consumption but still – *trees are dancing*.

As for misogyny, this charge always seems to be based on a disdainful reference in *The Last Battle* to elder sister Susan succumbing to the lure of face powder and stockings. But her brother adds regretfully, 'She always was in too much of a rush to grow up.' This is not an objection to femininity – it is the author sorrowing over the passing of innocence, making the point that to wish childhood away is, Christian or not, a terrible sin.

Oh, and the films are perfectly acceptable, denatured,

deracinated pabulum, filtered through Disney's bean counters instead of the roving imagination of one of the greatest masters of English fantasy fiction. I should have broken every DVD I could find in that wilfully impoverished house.

English children's literature is considered a treasure trove of high fantasy, but Narnia was as far as I wanted to go. I liked – still like – my flights of fancy firmly rooted in reality. I needed to be able to get back through the wardrobe, or out from under the floorboards. The Borrowers were welcome to share my world but I did not want to be a visitor stranded in someone else's universe entirely.

Which means, of course, that I have never got to grips with Tolkien. I just can't. The mere thought of that maniacally detailed world exhausts me. I got through *The Hobbit* – or 'Bilbo bloody Baggins' as I still quietly refer to it, despite the world filling over the last ten Peter Jackson-infused years with diehard fans of the whole thing – under duress at secondary school, but a) it never took, and b) *The Hobbit* is to the rest of the saga as a jog around the block is to back-to-back Tough Mudders. If the first nearly kills you, you don't go looking for more pain. And I feel very bad about this, not just because I have body-swerved a major literary landmark but also because I feel, obscurely, that I have let C. S. Lewis down.

He and Tolkien were, with Charles Williams, the Inklings – a part club, part literary society that met in Lewis' or Tolkien's college rooms at Oxford, or less formally at the Eagle and Child pub nearby, to read and discuss their latest (not-yet-published) writings. The likes of G. K. Chesterton, George MacDonald and Roger Lancelyn Green used to swing by too. So did Dorothy L. Sayers, though she was never allowed at the college gatherings because she was A Girl.

(Top tip: if reincarnation is a thing, you really should try and get reborn as a white, male Christian in the vicinity of 1950s Oxford. Nothing will go far wrong for you after that.)

It's possible that I am actually Inkling-opposed and that C. S. Lewis was in fact an exception to my unsuspected rule. I've still not read Chesterton or Sayers, and George MacDonald is a victim of my animus towards all fairy tales bar the ones on the Ladybird library carousel of yore,* and Roger Lancelyn Green

* The rule is that I don't read fairy tales. 'But that is completely – and I mean completely – stupid!' I hear you cry. 'Are you a full idiot, or what?' To which I can only say – I know, I'm sorry, and yes, probably. I have tried to break my self-imposed embargo many times over my reading career, with various Andrew Lang collections, and Grimm treasuries, and Hans Christian Andersen compilations but it has never worked. Beyond Ladybird age, everything that had recommended them suddenly became infuriating. I was never again seized by the elemental simplicities, the eternal truths enshrined by enduring symbols and archetypes. I just got frustrated by the lack of detail, the implausibility, the unrealism. Instead of evoking a sense of wonder and limitless possibility, they just left me wanting more. Maybe I never had the imagination that should rush in to fill the gaps. Maybe I started my degeneration into the awful, literal, unromantic, cynical, canker-hearted beast I have become earlier than I ever suspected. I feel similarly about short stories now. If you've got a good idea and a plot, give me more! Give me all of it! I am aware that this is to miss the point of short stories entirely. Being a bookworm does not necessarily mean being a good reader.

was the author of the first book I was ever defeated by despite actually wanting to read it.

A Tale of The Tale of Troy

I recently came across the fact – or possibly factoid, but it rings true to me so I am going to consider it so until persuaded otherwise – that we learn the vast majority of our vocabularies by the age of eighteen. After that, you doubtless will accumulate a few more dribs and drabs but they will never become part of your working semantic database or, for the more romantically inclined, your soul. You will not have easy mastery of them, never deploy them as often, willingly or confidently as you do the ones you imbibed before your post-pubescent brain started to calcify.

What is true for words is, I think, maybe even truer for stories.

I opened up Dad's latest offering, Roger Lancelyn Green's *The Tale of Troy*, and couldn't make head or tail of it. So many polysyllabic people (Philoctetes and Neoptolemus? Are you sure?), places, battles to keep track of, and the bit about the hollow horse took an age to turn up . . .

None of it would 'go in'. I felt, reading it at the age of eight, the way I feel when I read about economics now. I simply don't have enough background knowledge (Special purpose entities? Synthetic collateralised debt obligations? Are you sure?), enough pegs driven sufficiently securely into my mental wall to hang the new information on. I can follow it, just about, as I'm reading, but the minute I finish a chapter or turn a page the whole lot just slips to the floor in an untidy heap.

Maybe if I had got on with *The Tale of Troy* – or if, as less mud-turtley children might have done, sought out something that could bridge the gap between those two volumes of Ladybird Famous Legends and Lancelyn Green's retellings – it would have been my gateway to yet another world. I would have been plugged in to that hidden realm of classical influence and knowledge that still infuses, though most of us barely realise any more, everything around us. I might have become aware of a heritage that was, at least as far as state-educated, 1980s south-east Londonworld was concerned, only being handed down in random fragments now.

I finally read *The Tale of Troy*, along with all Roger Lancelyn Green's other retellings – versions of Arthurian, Norse and Ancient Egyptian stories alongside the various books of classical myths and legends – about ten years ago, and they were as powerful and thrilling as anything I have ever read, a cluster of potent, intoxicating tales which escaped my prejudice against fairy tales (which I had half expected to envelop them) by being so devoid of whimsy, so detailed and altogether so authoritative and convincing. His *King Arthur and His Knights of the Round Table* was the springboard from which I dived back into the pool of medieval literature I had only dipped a fearful toe into at university – *Sir Gawain and the Green Knight*, the *Pearl in the Myddes*, Chaucer, and of course Malory himself. It was a wonderful few months.

But it was also too late. Not for pleasure – as I say, it was wonderful – and not for gleaning a few reference points with which to orientate myself slightly better as I plough on through my library and, secondarily, life. But it was too late to make the books – and the legends – part of me. They are not and never will be. I had hoped I would feel like Susan Coolidge's character Katy Carr arriving in Europe. 'She had "browsed" all through her childhood in a good old-fashioned library,' writes Coolidge, '[and] had her memory stuffed with all manner of little scraps of information and literary allusions, which now came into use. It was like owning the disjointed bits of a puzzle, and suddenly discovering that properly put together they make a pattern'. But in fact what I have is just a few more bits of the puzzle.

'What you've never had, you'll never miss' they say, and of course we all know this is nonsense. I feel the loss of missing out on the illuminating power of Roger Lancelyn Green's books quite specifically and acutely. Every volume is a more hardcore version of what Lewis did in each Narnia chronicle – an effective condensation of a country's folklore and archetypes that are also (centuries of cultural cross-currents being what they are) our own. They should be part of everyone, and that means bringing them together at as early an age as possible so that they are a pattern ingrained rather than a puzzle forever.

Fashions in education and in reading change, but *King Arthur, The Tale of Troy, The Saga of Asgard* and all the rest are eternal. That is what legend provides: the sense of a connection reaching back through time, deep into the ancestral wildwoods, where an unacknowledged part of each of us still lives. Something visceral, elemental and, given the right teller at the right age, something understood. No wonder Lewis loved them so. I wish I'd been able to make the leap between him and the rest in time.

But I didn't. I turned without demur from the Age of Heroes to the Age of Heroines. I discovered Noel Streatfeild.

Streatfeild

All children are, at a certain age, consumed by a ravening lust for stardom. In my playground, girls tended to express it through the re-enactments of great moments in social history (Bucks Fizz's skirt-ripping, Lady Diana's wedding, Jane's transformation in *Neighbours*) while boys went more for sporting glory. In the football games that went on every playtime, they were all Kevin Keegan on the inside.

Noel Streatfeild has been sating this egomaniacal hunger (in girls, mostly) since 1936, when she wrote her first book for children, *Ballet Shoes*. 'The story poured off my pen, more or less telling itself . . . I distrusted what came easily and so despised the book.' Her readers had no such compunction – *Ballet Shoes* was an instant hit and is probably still her most famous and popular novel today.

It is the story of three orphan children, Pauline, Petrova and Posy Fossil, who claw their way up from nothing but a comfortable, upper-middle-class, post-war background to train at Madame Fidolia's Children's Academy of Dance and Stage Training and become the most renowned dancer, theatre actor and – er – engineer of their generation.

But the Fossils weren't who I first met. My heart belongs instead to Sorrel, Mark and Holly Forbes, the protagonists of *Curtain Up*. This is the story of three orphan children who claw their way up from nothing but a comfortable, upper-middle-class, post-war background to train, thanks to scholarships from the Fossil sisters, at Madame Fidolia's Children's Academy of Dance and Stage Training and become the most renowned dancer, theatre actor and – er – impressionist of their generation.

I'm teasing of course. A little. Because although Streatfeild's books do tend to adhere to the rags-to-riches formula, they also depart from traditional wish-fulfilment stories in important ways. For a start, all her characters are realistic children – like those of her idol E. Nesbit, Streatfeild's heroines (and occasionally heroes) are all fresh, natural, lively personalities. In *Curtain Up*, Sorrel is the responsible, anxious oldest child, Mark a bit of a sulker always in need of cajoling and 'managing' by those around him, while the baby of the family, Holly, has a sunny self-belief and the kind of imagination that easily leads her to become convinced that she did not steal a coveted attaché case from her cousin Miriam but that Miriam gladly lent it to her instead.

Streatfeild's children are beset by the same worries (frequently half-understood percolations down from the mysterious adult world above, or the insecurities that come with needing to make your way in a new school and negotiate relationships with people not immediately willing to offer friendship) as their readers are in real life. And they are capable of great loyalties and tendernesses, yet still prone to the same heart-squeezing jealousies (we have all been Holly at one time or another, even if our heart's desire was rarely a pre-war quality briefcase – though I'd love one now) and petty squabbles as their readers. Streatfeild is always particularly good on the agonies of not having the right clothes to wear – not to stand out, but to fit in; a legacy of her upbringing as one of three daughters of a high-minded, impoverished vicar and a mother who came down hard on anything she interpreted as a sign of vanity. In *Curtain Up* Sorrel longs for a party dress that 'rustles and sticks out . . . Suppose it could be yellow. Crepe de chine or silk net over taffeta' and in the book I loved almost as much, *White Boots* (which is basically *Curtain Up* on ice), Lalla has an array of beautiful skating outfits, while Harriet must wear her mother's old pink coat – a humiliation made worse by the fact that she has violently clashing ginger hair. I warmed deeply to this aspect of Streatfeild's work. My father wasn't a vicar, but my mother cleaved immovably to the belief that wanting to be anything more than decently covered by burlap sacking was a sign of moral depravity and shopped for our wardrobes accordingly. I was twenty-five before I owned an outfit that I liked. I didn't wear it. I'd never go that far.

The other major departure from tradition is that once the improbable circumstances have combined to get you to the dancing/singing/acting/sporting/skating/uh . . . engineering/uh . . . impressionism-ing institution of your choice, dreaminess is replaced by discipline, and sharpish. Once you are there, you have to knuckle down. It is the willingness to work, to be disciplined, and practise, practise, practise until you have mastered whatever techniques are necessary that turn Streatfeild's heroines (and occasional heroes) from merely talented individuals into stars. This is the lesson Streatfeild learned during her own ten years treading the boards, during which she enjoyed all the seediness, glamour and hard graft that came with being a member of the Charles Doran and Arthur Bourchier companies. (She bought as many lovely clothes as she could too.)

Streatfeild's insistence on a causal link between hard graft and success is actually quite a shock to the unwary reader – or at least it was by the time I was reading the books in the 1980s. I had been primed by at least two stories a week in the *Mandy* comics which Lauren Jones (lovely, kind, generous Lauren Jones to whom I owe a debt of happiness I can never repay) passed on to me once she had finished with them to believe that all you had to do was dance well at your local disco or do funny voices for your friends at school to be plucked from obscurity by a passing agent and hurled into the big time.

Now, of course, the two concepts have been uncoupled for so long that Streatfeild's books may be starting to read like medieval runes. *Kardashian Shoes* would be a book with a very different message. But I suspect that if today's star- and stage-struck youngsters give them a chance, they will come to life once more.

Torridon Library was also providing a plethora of practical, hardworking, morally and economically sound heroines. I had discovered pony books – my first taste of the delights of genre fiction (at least if you discount Enid, who was a genre unto herself). I had recently left the wooden bins and small shelves of slim paperbacks behind and, after a few weeks of research in the older children's section, had mustered the courage to choose my first 'proper' book there and seat myself at the big boys' and girls' table.

It was a a chunky hardback with line drawings only – I checked – so everyone could be very clear that it had not come from the infants' section and it was called *Jackie Gets a Pony.* It was by Judith M. Berrisford and in it, Jackie gets a pony. I was thrilled for her. And for me, because it was clear from the proliferation of similar hardbacks on the shelves that there were many more pony-based adventures to be had by her and many other remarkably and delightfully similar heroines.

I'm not quite sure why all the greats who had invented and fuelled the genre during its 1940s and 50s heyday were still, in the early to mid-1980s, so well represented on the shelves. Possibly the librarians were reliving their youths, or maybe there was some belief amongst Authority in proffering characters who lived for tack and mucking out instead of television and boys as a hedge against contemporary frivolity. I can't believe genuine readerly demand abounded. Certainly *Jackie and the Pony Thieves* (pony thieves steal Jackie's pony) was always waiting for me when I had read my way through her other fifteen adventures and returned, eager to begin the cycle of bran-mash-based adventures again. It may simply have been the case that so many pony books had been accumulated during the feverish peak decades that to have swept them all away once appetite had diminished would have left the place too bare.

Pony-book authors had many things in common (they were often from the same family for a start – Christina, Diana and Josephine Pullein-Thompson were sisters, and their mother was Joanna Cannan, one of the pioneers of the genre with *A Pony for Jean* in 1936, in which Jean gets a pony) but their foremost shared characteristic was their fertility. They were, in the main, writing about what they loved – horses, ponies, occasional dogs, horses, ponies, ponies – and genre fiction does not require intriguing new plots to be laboured over or emotional conflicts to be wrenched from your soul and rendered in exquisite prose. You can just get on with the job. All were capable of turning out a highly readable book a year. Berrisford wrote at least forty others in addition to her Jackie series over her thirty-seven-year career and the Pullein-Thompson sisters were virtually unstoppable. Christine probably takes the crown – though she would probably have preferred a properly soaped saddle – with at least 101 volumes published between 1948 and 1999.

I read all that were there – *A Pony for Jean* and its sequel *Another Pony for Jean* (I discover only now, alas, that there was a further instalment called – you'll never guess – *More Ponies for Jean*. Truly, the 1950s were a reassuring time), the Jackies, numberless Pullein-Thompsons, and I managed to buy a few Ruby Fergusons (pony books were nowhere near as prevalent in bookshops as they were in the library) for myself: *Jill's Gymkhana* and *Jill Has Two Ponies*. It's possible Ferguson's Jill series stayed in print longer than some of the others because Jill has a much more modern sensibility than most of the others, even though some – like the Jackies – were in fact written later. Chapter One of *Jill's Gymkhana* (first in the series of nine written between 1949 and 1962 – bit of a laggard, our Ruby, evidently), titled 'My Dream', opens like this:

> JUST look at that title! You see, I am the Jill concerned, and quite honestly if anyone had told me three years ago that anything so terrific as a gymkhana would ever be associated with my name I should have thought them completely mad. Yet such was to be my destiny. (That lovely phrase is not my own, I got it out of a library novel that Mummy is reading.)

Who could fail to be warmed, charmed and in immediate need of the remaining octet of adventures? A bit later on, her status as a child for all post-war ages is confirmed by her thoughts on the books her mother has been penning (à la *The Railway Children*'s mother, had I known it then) to keep penury at bay since Jill's father caught a fever on business in West Africa 'and never came back to us'.

> It seems awful to say it, but I never could get on with Mummy's books at all. They are all terribly up in the air and symbolic, about very whimsy children who are lured away by the Elves of Discontent to the Forest of Tears from whence they are rescued by Fairy Hopeful, and so on. I suppose some children must like these books and buy them or Mummy wouldn't get the cheques she does get; or perhaps it is that their aunts buy them and give them to the children for birthday presents. Anyway, so as not to hurt Mummy's feelings I always read every word of her books as they come out,

and try to say something appreciative, but honestly they leave me cold. I would rather have *Out With Romany*, or *The Phoenix and the Carpet*, or even something highbrow like *The Horse in Sickness and in Health*.

I can hear touches of Oswald Bastable, Cassandra Mortmain and assorted Fossils in there now, but at the time I loved Jill for herself alone.

The library's stable of pony books provided all the pleasures of Enid Blyton – formulaic comfort, certainty, ease, a lot of reward for your reading buck – with a new, equine twist and a much more satisfying amount of detail. The authors knew that they were writing primarily for 'outsiders' (children who actually have ponies tend to be out and about on them, living the pony-having lifestyle instead of reading about it) and so were careful to explain not just about the strange world of 'tack', the points systems at gymkhanas, the finer points of dressage and so on, but also to provide plausible (enough) explanations of how the money was earned and saved* first to buy the pony, then to furnish the kit,

* Pony books also, incidentally, completed the numismatic education that had begun with Milly-Molly-Mandy and her confusing insistence that two sixpences made a shilling. In my childhood, the old shilling pieces were still in circulation but being used as post-decimalisation five pence pieces (alongside the shiny new five pence pieces). So in my mind, a shilling was – clearly – worth five pence, not twelve. And yet she kept getting over five pence in change every time she spent a shilling (Milly-Molly-Mandy's outlays were never large). It baffled me, until I actually asked Dad for 'a shilling' to spend at the summer fete at my infants' school and my confusion somehow became apparent to him. He patiently – do I need to keep saying 'patiently'

provide the stabling and of course the all-important feed. Oh, the horror of the unexpected vet's bill that could throw off months of careful calculation and wipe out weeks of earnings yet to come from mucking out the stables of richer school friends and pile on yet more pressure to win a cheque at the next county show!

But the young reader lives for that kind of granular stuff. Careful, detailed world-building tells you that the author takes you seriously, that they want you to be right there, inside their vision with them. It's an implicit acknowledgement that you might have gaps in your knowledge and an absolute absence of contempt for that. This is a great gift, and relief, to any child.

I also adored the fact that, unlike Blyton's children, pony books' protagonists lived in the countryside full-time, not just during the holidays. I don't think I had realised that was possible before then. I didn't hanker after a pony of my own, specifically, but the lifestyle generally. I still yearned to be surrounded by fields instead of houses and lanes instead of roads full of traffic. No bookworm wants to live in London. It's noisy and

---

when I tell you my dad's doing something? It feels virtually tautologous at this point – explained that she was working in old money, when there were twelve pennies to the shilling, but that those twelve were now worth a modern five, so the coins had been pressed into alternative service. On this basis was I able to proceed with the fete, life and pony books, where funds were amassed in florins (two shillings! Twenty-four old pence! Ten new!), half crowns (two shillings and sixpence! Thirty old pence! Twelve and a half pence! Ask me another!), crowns (easy! Five shillings! 60d! Twenty-five new pence! You simply cannot stop me now!).

hectic and it just doesn't make sense. The past and the countryside. That's where our souls reside. What we really want is to retire to a tiny cottage somewhere unreachable to all but a chosen few as soon as we have accumulated enough books and money to be able to live out the rest of our days reading uninterruptedly from dawn till dusk and living on fried potatoes, eggs and the occasional rosy apple that had been due to be given to a lame pony down the lane. I'll give bran mash a try too maybe. I think it sounds delicious and have always chosen not to find out precisely what it is. If I hadn't given into marriage and motherhood, I reckon I would be about five years away from my goal by now. Ah well. At least I've got the books. And I may win the lottery yet.

If I couldn't live in the countryside or the past there was another option towards which I was almost equally drawn: underground. Torridon Library's shelving system was not infallible and so within the Judith M. Berrisford section often appeared books by Elisabeth Beresford. They were about a set of short, stout, furry creatures who lived in a burrow beneath Wimbledon Common – the Wombles. The gentle but lively adventures of the irrepressible Bungo, greedy Orinoco, scholarly Wellington and lovely, loyal, athletic-but-dim Tomsk (overseen by Great-Uncle Bulgaria, Tobermory, Madame Cholet and Miss Adelaide) as they go about their business of picking up the litter human beings leave behind to recycle and adapt for their own use, were born of the first stirrings of the green movement in the late 1960s and a chance mispronunciation by one of Beresford's children as they walked across 'Wombledon

Common'. (The Wombles actually move to Hyde Park in later years; a crazy but true fact which I include here in the hopes that it will propel you to victory in more than one pub quiz over the coming years.) They had been embedded in the national consciousness since about 1973, when the stop-motion animation series voiced by Bernard Cribbins had begun its two-year run. The programmes had been repeated many times since, but I wasn't aware of this. My mother had full powers of veto over our television-watching and – for reasons now lost in the mists of time but which something tells me will have been the mad fruits of dictatorial whim – *The Wombles* didn't make the cut. I knew them only on the page, save the occasional glimpse on other children's tellies or in battered annuals skim-read at jumble sales. The rough-textured nature of the animation and the backgrounds (sets? They must be sets) and the Heath Robinsonesque quality of all the things they built was a perfect rendering of the world Beresford had created and I thoroughly approved. Most importantly, the series' creators managed to capture the warm safety and cosiness of the Womble burrow.

I remember one day on holiday at Grandma's in Preston walking over a cobbled stretch of street near the old marketplace and pointing to them, saying 'This is what I like! This is where I want to be!' because I couldn't convey my liking for the past – I didn't know the word 'history' or 'historical' which might have gone some way to explaining myself to her. As it was, she thought I wanted to live on cobbles and watched me closely for years afterwards for further signs of mental instability.

I had the same problem explaining my Womble 'n' burrow love until last year, when I finally came across the word 'hygge'. It is a Danish word for a very Danish concept that has no direct translation into English but seems to be a mixture of cosiness, security, comfort, kinship and familiarity, coupled with a desire to keep things simple, uncomplicated and unexaggerated. They live it. Bookworms find it down fictional burrows. But whatever works, y'know?

The Wombles' indefatigable industriousness was also deeply satisfying. The furry clan had the same pleasing purposefulness as all those pony-book children – and all children long for a purpose. And their dedication to recycling, to squeezing every last droplet of usage out of everything, seemed an immensely sensible way of life too. Newspapers, old envelopes and bus tickets being turned into papier mâché and used to make bowls and mend burrow-cracks, jumpers and scarves being patched or unravelled and reused, tin cans, jam jars and every other sort of detritus being pressed into service of some kind – this all feeds some deep need in the juvenile psyche.

I wonder – often, actually – about when we lose that aversion to waste. When does that receptive little corner of our minds start to harden and grow impermeable to such simple common sense and make us into the adults Great-Uncle Bulgaria will never understand, 'Not even if I live to be 300'? Are we born preprogrammed with the sound survival instinct that tells us to be careful and salt away our resources against times of scarcity which the shrieking messages of consumer capitalism eventually drown out? Or is it just another manifestation of the general process of calcification we know as 'growing up'? It's a bugger, either way. And now we live in a world where, as I embark on a nightly reading of Bungo et al.'s adventures to Alexander, Great-Uncle Bulgaria's* kindly explanations of the beastly 'Pollu' (pollution) and how to fight it, and Wellington's experiments in the greenhouse resulting in an organic mixture that destroys plastic, read like relics of a ridiculously optimistic bygone age. So, not only have we ruined the world, we have ruined *The Wombles*. The burrow is my refuge no more. Brilliant.

* Or Great-Uncle Gulbaria as Alexander has it, a mispronunciation I cannot bear to correct.

6

Grandmothers & Little Women

Both my grandmothers were great grandmothers. Not great-grandmothers (at least, not yet – they would become so before they died but not by my womb), but great grandmothers. My dad's mother – known as Nanny – had been a nurse in between having 800 children, but by the time I knew her she was Les Dawson. Chain-smoking, bosom-hitching, permanently smiling through a happy fug of smoke and booze ('all snug in their Crimplene and gin', I would hear the late, great Victoria Wood sing years later and be instantly catapulted back to Nanny's precarious – there's no friction with Crimplene – but coveted lap), her conversation was a thing of wonder. Up and down and round it went, taking in everyone she'd ever seen, met, chatted to in the bus queue, given birth to, loved, lost, never cared about to begin with. It ducked down side alleys about the shopping habits, scandals (actual, rumoured, and invented on the spot), pets, grandchildren, salaries (actual, rumoured, and invented on the spot), miscarriages and every other non-salient detail about everyone within a five-mile radius of her front door. By the end of the afternoon you were more closely informed about the lives of a thousand people you had never met than you were about your nearest relatives. It was impossible to tell how much was true and how much was the product of a lifelong conception of silence as a mortal foe. Alan Bennett once described his mother sitting in the lobby of a hotel they were staying in and speculating on the lives of the other guests she saw passing by. 'He must be her son,' she might say, before embarking on a series of speculations about his likely personal flaws and failures in life. The next day they saw them again and she would say 'There goes that son again, up to no good,' completely unaware of – or at least unconcerned by – the fact that it had all been invented from scratch the day before. That was Nanny. She was great. It was like having a television on all the time, but one that loved you and stroked your face and gave you biscuits whenever you liked. But it did explain much about my father's Trappist approach to life. We value most what we have never had. In his case, it was a moment's peace.

When I got a little bit older Nanny would curl my hair with her hot wand – I think she used it herself to warm up her night-time whiskey (gin's a daytime drink, in case you were wondering) – and give me her old powder compacts and various little pots into which she had scraped the ends of her lipsticks. They were all a weird shade of deep pink that somehow managed to be so fantastically unfeminine that it was basically a contemptuous V-sign to all social convention. It was worn only by ladies of a certain heft and vintage and I have never seen it on anyone or anything since.

She also gave me *Sam Silvan's Sacrifice: The Story of Two Fatherless Boys*, a leather-and-gilt-bound Victorian treasure. It was a 'reward book', one of the hundreds upon hundreds of morally sound nineteenth-century tales published first by the Religious Tract Society to give to deserving Sunday-school pupils (or distributed among poor households by parish workers, in the hope of making them deserving) but which gradually came to be distributed more widely, and published by more commercial, less devotedly Christian outfits.

Books specifically aimed at children – as an idea, as a genre, as a product – began in the mid-eighteenth century with an entrepreneurial publisher called John Newbery. The medal given every year by the Association for Library Service to Children for the most distinguished contribution to American children's books is named after him in recognition of his achievement in making children's literature a respectable and profitable field of endeavour.

Before Newbery, there had been a few stray bits and pieces for da kidz, such as John Bunyan's *A Book for Boys and Girls* in 1686 (which was about as much fun as its 1724 retitling – *Divine Emblems, or Temporal Things Spiritualised* – suggests), James Janeway's *A Token for Children: being an Exact Account of the Conversion, Holy and Exemplary Lives, and Joyful Deaths, of Several Young Children* (again, not heavy on the laughs) in 1671 and Isaac Watts' *Divine and Moral Songs for Children* (in 1715), alongside religious tracts that saw pious orphans being rewarded with new, godly families, naughty protagonists despatched to eternal hellfire or tiny shriven souls being vouchsafed redemptive ecstasies on their little deathbeds. But their main aim was pedagogic (and salvatory). In the main, children made do with the lighter end of adult fare, much of which still survives (in more or less attenuated forms) as children's literature today: Arthurian tales, for instance, the legend of Robin Hood, Aesop's Fables, *Robinson Crusoe*, *Gulliver's Travels*, classical and regional myths, and the more interesting parts of the Bible.

Newbery saw an opportunity and took it. He started producing volumes like *A Little Pretty Pocket Book*. This, published in 1744, is generally held up as the first 'proper' children's book – to be read for enjoyment, not under duress for the good of your immortal soul. It cost sixpence, and for tuppence extra the infant owner got a toy with it: a red and black ball or pincushion (for boys and girls respectively – the publishers of *Sugarpink Rose* are not yet around to object). With them they could record the day's progress, adding a pin to the red side for instances of good behaviour, to the black for bad.

The sequel was called *A Little Pretty Pocket Book Identifying the Symptoms of Blood Poisoning Arising from the Conjunction of Dirty Pins and Imprecise Wieldings Thereof by Tiny Hands*. No, not really. But I imagine it would have sold well.The book itself contained letters from Jack the Giant-Killer exhorting Little Master Tommy and Little Miss Polly to be good, and poems about common children's games, followed by a moral extracted (often very dubiously) from each. 'Baseball' – the first documented use of the word, incidentally, though it's being used to refer to modern baseball's ancestor, rounders – runs:

> The Ball once struck off,
> Away flies the Boy

To the next destin'd Post,
And then Home with Joy.

MORAL

Thus Seamen for Lucre
Fly over the Main,
But, with Pleasure transported
Return back again.

Still more fun than reading about dying orphans, okay? Context is all.

By the second half of the eighteenth century, religious tracts had developed into the more narratively coherent and compelling moral tales that would eventually give rise to the reward book industry. Written mostly by women, the first of these is generally thought to be Sarah Fielding's *The Governess*, in which various students are encouraged to identify and reflect on their individual flaws and all pledge to do better on the morrow.

The aim of such tales was to train the childish mind out of frivolity and into sober, adult ways – an aim which reaches its apogee in a book called *Fabulous Histories* (later *History of the Robins*) about being kind to animals, by one of the most redoubtable, prolific and dogmatic of the moralists, Mrs Trimmer. Having given in, despite the era's and genre's fear of the power of fiction to corrupt, to the temptation of writing a book about talking birds, she goes to great lengths to strike pre-emptively against all possible harm. Readers should consider the tales 'not as containing the real conversations of Birds (for that it is impossible we should ever understand)' and her fables are designed 'not merely to excite compassion and tenderness for those interesting and delightful creatures on which such wanton cruelties are frequently exercised; but also to convey moral instruction to the young reader; and, in particular, to recommend the practice of general benevolence'. Are we all quite clear? Good. Then let the story, at last, commence. There are footnotes along the way to keep you from straying from the path of righteousness. 'The Mock-Bird is properly a native of America,' reads one, 'but is introduced here for the sake of the moral.' Duly noted, Mrs T.

Over the course of the century after *The Governess* first appeared, the bonds of propriety loosened, fiction ceased to be quite such a dread force in the minds of the good lady writers, and they gradually allowed the tale rather than the moral to come to the fore. In 1818, the first of three volumes of *The History of the Fairchild Family: The Child's Manual, being a collection of stories calculated to show the importance and effects of a religious education* was published, replete with dying children gloriously redeemed/emphatically not in their final hours, depending on how godly their tiny lives had been until then. Further volumes followed in 1842 and 1847, with a notable softening of attitudes each time.

This alteration in children's fare was partly because religious attitudes became a bit less blood-and-thundery, and partly because of the sheer weight of social change. The first half of the nineteenth century brought with it compulsory education for children and the invention of mass manufacturing, which meant books could be produced relatively cheaply for the first time. Now, suddenly there was a market of 3 million newly literate, story-hungry children to cater for, and catered for they certainly were.

The fanciful and fantastic were increasingly welcomed, and fairy tales, which for a long time had been judged the greatest possible pollutant of innocent, impressionable minds, were fully welcomed into the fold, in both their traditional forms and in new, such as Ruskin's *The King of the Golden River.* Charles and Mary Lamb wrote *Tales from Shakespeare* for young readers, and Catherine Sinclair even let the children in her 1839 tale *Holiday House* be unequivocally naughty without being eternally damned. GOOD TIMES.

By the middle of the century, the fashion had moved from strictly virtuous exhortations to stories about virtuous (or learning to be virtuous) children, and within another few decades the market and notions of acceptability had broadened further to include historical fiction and (for boys especially) adventure stories and relatively secular melodramatic tales, albeit with an 'improving' moral in there somewhere. It was to this later school that *Sam Silvan's Sacrifice* belonged.

It had also belonged to my dad. Inside on the flyleaf was written 'For Richard – see how long you keep it nice. Granny Mangan'.

I was speechless. It was old enough, Dad pointed out, for her to have owned it before she passed it on to him just as Nanny was now passing it on to me. I was holding HISTORY IN MY HANDS. Real history, family history in my hands. The flyleaf message was covered in crayon. 'Did you do that?' I asked Dad. He nodded. I was awed and appalled in equal measure. It gave me a new measure of the man. My quiet, gentle dad – a born recidivist. I'm reeling still.

Sam Silvan's Sacrifice was my first exposure to untrammelled Victorian melodrama. It's quite a thing, you know. The 'two fatherless boys' are Sam and his younger brother Fred. Fred is selfish. Fred is selfish, greedy, thoughtless and always being hauled out of scrapes or given extra crusts of bread or having his general mess cleared up by the ever generous, noble, selfless Sam. Fred is, frankly, appalling. Eventually, we reach the climactic set-piece of our morality tale. Fred's ineluctable . . . Fredness has landed them in a field with a snorting, maddened bull. The bull turns on them. The bull runs towards them. The boys run towards the high wall around the field. There is only time for one of them to boost the other one over. This, I knew, would be the moment when all that Sam had done for him over the years would suddenly overwhelm Fred and he would choose to boost his brother over the wall to make up for a lifetime of sin.

I don't know what part of *Sam Silvan's Sacrifice* I didn't understand.

Because of course, the Victorians being what they were, Fred has no such epiphany. He gladly accepts Sam's shove over the wall and then looks down in horror as his saintly brother is gored to death below him. He sure feels bad then! But IT'S TOO LATE! I mean, like, REALLY too late! Because Sam's dead! *Completely* dead. I really cannot convey to you how dead he is. The finality of it was terrible. I didn't grieve for Sam. You're dead, you're dead, I reckoned, and the keen edge of my compassion for him and his innards was further dulled by the slight contempt in which I continue to hold all pushovers and softies. But the contemplation of the infinite punishment Fred's now-awoken conscience had in store for him held me completely in its thrall. My own conscience was an overactive organ that had already colonised large parts of my mind and was pursuing the rest relentlessly, and my own sins, I knew at least in the rational part of my mind, were small. But what it would be like to live with something so awful pressing down on you, such guilt abrading your very soul . . . I shrank in horror from the idea and yet could not resist tiptoeing around it, trying at least to gauge the size and shape of such a burden.

Fred and Sam, you live in me still, every time I think of taking the easy route out of a difficulty or am tempted to let someone else deal with the consequences of some stupid thing I've set in motion. Well played, Victorian moralists, Granny Mangan and Nanny. Well played.

My other grandmother – Mum's mum, known as Grandma – was equally great. She was born and bred in Edinburgh but moved to Lancashire when she got married and gave birth to a child every year or so there until her husband David contracted rheumatic fever while serving as a naval doctor in the war, and died. 'Good job,' my Auntie Nancy, looking at the five children under seven, told her.

When we went to stay with her, which we did at least three times a year, she fed us Hawaiian sandwiches, Club biscuits and Wine Gums without surcease and when Mum tried to object, she would say 'For heaven's sake, Christine, they're on their holidays!' It was the only time I ever saw my mother cede any kind of ground. When Grandma came to stay with us, which she did at least three times a year, she would sneak us toffees in between playing 'Bobby Shaftoe' and 'Soldier, Soldier, Won't You Marry Me?' on the piano 800 times a day for us while we marched up and down the carpet pretending to be silver-buckled sailors and treacherous soldiers, and as soon as my parents left for work in the evening we would play pontoon and three-card brag for pennies and tuppences until pleasingly far past bedtime. She would bet on a six high 'just to make a game of it'. You would not have known from her cavalier attitude to her rapidly diminishing purseful of coppers that this was a woman who came fifth in the national Civil Service exams in 1930-something and knew the entirety of Scottish history like the back of her hand.

Whenever she left to go home it was an occasion of much lamenting on our parts. So she started leaving 'a wee present' for each of us in the top drawer of the chest on the landing. We would say goodbye to her in the morning before we went to school but have the thought of the gift to distract us from finding her gone when we came home.

One day after Grandma had done her disappearing act, Emily and I rushed upstairs to open the drawer. A box – an entire box, not plastic packet! – of Maltesers for her. And for me – something even more incredible. The most gorgeous book I had ever seen. She would give me many over the years, from Josephine Tey's *Brat Farrar* to George Eliot's *Silas Marner* and I will regret forever that she died before I discovered my own liking for the Waverley novels, which she loved with a passion befitting a Caledonian expat, but this was by far the most beautiful. A hardback, bound in red leather with gold curlicues all over it, and inside were onionskin pages covered in an attractively quaint font. The title – on the spine of the book only, not the front cover lest it interrupt all those gold curlicues – promised they would tell the story of *Little Women*.

It would prove to be a great story when I got to it, but there was much to detain me first. Beautiful endpapers – those flourishes repeated in a duller gold on a chocolate-brown background – gave way to a strange thing called 'a biography of the author' (a Louisa May Alcott, apparently), which lasted three and a half pages and was almost as good as a story.

In fact, it was such a heavily bowdlerised version of the author's life that it did almost amount to a story. According to this brief outline, the Alcott family were as gently and picturesquely impoverished as the Marches and almost as content. It glosses almost entirely over the fact that Louisa's father, Amos Bronson Alcott, was a relentless narcissist who put his family through hell with his commitment to his Transcendental ideals and who had a messiah complex that precluded him ever doing a proper day's work and providing for his growing family. In 1840 he abandoned the little school he had set up, in order to preach and write full-time. This was about as bad an idea then as it would be now ('I wait not for the arithmetic of the matter,' he cried, the sentiment of the incurably selfish everywhere), and it marked the last time he would ever bring in a regular wage.

He never liked Louisa very much. She was too outgoing, impulsive and opinionated. He called her and his wife Abba 'my two demons', and much preferred his docile oldest daughter Anna who would often greet him at the door with a list of her 'sins' and ask forgiveness.

I know. Unpick that at your leisure.

It was his two 'demons', however, who kept the family afloat via their various labours, though they both became – understandably – embittered by the process over the years, and it was the success of *Little Women* in 1868 that finally brought them some true financial relief and Louisa a measure of personal freedom.

Or, as my copy's biography puts it, 'Henceforth she was her own master, able to live where she liked and the way she liked, and – and this had always been one of her fondest dreams – minister to the well-being of her family.' Okay . . .

After those pagefuls of factoids, there was an even stranger thing called an 'Introduction', which was about the book itself. I skipped that. Why would I read ABOUT the book when the actual book was there, waiting to be read just a few pages on?

And what a book it was. In the story of the March family grappling with genteel New England poverty and finding ways to keep themselves happy and busy while their beloved father is away fighting in the war, there is something – and someone –for everyone.

Stay-at-home types can take comfort in Meg's story. She is the eldest sister and therefore Terribly Sensible, except for one never-to-be-forgotten chapter when she throws caution and New England Puritanism to the wind and gets her shoulders out for the lads at a ball. An evening of wild champagne-sipping and fan-waving are enough fun for one lifetime, however, and she is then able to settle down happily with John Brooke and a linen cupboard.

I had and still have a lot of time for Meg. I too would discover once adolescence hit in a few years' time that one evening's excitement was enough and retire from the fray thereafter. In my case, it was not at a ball but a grimy nightclub in New Cross, south-east London, called the Venue. It was too loud to talk and there was nowhere to sit except for the filthy floor – you were supposed to be up and dancing, of course, but I mimed a resounding 'No' to that – and a single drink cost twice what I was earning an hour at the local supermarket and everything was awful. I sat – gingerly – in a corner and thought fondly of linen cupboards until it was time to go home.

For readers of a less hermitic stripe there's Amy – an admirably proto-modern girl who has to be beaten over the head with the family copy of *The Pilgrim's Progress* before she can remember to pretend that people are more important than money and that her Aunt March's rosary is not, in fact, simply a statement necklace. Attagirl.

Romantics can have Beth, and even from my very first reading were welcome to her. I was profoundly perplexed when a family friend saw what I was reading and asked if I had cried at her deathbed scene. It had not even occurred to me to mourn the passing of such a relentlessly angelic, bloodless nothing – a lack of feeling the years have done nothing since to remedy.

Tomboys of course have – once you've made allowances for various nineteenth-century handicaps – a glorious heroine in Jo. From her they learn that they can make money in unfeminine ways such as writing (as long as they a) spend their hard-earned cash on sending careworn Marmee to the seaside and b) eventually stop it to marry ancient German men with beards and open orphanages for boys in none-too-subtle exercises in wish-fulfilment).

Writers-to-be love Jo perhaps even more passionately. She was the character Louisa May based most directly on herself (the others were idealised portraits of her own sisters and parents) and her longing to write and the fulfilment she finds in doing so provide the most vivid moments in an already vivid book. Her description of Jo 'falling into a vortex' and giving herself up to 'scribbling' in the attic for as long as a story held her thrilled me to the marrow. It was with great sadness I learned years later that the writing of *Little Women* itself rarely gave the author that vertiginous feeling of exhilaration. She enjoyed writing the gothic romances that had made her name (her first was published in 1854) and the more lurid tales she published pseudonymously in the 1860s because they offered her an escape from what was, by and large, quite a hardscrabble and miserable life. But *Little Women* was based on her real life and written at the behest of others; her father thought there should be more good, plain, morally uplifting stories for boys and girls, and her publishers wanted 'a girls' book' from her – so she found it more of a slog. As she put it in her diary, 'I plod away, though I don't enjoy this sort of thing. Never liked girls or knew many, except my sisters; but our queer plays and experiences may prove interesting, though I doubt it.'

Her publisher doubted it too when she sent him

the first dozen chapters – he found them 'dull'. But by the time the first proof of the whole book was done, both he and the author were more impressed. 'It reads better than I expected,' Louisa's diary records. 'Not a bit sensational, but simple and true, for we really lived most of it; and if it succeeds that will be the reason of it . . . Some girls who have read the manuscript saying it is "splendid"! As it is for them, they are the best critics, so I should be satisfied.'

Those early readers were an accurate bellwether. *Little Women* was an instant bestseller and has been loved by generations of (mostly) girls ever since.* The March sisters' adventures remain as fresh and moreish as the muffins that greet them when they wake on Christmas Day, and as satisfying. Their little universe is a well-ordered one. Sins are always expiated. Sacrifice is always rewarded (with spiritual growth, not money or extra limes or anything – that would kinda negate the whole concept) and so is kindness. Let someone use your neglected piano and a pair of bespoke embroidered slippers will soon be yours. Justice is always done – at least according to the 1868 lights of a woman working through some fairly major Daddy-'n'-Transcendental-theology issues. I was fine with Beth going to her reward but I thought Jo letting Amy plunge through the ice and nearly drown was entirely fair compensation for Amy throwing her manuscript on the fire. No need for Jo to sob for forgiveness afterwards. She would have been

* G. K. Chesterton was a fan, admiring *Little Women*'s realism and likened Alcott's work to Jane Austen's, but said he felt like 'a male intruder' on its grounds.

well within her rights to let her drown, I thought, and I stand – as the anxious guardian of my own manuscript 'ere – even more firmly by this today.

I also remain undecided about the whole Jo/Laurie/Amy/Professor Bhaer imbroglio. Between the publication of the first part of *Little Women* and the publication a year later in 1869 of the second – known as *Good Wives* – readers begged Alcott to have Jo marry rich boy-next-door Laurie, who befriends the whole family but Jo in particular.

They were out of luck. This was, after all, a woman who once lauded spinsterhood in an article entitled 'Happy Women' on the grounds that 'liberty is a better husband than love to many of us', which is nineteenth-century feminist speak for 'Have you SEEN the state of most of them? JESUS.'

Her diary entry for 1 November reads: 'Began the second part of "Little Women" . . . Girls write to ask who the little women marry, as if that was the only end and aim of a woman's life. I won't marry Jo to Laurie to please anyone.'

Perhaps if the pressure from her public and her publisher hadn't been quite so great she would have let Jo go unmarried entirely. As it was, she at least resisted the easy option and invented the professor instead. He has no real ancestor in (juvenile) fiction – he was created especially for Jo. She meets the Berliner – 'neither rich nor great, young nor handsome, in no respect what is called fascinating, imposing, or brilliant, and yet he was as attractive as a genial fire, and people seemed to gather about him as naturally as about a warm hearth' – after she has turned down Laurie's proposal of marriage and gone to New York City to write and teach. They form a friendship that deepens gradually and diffidently into love. They marry and once Aunt March dies, turn her huge home and grounds into a boys' orphanage. Yes, there are shades of Louisa's father in idealised form in there – a teacher who sticks at it, an older bearded man who puts his orphanage-wide family and his wife before everything and can be relied on at all times – but he is right for her. And more of a man than Laurie will ever be, I'm telling you.

Look, I liked Laurie, okay. He was fine. He just . . . well, he wasn't much, was he? He was too light and bright – when he wasn't being spoiled and sulky – for Jo. He was a much better fit for Amy. They could waft around Europe insubstantially together. Jo needed something more stolid altogether. So yes, I'm a Bhaerite. I rate the prof.

I have had many arguments about this over the years. Not as numerous as those I've had about *Anne of Green Gables* (sickening? Or charming beyond measure? We will get to this), but still – many.

Those not on Team Bhaer find him smug, patronising and – as a friend once shrieked at me in a moment of particularly high emotion – 'He kills her dreams!' because she ends up running a school at which he can teach, instead of carrying on writing for a living. I still do not see it. I think he's wonderful. And she *wants* to run that school. She's just lucky she fell in love with a man who can also teach. It's all good.

Whatever your view of particular events or characters in the book, taken all together what *Little Women* does give the reader is a picture of four different girls (and a

Marmee) working to cultivate, subdue and repress various aspects of themselves to fit a preordained model of femininity. Which leads you to the very dimmest beginnings of a shred of a scintilla of awareness that there is a model. And that that's . . . that's a bit mental.

Elizabeth Janeway wrote in a *New York Times* book review in 1968 that '*Little Women* was written by a secret rebel against the order of the world and woman's place in it, and all the girls who ever read it know it.' It gave me another link in a chain of thought I was not quite consciously developing. I tucked the Marches in beside Ramona and felt able to set my face a little more firmly against 'twirly' girls at school, who – at eight-going-on-nine were growing twirlier by the bloody day.

Classics

Little Women had another welcome effect too – it introduced me to the hitherto unknown world of The Classic.

I wanted to know why this book had had so much effort put into it. The red leather! The gilding! The very, very thin, very, very white paper! The introduction and biography! It seemed to fall under the heading of material rather than philosophical conundrums, so instead of running to my usual fount of book-wisdom, I presented it to my own Marmee for consideration.

It was an old book, she explained. But Grandma had only just given it to me, I pointed out. No, not in that sense, she said. In the sense that it had been written a long time ago and been printed and reprinted ever since because people kept wanting to read it. It was considered A Classic. There were lots of them – books that had endured and which everyone had either read or at least heard so much about that they had absorbed the essence of them almost by osmosis.

What was osmosis? I asked. But she had run out of time for explanations – I think the house needed repointing before our swimming lesson or something – so I spoke to empty air.

No matter. The next time Dad took me to Dillons in Bromley, I scanned the shelves until I found the title *Little Women*. It was part of a series which all had similar covers – the Puffin Classics livery. Over the next few months Dad would add many volumes to my shelf at home. I weeded out first anything too adventurous (*Treasure Island*, *Journey to the Centre of the Earth*, *Coral Island* and so on) and second, all the animal stories.

I had an early, strict and enduring rule against books in which animals – especially talking animals – were the predominant feature. Thus to the oblivion to which I had already consigned Beatrix Potter, Winnie the Pooh, the inhabitants of Brambly Hedge, Rabbits Peter and Brer and Tales of Farthing Wood I now added, with an equal lack of compunction, the likes of the *Just So Stories* and *The Wind in the Willows*. What an idiot. I do not know where or when this mindless prejudice was formed, but in the coming years it would also set me against classics like *Tarka the Otter* and *Ring of Bright Water*, and the Whitbread Award-winning *The Song of Pentecost* and countless less famous others. What. An. Idiot.

Never mind. What's done is done, and even after a

purge of fur and feathers, there was still a fair portion of the canon to devour. I set to work with a will.

The canon, for children, generally means books written between (roughly) the late Victorian era and the end of the Edwardian age; products of what's traditionally been considered the golden age of children's literature, bookended by *Alice in Wonderland* (1865) and *Winnie the Pooh* (1920). Any later and you're into upstart, Modern Classics territory. Any earlier and you're back in moral-tale territory and a world too different for its stories to have endured.

But by the middle of the century, as we have noted, entertainment had largely supplanted education as the driving force in children's books. Most of the categories and genres – including adventure, school and family stories – into which children's books still fall today had been established, and the machinery for producing, bountifully illustrating and distributing writers' wares was becoming ever more smooth and sophisticated. Authors could make decent livings writing for children, which attracted more and more contributors – good and bad – to the field. Still, they hadn't quite managed to shuck off the last vestige of the moral tale – the tendency to talk as an adult, slightly down to children. A faintly pedagogic tone and a teacherly distance remained between the author and his or her reader.

And then came Alice.

7
Wonderlands

> Many a day we rowed together on that quiet stream – the three little maidens and I – and many a fairy tale had been extemporised for their benefit . . . yet none of these tales got written down: they lived and died, like summer midges, each in its own golden afternoon until there came a day when, as it chanced, one of my little listeners petitioned that the tale might be written out for her . . . In a desperate attempt to strike out some new line in fairy lore, I had sent my heroine straight down a rabbit hole, to begin with, without the least idea what was going to happen afterwards.

The quiet stream is the Thames in 1860-something, the tale teller is the Reverend Charles Lutwidge Dodgson and the petitioning maiden is Alice Liddell. The tale itself became known as *Alice's Adventures in Wonderland*, which Dodgson – not wishing to damage his scholarly reputation as a mathematician at Oxford – published under the nom de plume Lewis Carroll.

I did not read it when I was a child, though it has been so thoroughly embedded in the national psyche since it first sold out on publication that for years I believed I had (that of course being Alan Bennett's famous definition of a classic – a book everyone is assumed to have read and often thinks they have). It wasn't until I started reading it to Alexander last year* that although I knew about the white rabbit, the bottle labelled 'DRINK ME', the cake labelled 'EAT ME', the growing and the shrinking, the encounters with the hookah-smoking caterpillar, Cheshire cat and its grin, the Mad Hatter, tea parties and croquet with the Queen of Hearts with flamingos for mallets and hedgehogs for balls and the frankly rigged trial of the Knave of Hearts who stole some tarts, I hadn't actually experienced them first-hand. I had just absorbed the basics through the ether.

And what I hadn't appreciated from a distance was the very thing that makes *Alice* such a landmark in children's literary history – the directness of Carroll's voice; the alternating stoicism and stroppiness of his protagonist (who completely steps outside the hitherto unbroken tradition of polite, delicate, submissive heroines) as she navigates her way through this world of irrational

* This wasn't the reason I chose it for a bedtime story, but the writer Roger Lancelyn Green once suggested that the ideal was for a child first to get to know Alice by hearing her adventures read aloud anytime between the ages of four and eight, before 'the Gradgrindian fact-pushing at school' eroded the willingness to suspend disbelief. He was writing in the pre-league tables, pre-SATs, pre-unspeakable, ridiculous rest of it 1960s, so God knows how much more our children need her these days. The window of opportunity for tumbling rewardingly down the rabbit hole together is probably only moments away from slamming shut completely.

creatures, mad royals and untrustworthy labels on attractive foodstuffs; the all-pervading sense of a writer at one with his child-self instead of writing down to a half-remembered state; the sheer modernity of it all.

Also – it's an absolute rush. A delicious, borderline hallucinatory, confection. Alice is a riot of nonsense, parodies, wordplay, twisted and dreamlike (il)logic, invention and imagination tumbling over each other in the excitement. There is something in there for everyone. I like the semantic shenanigans (the Mouse giving a very dry lecture on William the Conqueror to restore those who have been soaked by Alice's gigantic tears pleases me most), while Alexander is as yet more entranced by the cat that leaves its grin behind. I do wonder what the mother of a more mathematically inclined friend of mine thought when her son's interest snagged on the EAT ME and DRINK ME scenes because, he recalls delightedly now, 'they introduced me to the concept of absolute scale!' She was probably used to operating at a certain level of bewilderment by then.

It reads completely differently from everything that came before it. There is no question that it is meant purely to entertain and to entertain unstoppably – a stream of nonsense (in the best possible sense) designed to carry every reader away. Way to inaugurate a golden age, Mr C! Thanks!

Frances Hodgson Burnett

Although I missed out on Alice, my actual introduction to the Edwardian classics was an absolute belter. The writer and critic Marghanita Laski once said that she had loved it because it was 'a book for introspective town children'. As one of that happy, if pallid, breed I can confirm that she was absolutely right. It was *The Secret Garden*, and it had absolutely everything you could possibly want in a story. An admirably sour-faced orphan – Mary Lennox, whose parents die when cholera sweeps through their home in India. A country house – Misselthwaite Manor, to which Mary is sent to live with her even more sour-faced uncle who is still mourning the death of his wife. An invalid boy – her cousin Colin, who has a non-specific spinal problem and is the source of the mournful cries that have been keeping Mary up at night and improving her temper not at all. A SECRET GARDEN – the key to which Mary discovers as she begins to warm to and explore Misselthwaite Manor. And finally a proto-sexgod called Dickon, brother of the manor's friendly maid Martha Sowerby, who knows all about gardening and how to roast eggs in a tree hollow. Together in the peaceful privacy of the garden they bring hope, Mary's tender side and Colin's legs back to life. Who could ask for anything more?

Judging by its relative lack of success on publication, the answer seemed to be – quite a lot of people. *Little Lord Fauntleroy*, Frances Hodgson Burnett's first children's story (about Cedric Errol, a poor little boy in New York who turns out to be an English earl – a rags-to-riches story that echoed Frances' own and was a plot she used many times in her adult and children's fiction), had been a critical and commercial triumph. Adults, in particular, loved it and a generation of young boys were forced into velvet suits, lace collars and curl papers until their fond mamas emerged from their collective passion to ape the sartorial fashions of the eponymous hero. The mobcapped shades of Kate Greenaway's generation must have hovered round and laughed. The little lord himself, to be fair, is far less nauseating in the book than in the various screen adaptations that have come to dominate our memories of him – but the clothes . . . the clothes were always terrible. They – and the accompanying long, curled hairstyles – were based on those Hodgson Burnett herself created for her own two sons. All great women have their blind spots.

And she was an amazing woman. She was born into a well-to-do family in Manchester in 1849 but when her father died of a stroke in 1853 they began a descent into poverty that – despite her mother's Stakhanovite efforts to keep the family ironmongery business going – eventually forced them to emigrate to America in 1865. A rather incongruous fact considering how firmly associated she is with the quintessential Englishness embodied in *The Secret Garden*, but fact it be. At sixteen, Frances arrived in Knoxville, Tennessee and would not even visit England for the next twenty-two years.

It was all hands to the pump in the New World – or, in Frances' case, to the pen. She had always loved making up and enacting stories as a child, and so she began writing some for magazines. She was soon a frequent contributor to the prestigious likes of *Godey's Lady's Book* (the magazine pored over by the Ingalls women in the Little House on the Prairie books), *Harper's Bazaar* and *Scribner's Monthly*.

In 1873 she married Swan Burnett, a doctor whose medical training she paid for and whom she would out-earn with the success of what she called her 'potboilers' ever after. A few years later she published a full-length book set in Lancashire (*That Lass o' Lowrie' s* – still a good read, if tha c'n cowpe wi' t'excruciatin' phonetic renderin' o' t'characters' dialogue) and began to build a reputation as a romantic novelist. In 1879 she went to Boston and met Louisa May Alcott and Mabel Mapes Dodge, the editor of children's magazine *St Nicholas*, which inspired her to try her hand at children's fiction. *Little Lord Fauntleroy* began as a serial in Dodge's esteemed organ in 1894.

Years of prolific writing for adults, extravagant living and – once income allowed – annual trips back to Blighty followed, interspersed with periods of exhaustion from overwork, struggles with depression, and recuperation. In 1890, her beloved oldest son Lionel died of tuberculosis, a loss from which she never really recovered. Amongst other things, it caused her to retreat from her Anglican faith and look for solace in spiritualism and Christian Science. She and Swan unofficially separated and would divorce in 1898. She kept on their house in Washington DC but gradually moved herself back to England, though she continued making trips back across the Atlantic to stay in touch with her other son, Vivien, who was now at Harvard (and inconspicuously dressed).

In England she made her home at Great Maytham Hall, which was exactly what it sounds like – a huge, beautiful country house, in Kent, whose large grounds included several lovely, peaceful walled and rose gardens in which Frances could write. And, in between remarrying (a wrong 'un called Stephen Townsend who was basically only after her money) and divorcing again, she did. Her adult readers got several novels and in 1905 it was the children's turn. She gave them *A Little Princess*, an expanded version of a story that she had written a few years before for *St Nicholas*, called 'Sara Crewe; or, What Happened at Miss Minchin's'.

I didn't come to *A Little Princess* until after *The Secret Garden*, but I loved it almost as much. It is a much simpler story, in content and execution. Sara is the beloved only child of her widowed father who enrols her at Miss Minchin's boarding school for young ladies so that she can acquire some education and polish while he goes off to acquire some diamond mines and polish his fortune.

Can you see where this is going yet? It's great, isn't it?

Sure enough, father loses his fortune and his life out in diamond-mine country and Sara is left a pauper. From being feted by the awful Miss Minchin and her equally awful pupils, Sara is suddenly cast out. Miss Minchin banishes her to the attic and makes her work as a servant. Oh, the glorious horror of it all! But Miss Minchin has reckoned without Sara's fortitude and imaginative resources. She pretends that she is a princess disguised as a servant, or sometimes a prisoner in the Bastille and this – together with her friendship with Becky (a real servant girl, with the lumpen, lower-class face and nervy manner to prove it) and the mouse in her garret – gets her through her cold and unloved days.

After many trials and tribulations – and one incredible sequence that pierces me still with the same degree of exquisite agony now as it did when I first read it over thirty years ago, in which a starving Sara finds a sixpence in the slush-filled gutter one bitter winter's day, buys twelve buns and ends up giving them all, one by painful one, to a beggar girl in the street ('She is hungrier than I') – justice is done. Mr Crewe's friend, complete with her father's lost fortune which was not so lost after all, turns up to rescue her. And Becky becomes Sara's personal maid, because this is justice, sure, but 1905-style.

I will be honest. You can come to *A Little Princess* in a mood that leads you to find it faintly sickening. The legacy of the Victorian love of sentiment regarding childhood is sometimes too plain to see. The testing of Sara's magnanimity and patience is constant and her saintliness sometimes verges on the absurd. The baker who watches Sara give away all her buns is so uplifted by her example that she employs the beggar girl as her assistant on the spot, FFS.

And yet, and yet – it is lovely. Overall, it stays on the right side of the line – charming, not preachy, with an earnest, not pious heroine whose chosen survival tactics read, especially to someone of an age at which he or she is acutely aware of children's very real powerlessness, as bravery not passivity.

But it is undoubtedly *The Secret Garden* that is Hodgson Burnett's masterpiece. The seed of the tale of lonely Mary and Colin, upon whom nature and the gradual gathering of friends slowly work miracles, was sown at Great Maytham Hall but its full flowering took time. It was published in 1911 to good reviews (most along the simple lines of *Outlook* magazine's 'a more delightful mystery for the child mind could not be imagined than that of this long locked up, deserted, almost dead garden', though one did say that '*The Secret Garden* is more than a mere story of children; underlying it there is a deep vein of symbolism') but no great fanfare. When Hodgson Burnett died in 1924 it was – unlike *Little Lord Fauntleroy* – barely mentioned in her obituaries.

But fate, as Sara Crewe will tell you, is a funny thing. Over the years, Cedric's star faded and *The Secret Garden*'s has only risen. It was a book children loved and kept passing on to their own children in turn. Thus it survived until 1949 when a beautiful illustrated edition was published on the twenty-fifth anniversary of Hodgson Burnett's death. Buoyed by and resonating with the post-war atmosphere of optimism – and what was a blasted Europe but a giant garden just beginning to put out new shoots again? – it was granted a second more public lease of life and entered firmly into the cultural consciousness, from where it is frankly unlikely to be dislodged.

It is a book that lends itself brilliantly to whatever sociocultural concerns the age happens to be gripped by. The religiously inclined can see the story of Mary, her character remoulded gently but firmly as she digs and prunes the forgotten garden, as a lament for our lost prelapsarian innocence. Or, if you are still shaking your metaphorical fist at the Industrial Revolution, a paean to England's bucolic golden age. Alternatively, if you're a Freudian, I'm sure you can interpret it in all sorts of ways unsuitable for this book.

Many have seen the garden as a symbol of motherhood – Mary nurtures it and brings it back to life and it does the same right back to her. Or perhaps it's a story of exile and homecoming, or the journey through grief.

It was written when the bereaved Hodgson Burnett

had become interested in Christian Science and various forms of spiritualism that perhaps offered her more comfort than more inflexible, established religious doctrines did, and perhaps the magic that Mary, Colin and Dickon come to believe is at work in the garden is her attempt to depict or grasp hold of them. But I suspect that for most children the characters' faith in the garden's magic reads, as it did to me, as a simple appreciation of the wonder of nature. That plants push up through the earth at certain times of year, bloom and fade in unison without any outward instruction is, when you first become aware of it, utterly extraordinary. A rose is always a miracle, but you only appreciate that when you're young. You don't need to reach for an external God looking down and orchestrating everything. But you might just reach for a trowel.

I actually did. *The Secret Garden* was one of the few books that inspired me to get off the sofa and do something to try and bring some of the glory of that imagined world into the real one. I hadn't had a doll's house or a knackety-kneed owl or a vortex-friendly garret to try other things out in, but I had a garden. My mother was thrilled. I was DOING something! Bending at the waist, moving limbs, using muscles we had all presumed atrophied long ago. She bought me seeds, a little bag of compost and showed me how to dig it into the soil to prepare the ground for sowing.

For a few days all was well. But the thing about gardening, it turns out, is that it is very slow. Very, very slow. Slow even for a child who was usually so inert she was technically a mineral. You have to dig for ages and then you scatter the seeds and instead of just turning the page to find them bursting into bloom, fuck all happens for months. No robins come to visit you. Or sex gods. Just your mother and your sister, who are out every five minutes to see what you're doing and explain how you're doing it wrong. I began to understand why you needed a *secret* garden.

And you have to do it all out in the fresh air. There was nothing to redeem the experience at all (Mum rejected the idea of hollowing out the apple-tree trunk so that we could try roasting eggs, with a firmness that was surprising even for her) so I returned to the sofa and the book, in which seasons and events unfolded quickly, pleasingly and reliably. I would not make the mistake of trying to find contentment in real life again anytime soon.

E. Nesbit

Next on my canon-run came Edith Nesbit. I suspect, given how often I still mix them up, that I thought they were the same person. In fact, they do have many similarities. Like Hodgson Burnett, Nesbit was a sociable, extrovert, unconventional woman (Hodgson Burnett with literary and Edwardo-hippy types, while Nesbit favoured the Fabians whose formal society she and husband Hubert Bland co-founded). They were both wildly imaginative since youth and prolific producers of potboilers and other hackwork (which here does not mean bad – neither of them ever produced anything unreadable – but simply done to a brief, for a particular market, not wrenched from the heart), writing at least as much for money as out of natural desire and inclination. Like Hodgson Burnett, Nesbit was less strait-laced than we generally think of late-Victorian ladies (let alone our favourite children's writers) and only got away with several extracurricular activities – including a relationship with a lover ten years younger than herself, Oswald Barron, who inspired *The Treasure Seekers* and to whom the book is dedicated – because of her wealth and status. She also had to deal with an unsatisfactory husband – though Bland was much worse-behaved than Swan or even Stephen. He carried on several affairs, including one very long one with their good friend and housekeeper Alice Hoatson. She got pregnant twice and Nesbit adopted both children. She was much happier in her second marriage. In a letter to a friend at the age of fifty-nine she said she finally knew 'what it was to have a man's whole heart'.

But this is all faintly distressing. Let us stop letting daylight in upon magic and turn to the books. *The Railway Children* was the one I revered beyond all else.

The comfortable, complacent world of Roberta (Bobbie, or Jenny Agutter forever if you saw the film at a formative age), Phyllis and Peter is suddenly shattered when their father is mysteriously forced to leave them. They must abandon their lovely house in Edwardian suburbia and go to live in a small cottage in the country near a railway line. As this is 1906 and Sunday lifestyle supplements have yet to be invented, this counts as a Bitter Blow rather than Living the Dream.

The children must learn a new mindset ('Jam OR butter, dear – not jam AND butter. We can't afford that sort of reckless luxury nowadays!' counsels their mother, whose superb cheeriness and pluck are the tools with which we truly built the empire), and seek out new friends and entertainments.

As luck would have it, it is not only lifestyle supplements but the Health and Safety Executive, paedophiles and tabloid scaremongering that have yet to be invented, so the children are free to wander up and down the railway line, befriending all the people they come across. These include Bernard Cribbins – I mean Perks, sorry, that film really did get to me – the stationmaster, and the Old Gentleman, a regular commuter on the 9.15 a.m. down train. When Bobbie, the eldest of the children, eventually discovers that their father left them because he was falsely accused of selling state secrets to the Russians and sent to prison, it is the Old Gentleman she asks for help and who eventually succeeds in proving Mr Railway-Children's innocence.

The arrival of the vindicated Mr R-C at the railway station has been made famous by the film – Jenny Agutter's cry of 'Daddy! Oh, my daddy!' is still capable, nearly forty years on, of pulverising all hearts within a three-mile radius – but the ending of the book (a version of which is used in the film but you are still sobbing too hard to appreciate it) is sweeter still. Bobbie leads him back to the house and tells him to 'Come in! Come in!', and the narrator turns the reader, with exquisite Edwardian politeness, gently but firmly away.

'He goes in and the door is shut. I think we will not open the door or follow him. I think that just now we are not wanted there. I think it will be best for us to go quickly and quietly away. At the end of the field, among the thin gold spikes of grass and the harebells and Gipsy roses and St John's Wort, we may just take one last look, over our shoulders, at the white house where neither we nor anyone else is wanted now.'

I had long been banned from reading books at mealtimes – at breakfast I would hungrily read and re-read the cornflake packet instead – but because I was now permanently immersed in a book at all other times and had effectively withdrawn from family life (and all other sorts, but it was family with which she was mainly concerned) Mum had issued a decree: I could only do it downstairs. I was to be within the sphere of family activity even if not part of it. Which meant, in effect, that I could only read in the sitting room, because that was the only place – the clue was in the name – that you could sit. (Though even there, not if the sofa cushions had recently been bumphled. You had to give it an hour or two, until the bloom was off the recently plumped rose.) I'd like to say I protested, but I'd met my mother before and knew it would just be a waste of valuable reading time. So I took up near-permanent residence on the sofa, moving to the armchair by the window at bumphling times and on the odd occasions when the sofa was fully occupied by people wanting to watch telly.

It didn't really matter. At that age, once I was reading, my concentration was total, my immersion in the book complete. A few sentences was all it took for the world to fade away and fiction to assume reality. Short of my sister dragging me off by the hair to play snap or hide and seek with her every so often, I was as happily isolated as I had been up in my room, but my mother's sense of decorum was satisfied.

But I must have escaped the sitting room occasionally

because I remember reading that final paragraph of *The Railway Children* for the first time up in my room, lying on my bed in front of the window one late afternoon, tilting the book to catch the last of the light as the sun went down. It was the perfect setting for a perfect last page. I went downstairs in a haze of happiness. Probably to be shouted at for absenting myself without filling in the relevant permission slips, but it was totally worth it.

Despite my ongoing disagreement in this matter with Mum, I identified keenly with Bobbie, the ceaselessly vigilant and responsible oldest sister, because I felt very much that of my mother's two offspring, I would definitely be her chosen confidante at a time of familial distress. I had just got glasses and felt they gave me an air of gravitas with which my sister's ability, fully developed even at the age of six, to identify, dissect and solve any practical, physical or emotional problem within thirty seconds simply could not compete. Yes, were our father to be wrongly accused of espionage and national treachery, she would come to me. I would tell her to let him serve his time – as a fellow introvert, I could imagine nothing nicer than a stretch of solitary confinement somewhere with three guaranteed and silent meals a day – and she would go away comforted, and I would be her favourite. Dad's too, when he found out how well I had arranged things for him. I could make a go of genteel poverty and manage without buns for every tea, as long as I was guaranteed a happy ending before the deprivation became too unmanageable.

It was all very satisfying. *The Story of the Treasure Seekers* did not please me half as much, even though it was set just down the road in Lewisham. I read it, liked it, but not enough even to pursue the family through the two sequels – an admission that pains me greatly to make as it is so clear to me now that from almost its opening line the volume of the Bastables' adventures is (as well as being formally innovative, as the first time such a book had been written in the first person) a comic masterpiece. 'There are some things I must tell before I begin to tell about the treasure-seeking,' says the narrator, soon revealed as Oswald despite his attempts at omniscient neutrality, 'because I have read books myself, and I know how beastly it is when a story begins "Alas!" said Hildegarde with a deep sigh, "we must look this last on our ancestral home" – and then someone else says something – and you don't know for ages and ages where the home is or who Hildegarde is, or anything about it.' It's Teddy Robinson and Plop all over again. At the time I thought Oswald was a bumptious fool (and to be honest, I would still love to read a book that opens with Hildegarde looking her last on the ancestral home), but now the whole thing has me hysterical, as well as in awe of Nesbit's deftness in keeping the comedy rolling while shooting it through with shafts of sadness. 'Our mother is dead,' says the narrator in that same opening paragraph. 'And if you think we don't care because I don't tell you much about her you only show that you don't know very much about people at all.' Wonderful.

Twain – Coolidge – Montgomery

Then I took a little break from my native land's golden age and moved temporarily back to America, courtesy of Mark Twain's *The Adventures of Tom Sawyer*, that glorious jumble of scrapes and japes that were apparently naturally a boy's lot if he were able to bowl round a tiny Missouri town on the banks of the Mississippi in the middle of the nineteenth century. Tom explored caves, outwitted everyone from sheriffs to Sunday-school teachers and had as his best friend the only boy in St Petersburg with greater liberty than he: Huckleberry Finn, the motherless son of the town drunk.

The boys' audacity left me breathless. Daring enough to slip out at night to try a new cure for warts (involving moonlight and a dead cat), but to discover that you were presumed dead and keep quiet thereafter so that you could attend your own funeral – well! That took my breath away for longer even than the threats issued by the murderous Injun Joe. Alongside that was the touching evolution of Tom's conscience and the glory of Twain's wit and prose more limpid than the streams forever tempting Tom astray. I had never met an author who delivered so many revelations so accessibly. So accessibly in fact, that they didn't even feel like revelations – they simply felt like things I had always known, hovering about on the edge of my consciousness until this kind man took the trouble to resolve them for me into words. The most interesting (and famous) one, perhaps, came in the very first chapter, when Tom, by pretending that it's fun, persuades his friends to pay him for the privilege of painting the fence Tom has been told by his long-suffering Aunt Polly to whitewash as a punishment for stealing jam from the pantry. 'He had discovered a great law of human action, without knowing it – namely, that in order to make a man or a boy covet a thing, it is only necessary to make the thing difficult to attain. If he had been a great and wise philosopher, like the writer of this book, he would now have comprehended that Work consists of whatever a body is *obliged* to do, and that Play consists of whatever a body is not obliged to do.' It was a book both funny AND informative. I hugged it hard to my breast until it was displaced by another cornerstone of American children's literature; Susan M. Coolidge's 1872 classic *What Katy Did*.

What Katy Did followed in the wake of Alcott's *Little Women* and was possibly suggested to Sarah Woolsey (Coolidge was a pen name) by the editor of *Little Women* himself, Thomas Niles, to capitalise on the newly forged appetite for lively, realistic girls and their exploits.

The freckled tomboy in petticoats and heavy boots on the cover piqued my sister's interest and it became one of the three books she read as a child. The other two were the BBC Micro computer guide and a Haynes car manual. It should have come as no surprise, perhaps, that when she reached the end of Coolidge's tale, she hurled it across the room shouting 'Katy did nothing!' before stalking off to finish the kit car she was coding an automated build for behind the sofa.

She had a point, in a way. Katy is the eldest but the most rambunctious of the Carr siblings when the story begins. After a few chapters of delightful adventures and mischief-making, she decides to play on the new swing Papa has put up in the barn, even though this has been Expressly Forbidden by Aunt Izzie, who has looked after them all since their fond mama died.

Katy swings high. Too high. Astute reader spots metaphor. The swing breaks and Katy lands in a crumpled heap, injuring her back so badly that it is understood she will never walk again. Confined to bed, Katy rages impotently against fate until one day, the similarly physically afflicted Cousin Helen (the question of whether this is a coincidence too far even by the forgiving standards of nineteenth-century children's fiction, or whether paraplegic women were in fact a common feature of shabby genteel Connecticut families in the 1870s strikes me only now) comes to visit her. By quiet example she shows the shamefully resentful Katy how she can transmute suffering into feminine grace, patience and understanding. Over the succeeding months and years, Katy learns to accept her lot and gradually transforms herself into a Good Girl, becoming the loving centre of the family – the wise, gentle, self-abnegating woman to whom all turn for comfort, advice and a deal of hair-stroking. And then, one day, she learns to walk again! Hurrah!

After the first few chapters then, it is, as my sister indirectly pointed out, not so much what Katy did but what process of inner transformation she underwent. Naturally some of the ideals held up to Katy have dated – the cultivation of womanly passivity is now no more recommended than is the confinement of those with disabilities to a single room upstairs. Likewise the idea that disabilities will be lifted from you if you behave well enough is outmoded (and something Jacqueline Wilson was particularly careful to reject when she published a contemporary rewrite of the story a few years ago). But the idea that good can come of suffering intrigued me, and sowed a useful attitudinal seed for later life and the advent of maths homework that required you to do more than sort apples into groups of five. Whether its other lessons about the feminine virtues of choking down your inner torments and subjugating your every desire to the whim of God are quite so helpful to readers, I doubt.

My sister, incidentally, now programs computers for a living and makes a fortune. She has no understanding of the human condition, but it turns out that this matters far less than you were ever promised. She gives me money for books. So the world turns.

I was reading so much and so quickly by this point that it was only if a volume triggered a truly obsessive number of rereads that my dad's attention would be caught. So it was with Katy and soon that god amongst men supplied two sequels, which followed the now-ambulant heroine on adventures further afield.* *What Katy Did at School* sends her and Clover off to boarding school in New Hampshire where they make firm friends with lively, plucky Rose Red, politely distance

* And a little after that I would find on the back flap of a hardback edition of *What Katy Did* in the library mention of another sequel – *Clover*. I ran to the librarian to beg her to track down a copy. But she had never heard of it, it wasn't on the system anywhere and there my quest – pre-Internet, children – ended. We were all undemocratically at the mercy of institutional caprice and unreliable gatekeepers in a way that hardly exists now. However. A few years ago, both *Clover* and the final, even-more-thoroughly-forgotten book in the series *In the High Valley* were republished. The good news is that I now have the full set. The bad news is that *Clover* and *In the High Valley* went unpublished for decades for a reason. They are not a patch on *Katy* one, two or three. But I still think they are happy to be all together again.

themselves from their awful cousin Lily and gradually thaw the icy demeanour of one of the mistresses with their warm, unaffected Midwestern ways and good hearts. The sequel to the sequel, *What Katy Did Next*, is the tale of her year's tour of Europe as a companion to her father's patient, Mrs Ashe. I, having no urge to travel myself, didn't like this one as much but I was happy for Katy and I did enjoy seeing London through the eyes of a nineteenth-century American. She is particularly impressed with Westminster Abbey and my sense of time and scale warped with hers as we gazed together at its 'dim, rich antiquity [with] eyes fresh from the world which still calls itself "new" '. It was a tiny illustration, though as neat a one as you could hope to find, of reading's limitless power to expand and transport you through history, space and in and out of others' consciousnesses, and I sighed with satisfaction.

Soon after that, handsome young naval officer Lieutenant Worthington arrives and the book lost a great deal of its hold for me as Katy fell in love. Nevertheless, I persevered to the end, noting in a detached way that if you *had* to fall in love, their stiff, unsentimental method was probably the way to do it: one mention of it being 'very nice' if the lieutenant were to escort them to Genoa, one off-screen conversation before she heads back to Connecticut, and a single telltale blush when Clover mentions 'that brother' of Mrs Ashe once she's home, and they were done. But overall *What Katy Did Next* definitely took the bronze, *What Katy Did* the silver and *School* the gold.

Somehow, somewhere – I can only think there must have been a biographical or autobiographical gobbet or two about the author in my copy of Tom Sawyer*, chosen to encourage us to pick up other books – I read Twain's assertion that the eponymous heroine of *Anne of Green Gables* was 'the dearest and most loveable child in fiction since the immortal Alice'. I tracked a copy down at the library and read it eagerly, only to discover that my idol had steered me wrong. Anne Shirley made me as sick as a dog.

At first she had my sympathy. She was an orphan and, while I was prepared to hope that they arranged things slightly better in Canada, I knew from *Mandy*, *Bunty* and Sarah Crewe that this was a grim lot to be handed in life. But this sympathy rapidly wore off. Relentlessly cheery was Anne Shirley. Relentlessly talkative. Relentlessly uplifted by the sight of apple and cherry blossom. Relentlessly enthusiastic about poetry and puffed sleeves. I returned my copy to the library after an unprecedented single reading and went to tap Grandma for whatever medications she had in her capacious handbags for treating childhood nausea.

We must reach for another Mark Twain quotation. 'When I was a boy of fourteen, my father was so ignorant I could hardly stand to have the old man around. But when I got to be twenty-one, I was astonished at how much the old man had learned in seven years.' I had come to the book too young. When I picked it up again a few years later, I too was astonished at how much it had improved – and shortly thereafter secretly

* I have most of my childhood books still – at least from the days of Plop onwards – but *Tom* is one of the few to have been lost along the way.

devastated by the fact that not only could I be an idiot in all matters sporting, artistic and practical I could also be so when it came to reading too.

On rereading, then, I learned that Anne Shirley is indeed a dear and most loveable child. Who could not, after all, adore anyone who insists that her name be spelled with the 'e' – 'so much more distinguished. If you'll only call me Anne with an e I shall try to reconcile myself to not being called Cordelia.' However could I have not? She is not twee and Pollyanna-ish (it suddenly occurs to me that I should almost certainly reread *Pollyanna* too) but a doughty survivor of a harsh upbringing who has refused to let circumstances crush her spirit. She arrives at Marilla and Matthew Cuthbert's farm in Avonlea with the odds stacked against her – orphaned, unwanted (they are expecting a boy) and, her greatest and most lamented trial, red-haired and freckled.

She proceeds, through her odd way of seeing things, through her patently honest love of beauty and endearing attempts to master her various jealousies and yearnings, to win over the Cuthberts, their neighbours and millions of readers who have met her over the years since the book was first published. When I settle down with it these days, it is the gradual softening of Marilla that seems to me the true miracle of the book, but this only reminds me again of the great truth that you are never too young to start rereading.

As my cornflake-packet dependency attests, by this point reading had evolved from a simple pleasure to an actual need. It wasn't just my preferred activity any longer but an addiction, albeit of the most benign and valuable kind. It was almost physically painful to be kept from it. Every other activity was an interruption, a depredation on time that could be better spent. Birthday parties and going for tea at people's houses was always awful. School was a necessity, playing with my sister was okay and television had its moments (not many – there were only three channels and Mum naturally had entire charge over what we watched and when) but . . . I was just always happiest reading.

Dad understood entirely.

Mum didn't, quite, but rolled her eyes and tried to accept that there were some things even she couldn't change and her child's constitutional make-up was one of them. I'm not saying she wouldn't have dived into my DNA and started replumbing my double helix if technology had allowed, but as things stood it was one of the few things in life she had simply to grit her teeth and bear. She would wear those teeth down to nubs over the next ten years.

Other people, however, got strangely angry. A certain percentage of adult visitors would greet me with a disapproving 'Every time I see you, you've got your head in a book!' or 'Don't you ever go out in the fresh air?' or some variant thereof. A much higher percentage of children hated it. If I tried to read at playtime, the book would be batted out of my hand. If I tried to read secretly during lessons with the book hidden on my lap, it would be reported with undisguised glee.

I have far more sympathy with my enemies – as I unequivocally categorised them – now than I did then. I used to argue (inwardly. I did everything inwardly) that everyone should be free at playtime to pursue their own favoured hobby. Those who wanted to skip could skip,* those who wanted to play British Bulldog, kiss-chase or Feet-Off-London could do that and those who wanted to pinball round the place screaming for forty minutes could do that. I wasn't stopping them. Why were they intent on stopping me? Let a thousand fucking flowers bloom, dudes. But of course this is asking too much of children. It is infuriating to see someone determinedly wall him or herself off from you, from the group, whether it's by books, headphones, video games, smartphones or anything else. It is absolutely a form of rejection and nobody likes being rejected.

The adults, I think, could have held their tongues. They got their due – I always stood up, said hello, answered questions politely. Then I escaped, like any child does, as soon as I could – just back to my book on the sofa instead of the garden or the television or a friend's house or whatever they would have preferred. I suspect their attitude was fed more by the hostility we feel for precocity (it seems to mess with the natural economy) and the anger or envy we feel for anyone getting pleasure from something that we cannot. I feel this for lovers of music and art – neither of which I 'get' – though I try to pretend to myself that it is a higher feeling; an appreciative longing to be like them, a yearning for their gifts and insights. But actually it's

* We still had skipping ropes in the playground. A girl at each end – don't get cross with me, it WAS always girls and I am just reporting – and a queue of skippers awaiting their turn in the middle. Does this still go on, or am I remembering a time that will vanish from living memory with my generation?

low-level, infantile (primitive) rage that I can't see what they see or hear what they hear. That these avenues of pleasure are, by as random a selection and arrangement of genes and circumstances that opened the way of reading to me, closed. It IS infuriating. But I do hold my tongue.

A generation on, things are different for my son because he is a different child from me, in a different time. Alexander can read, he likes to read, but it does not (yet? I cannot tell you how much aching longing I pack into that single syllable) have him in the vicelike grip that it did me by his age. He is not – *yet*? – a bookworm. The four minutes or so of reading he voluntarily does in a week are not likely to perplex or anger anyone (except me, and I am still holding my tongue). And so the idea of banning him from reading in certain places is laughable. If his father or I happen across him reading anywhere – bedroom, sitting room, bath, sitting naked in his own filth while strangling a cat – we brake hard and back away as silently and unobtrusively as possible. Then we run and find the other and deliver, in hushed, awed tones the joyful news: 'He's reading!' More often than not, I tiptoe back to watch. I can practically see the stream of glittering words flowing into his mind, giving him new names for new things, teaching him in some fundamental way that nothing else can manage how words fit together, how sentences work, how language can be bent this way and that to conjure worlds, feelings, arguments, everything. I want to find a way to grab it in my hands and join the book in stuffing more of it into him because I know it's not going to be long before he lifts his head and rejoins us in the real world. Whenever he shifts position I hold my breath – is the spell about to break, or will it hold? If it holds I sigh with relief. If it breaks, I scarper before discovery.

It is, I agree, pathetic.

And of course my son lives, like all children today, surrounded by temptations literally unimaginable in their parents' childhoods. 'Any sufficiently advanced technology is indistinguishable from magic,' the science-fiction author Arthur C. Clarke famously wrote. But I think that even if we'd been invited as children to think up the most extraordinary possibilities that could be afforded by the most powerful wizardries, we would have struggled to come up with the Internet, the iPad, smartphones. Portable screens that can show you anything you want, anywhere and anytime you like, for free (mostly), at the touch of not-even-quite-a-button. The world's art, culture and music accessible through a device smaller than a wallet. Even if you do only use it, in the end, for cat videos. Or, in Alexander's case, *Tractor Tom* and *Scooby Doo*.

We have kept him, so far, from video games and suchlike (adherence to principle here being massively aided by our genuine and total inability to download apps or hook up a PlayStation) but there is only so long we can beat back the waves. Soon they will engulf us and bear him away on their pixellated currents.

Sometimes I make an attempt to read through the research about the effects of screen time on children, but my heart is never in it. I know what screen time does to me, and unless someone in authority can prove to me that my brain chemistry is unique in the annals of human history, I will take my individual experience as representative of the whole. And my experience is that watching telly is easier than reading a book. Even for me, who loves to read, who finds it second nature, who is surrounded by books to suit her every mood and has literally only to reach out a hand anywhere round the house to pick one up. That's why at the end of the day, I switch on Netflix instead of opening a paperback. I have a restorative, mindless few hours on the sofa with a box set and then I go to bed and read. One activity is unavoidably passive, the other unavoidably active.

My near-pathological love of reading made me unnaturally resistant to the siren call of the screen (although that was markedly weaker back then, coming as it did via only three channels, only one and a half of which even acknowledged children as a viewing demographic) but which is a normal, healthy child today going to plump for, given the option? And given how hard and – though we forget this over the years – fundamentally unnatural reading is in your early years? Reading the simplest book is more difficult than letting the most complicated programme unspool before you.

Obviously in an ideal world you would be able to explain to children that while reading might be hard at first, the rewards throughout life are proportionately large. Unfortunately, most children stubbornly resist the concept of deferred gratification ('I'll take that double sundae now, Mother,' they insist, 'heedless of the consequences for my appetite for lunch'), and so you have to shape their world accordingly. Thus you learn not to let them see the sundae, the PlayStation or – oh, if I had my time again – *Scooby Doo* too early or too often.

Encouraging reading in this day and age is like trying to create a wild-flower meadow. Most of the job is just about clearing and preserving a space in which rarer and more delicate plants can grow, planting the seeds and just hoping to God they take root. As I say, they have not – yet – done so in Alexander. But I keep digging up bindweed and hacking back the brambles, trying to keep the way clear. What else can you do? Eh, Mary? Eh, Dickon? What else can you do?

8

Happy Golden Years

Puffin

Many people I have met in my adult life – friends, many of them, after I started to get the hang of people in my early twenties – have assumed I was a member of the Puffin Club. This was an institution set up in 1967 by the then new and indefatigably sociable editor of Puffin Kaye Webb when she took over from the (decidedly old-skool) Eleanor Graham.

I was not a member of the Puffin Club.

Webb set up the club to encourage like-minded children to get together. To this day, the idea of a sociable bookworm sounds to me like the oxymoron to end all oxymorons, but apparently they were out there and they descended on her club in droves. It promised – and delivered – all sorts of events, day trips and get-togethers and had soon gathered over 200,000 members, several of whom nearly drowned when Webb took them sailing round Lundy Island off the Devon coast after mishearing the skipper's advice not to set out.

Twenty years on, by the time I was reading about

membership in the backs of all my Puffin books, the original frenzy of activity had abated somewhat but the threat of companionship and conviviality – if not drowning – seemed to linger. 'Psst,' said a speech bubble issuing from the beak of a puffin in a cloak at the back of *The Borrowers, The Family from One End Street* et al. 'Heard about the Puffin Club?' He promised a badge, a membership book and delivery of a quarterly magazine called *Puffin Post*. 'It's a way of finding out more about Puffin books and authors, of winning prizes (in competitions), sharing jokes, a secret code, and perhaps seeing your name in print!'

Innately unclubbable anyway, and daily assured by my schoolfellows that bookworms were the lowest of the low, I could not imagine anything worse than being in touch with more of me. At the very least, talking to them would be almost as much of a waste of good reading time as entering competitions would be. And imagine a magazine largely made up of contributions from other children. My own creative offerings, be they drawing, writing or trying to bend pipe cleaners into recognisable shapes, left me profoundly depressed. I wouldn't shell out for either more of the same or – worse – evidence of others' far greater brilliance in the field. Although I probably didn't actually need to worry too much – *The Borrowers'* back pages were already out of date. *Puffin Post* closed in 1982, though the club itself continued in various relaunched forms until very recently.

That said, I now suspect that I was unwittingly some kind of proxy member of the club. My school had started holding a weekly book sale and although I have consulted both Puffin and their archivists and none of them can find any evidence for it, I think it must have been part of Webb's web. Every Friday lunchtime, a classroom's tables were pushed together and covered with books. Shiny, beautiful, mesmerising new books. You could wander round and browse for whatever remained of the hour after your lunch sitting (the dinner hall was small, we went in shifts) and no one would chase you out, insisting you got some stupid fresh air before afternoon lessons began.

You got a savings card and once you had chosen your book, the teacher in charge put a slip of paper with your name on inside it and it was reserved for you. No one else. Unless someone nefarious took that slip of paper out and had theirs put in instead. This happened to me twice. Yes, I know who did it. I won't say who, but when I die you will find the name 'Claire Stephens' engraved on my heart. Anyway. Every week thereafter you would bring in money towards it, and have your card stamped in 5p increments until you had paid in full. Then the book was yours.

I bought *Stig of the Dump* this way, which was Webb's own first commission for her new Puffin Originals series. She set this up in 1962, wanting to move on from simply buying the paperback rights to previously published books, and *Stig* was one of the books she always said she was proudest of publishing. It had been rejected by many other firms but became a bestseller for Puffin and hasn't been out of print since. It cost me 90p and took forever. I measured out my life in Fridays and 5p stamps. At last it was mine. And it was brilliant. The story of Barney and his befriending of a Stone Age boy who lives at the bottom of the local chalk quarry-cum-dump (what? Why, where would you live if you'd been left behind by the Stone Age? How else would you access the tin cans and jam jars you need for your flues and windows? Hmm?) was worth every penny and every exquisitely agonising minute of deferred gratification.

Then I was allowed to choose another book. The loosening of credit restrictions that was causing the property market to go nuts had not yet reached primary school economies and you had to pay off your first one in full before you could lay claim to another. Which to choose, which to choose . . . The one with the cartoon of the pig and the spider on the front looked interesting. I took a look at the first page. 'Where's Papa going with that axe?' Those six words – one of the most famous opening lines in children's literature – told me I was in the hands of a master and I demanded my reservation slip for E. B. White's *Charlotte's Web* forthwith.

Papa is about to kill Wilbur, the runt of a litter of piglets just born on the farm. After Fern's heartfelt protests, his execution is stayed and Fern is allowed to raise him. In the cosy barn he shares with an assortment of other creatures Wilbur's most constant companion is the beautiful, dignified, noble, intelligent spider Charlotte. She weaves glowing endorsements of Wilbur into her web, making him a valuable attraction at the farm and saving him from slaughter a second time when he grows up. In 1948, White – already famous as a contributor to American literary magazine the *New Yorker* and as the writer of another book for children, *Stuart Little* (about the adventures of a mouse born to a human family in New York City) – had published an essay entitled 'Death of a Pig', about his failure to save a sick beast that he had bought for his farm. Though he never admitted as much, it is hard not to see the book he started a year later, after resigning from his job at the *New Yorker*, as an oblique attempt at redemption. The idea of a spider as saviour came to White as he watched one building a web and hatch an egg sac on his dresser while he pondered a way to prevent his fictional pig suffering the traditional fate.

A farm. A cosy barn. A plump, endearing hero and a watchful, clever friend. Sounds charming, doesn't it? It is. It was. I set my prejudice against talking animals aside and read on delightedly. It was so clear, succinct and yet evocative (White was a famously elegant, economical author and essayist, whose rules for writing were enshrined in the language guide written by his former teacher William Strunk, *The Elements of Style*, which White later edited and updated so thoroughly that it has been known as *Strunk & White* ever since, at least amongst those of us nerds who like to chat about these things) and it seemed to speak directly to me. White once referred to his younger self as – and I think my heart will break as I type these words – 'a boy I knew', and *Charlotte's Web*, even more than the earlier *Stuart Little* or the later *Trumpet of the Swan*, seems always to be speaking through and to that child.

But TURN AWAY NOW, PLEASE, children who have not read this book – and adults who *have* read this book but whose prepubescent homunculus is not dead but only sleeping and will feel the wash of unbearable horror and misery anew if it wakes again now – because the end of *Charlotte's Web* is nigh and the truth of the matter is this: Wilbur lives. But Charlotte dies.

I. Could. Not. Believe. It.

Yes, the tone of the book had been becoming ever

more darkly suggestive. The barn had been filling with foreboding. But even unto the last twenty pages I had been deliciously anticipating the sudden twist that would surely swoop in and reprieve such a kind and valiant friend from what would in real life be her certain fate. Even if White had kept the original title of the final chapter – 'Death of Charlotte' – instead of changing it to 'The Final Day' I would have remained firmly optimistic.

The reprieve did not come. Though her children live on, thanks to Wilbur rescuing the egg sac she leaves behind at the county fair, Charlotte dies, as spiders do, at the end of the summer.

I was beyond appalled. I took the book and my outrage to Dad, who accessed his inner lay preacher and told me that Charlotte had lived well and died free, playing her part in the grand scheme of things. In the midst of life we are in death, apparently, and to everything there is a season. 'I know people die in real life,' I shrieked. 'But why do they have to die in books?' He couldn't answer me. Nor could he come up with a satisfactory balm for my secondary sense of authorial betrayal. Better to have axed Wilbur at the beginning, I raged, than allow me to grow to love the protagonists and then give one of them the chop in the end. But perhaps it was good to read a book that sought to prepare you rather than protect you from some aspects of life, he suggested. I suggested not.

It has taken thirty years for me to be able to contemplate this book with relative equanimity. I see now that the ending is as beautiful, bold and full of integrity as Charlotte herself. White wrote it as he turned fifty, as his son moved out of boyhood, as his beloved editor at the

New Yorker Harold Ross died and everything was changing. He saved the pig, but something had to give – or be given up – instead. White's story is agnostic but it makes plain that in the midst of life we are in death. But it also makes clear that life goes on. Charlotte's hundreds of children scrambling round the barn tell us so. I have gradually come to find comfort in its simple acceptance of the world the way it is and the lack of striving for an answer that would explain it all. It is what it is. We are born, we die and if we're lucky we make some good friends along the way who will remember us when we're gone. It's enough. Not least because it has to be.

Maybe this means that if Alexander ever comes up to me, book in hand and eyes wide with horror at what he has just witnessed and demanding explanations and justice, I will remain sanguine enough to use the opportunity to explore the notion that fiction can confer immortality of a kind – 'Look!' I say in my roseate dreams, 'Charlotte can be made to live again by turning back to page one! Such is the magic of books!' But I doubt I will manage it. I think we'll just have to sob wordlessly into each other's shoulders and wait for another quarter-century to do its healing work. A reader I knew tells me so.

Tolbooths And Gardens

But if the weekly book shop was my living pig – hurrah! – another school innovation lay on my soul like a dead spider. Boo! Boo to whoever it was decided that reading aloud in class was a way to inculcate a love of literature.

We murdered many books this way. They were mostly

school primers but also and bizarrely *The Starlight Barking*. Why on earth we were reading the semi-mystical, largely demented sequel to *The Hundred and One Dalmatians* instead of the brilliant original (Pongo! Missus! Perdita! 98 spotty puppies holed up in Hell Hall and waiting for rescue! Was there ever a more pleasing notion for a book? That, you know, wasn't about a race of tiny people under the floorboards?) I have no idea. Maybe they thought everyone would have read the book or seen the cartoon film of the original that had recently been reissued to cinemas. Maybe someone had bequeathed a job lot to the school. Maybe someone had a tiny bit of budget left over at the end of the tax year and had to get rid of it quickly. We will never know.

Anyway. It was utter torture. Torture when you were the one doing the reading (I at least didn't have to suffer the humiliation of not being a fluent reader, but I was pathologically monotonous and winced as every word out of my mouth fell dead. They were so wonderful in my head) and worse when you were sitting in silence listening to people struggling painfully through a story that seemed like it would never end.

Eventually, however, this black pall passed. Sunlight broke through. Someone, in his or her infinite wisdom, replaced reading aloud with story time. For half an hour every day, thirty children would sit cross-legged on a piece of thin polyester matting, and peace and a modest kind of communal rapture would reign. Being read to was not as good as reading to yourself, I reckoned, but it was a lot better than nothing. And maths. I did not then nor have I yet seen the point of finding the area under a graph.

I remember only two books from this glorious time, but what a pair they were. Do you know that e e cummings poem that goes 'i carry your heart with me (i carry it in my heart)'? More than any others, perhaps, I carry these books in my heart and my heart is in these books. They could hardly be more different, but they are two of the three poles (we'll meet the other one shortly) around which my prepubescent soul was – is now and ever more shall be – slung.

My beloved teacher Mrs Pugh was on maternity leave. I was unsure of her replacement, Miss Dobbs, until she began reading us Norton Juster's *The Phantom Tollbooth*.

Milo, a languidly bored, cynical child and the first unlikeable central character I had ever come across in fiction, is sent 'an enormous package . . . not quite square . . . definitely not round, and for its size it was larger than almost any other big package of smaller dimension that he'd ever seen'. It is, in fact, a miniature purple tollbooth and when he drives past it in his toy car, he embarks on a series of adventures in Dictionopolis (with a grand marketplace where letters are bought by the handful) and Digitopolis (whose land is mined for numbers, while rubies, emeralds and diamonds are thrown away with the earth). These are the two capital cities of the Kingdom of Wisdom, governed by two warring brothers – King Azaz the Unabridged and the Mathemagician – who have exiled their two sisters, Rhyme and Reason, for refusing to judge whether words or numbers were the most important. Since then, the kingdom has descended into chaos.

In thirty-minute chunks, we followed Milo and his

helpmeets Tock the faithful watchdog and the annoying but endearing Humbug through the Doldrums, up and down the Foothills of Confusion and Mountains of Ignorance, and jumped with him and his companions to the Island of Conclusions. On the way, they – and we – met, among many manic others, Faintly Macabre (the Not-So-Wicked Which), the tallest dwarf in the world (who looked remarkably like the shortest giant in the world), the Awful Dynne (who collects sounds for Dr Kakofonous A Dischord) and the .58 boy, who is the fifth member of the average American family (at least in 1961, the year of the book's publication) with its two parents and 2.58 children. With help from some and hindrance from others, Milo restores Rhyme and Reason to their proper place and returns home (whereupon the tollbooth vanishes) no longer languid and never again to be bored. His tollbooth may be gone but, he realises, the books he once regarded with disdain will function as portals to other worlds and adventures just as well.

There are obvious shades of Lewis Carroll here, although Norton Juster himself cites his father – an inveterate punner – and the Marx brothers' films as his greatest influences. At nine, I had never read or met any of these splendid entities. I came to *The Phantom Tollbooth* fresh and it rocked my tiny world.

In 1960 Juster was a 31-year-old architect living in a Brooklyn basement flat. He received a Ford Foundation grant of $5,000 to write a book for children about cities but instead he found himself scribbling down sections of Milo's story. Above his apartment lived an artist called Jules Feiffer. He became interested in Juster's writing and started to illustrate it with the drawings that are now as inseparable from *The Phantom Tollbooth* as John Tenniel's are from *Alice*.

Juster took Feiffer's illustrations with him when he went to show the first fifty pages of his book to various publishing houses. It was a tough sell because the received wisdom of the time was that children's books should not contain anything that children did not already know. 'Everyone said this is not a children's book, the vocabulary is much too difficult, the wordplay and the punning they will never understand, and anyway fantasy is bad for children because it disorients them,' remembered Juster half a century later. But Random House saw its merits and agreed to publish it.

Two decades on, that Brooklyn manuscript and drawings done on handfuls of cheap tracing paper ('Had Norton told me he was writing a classic,' Feiffer said in an interview years later, 'I would have used nicer paper') was still delighting children, especially one in a Faintly Dismal corner of a Definitely Dismal patch of south-east London.

The pace, the wit, the invention were dizzying – even if we did only fully understand about .58 of it at the time. There was action aplenty, and if you didn't get one joke or pun or piece of wordplay, another would be along in a minute. They fell from the pages like sweets tumbling from a bag. Maybe it was because Juster was a synaesthete who felt intensely intimate connections between words, colours and numbers, that his first book for children (he would not go on to write many more, alas) was so vivid and resonated so strongly even with readers more loosely wired. But it was a book that, aside from the obvious pleasures of the story, also revelled in and made gloriously explicit and true what I had previously only vaguely intuited: that words weren't just markings on a page to be passively absorbed and enjoyed but could be tools, treasures and toys all in one. They could be taken out and played with, and even bent to one's own will in their turn. At one point, travelling across the no man's land between Dictionopolis and Digitopolis, Milo comes across the orchestra whose music is what floods the world with colour, a different instrument for every hue. Violins tip the grass green, 'trumpets blare out the blue sea' and at dawn while the conductor Chroma sleeps, Milo dares to take the stand and crook a finger. 'A single piccolo played a single note and off in the east a solitary shaft of cool lemon light flicked across the sky.' I knew none of this could really happen. Violins couldn't tip grass green, a piccolo couldn't summon a single shaft of lemon light, but words, I saw for the first time, could conjure up both. Reading *The Phantom Tollbooth* was like watching the translucent paper being peeled off a transfer, revealing the true colours beneath. The world of every book would glow a little brighter ever after.

By its fiftieth anniversary in 2011 *The Phantom Tollbooth* was estimated to have sold about 4 million copies.

In 1983, however, none of these was being sold in the UK. I know this because as soon as Miss Dobbs had closed the covers on the final instalment, I begged my father to buy me my own copy (I had started searching school and local libraries as soon as the first chapter was over and found nothing). We went to the Greenwich Book Boat, which had become a recent favourite haunt – nothing there. We went to Dillons in Bromley – which had a COMPUTER! As if it was already the FUTURE! – that told us it was out of print. For some reason we didn't then start scouring second-hand bookshops – maybe Dad didn't think they dealt in children's books – so after the ensuing bout of panic and grief wore off, I accepted my fate. There was, in those benighted, Internet-free days, nothing to be done.

It is easy to forget how many gatekeepers there are between us and the books we want – or do not yet know we want – even as adults. And as children we are at the mercy of even more. In addition to every reader's dependence on publishers, buyers, stockists, retailers, knowledgeable sellers, librarians and friends (and of course on the writers at the very beginning of the process to come up with the lovely, lovely goods in the first place), children have parents, teachers and their own ignorance of how the world and its retail outlets work, and a lack of control over their own circumstances and finances. I wonder – if Miss Dobbs hadn't lifted the barrier, how many of the thirty of us sitting on the carpet in front of her would have come across this shiningly glorious book? Almost certainly after the perfect age to meet it and, more likely, never.

I have diligently acquired several copies since as a hedge against further deprivation. I can see three as I sit at my desk. There's the blue-covered edition I took out a parental loan to buy for £1.95 in 1986 when it returned to Dillons' shelves three seemingly endless years after my devastation, the red-spined edition identical to the one Miss Dobbs read from which I picked up for a pound in a second-hand bookshop in Norfolk a few years ago, and a 1970 hardback edition that I bought from another Norfolk dealer for £5 and turned out to be ex-Lewisham Library stock. It must already have been withdrawn from circulation by the time I was scouring the place, but clearly we were meant to be together. And it is a beautiful copy – perhaps the only attractive thing to have come out of the 1970s. Bury me with it please. It remains a masterfully wrought, glorious, hilarious, life-affirming read – a celebration of words, ideas, sense, nonsense, cleverness and silliness but also of a love of learning for its own sake. I suspect, in a world in which education is increasingly being reduced to futile box-ticking and forcible rendering into measurable quantities that which can never be made tangible, this is a message that will become only more revelatory and valuable to those lucky enough to hear it. The piccolo sheds light everywhere.

*

When we eventually finished *The Phantom Tollbooth* I was bereft. Back to spelling tests, to something called long division and to building a papier mâché trench to learn about the First World War. Oh, and we had to grow broad beans in jam jars filled with damp blotting paper. The paper held them against the glass, so they looked like eyes watching you balefully from the windowsill. You could see their roots reaching down, desperately sending out further tiny furry offshoots searching for greater sustenance than wood pulp and water. I looked back at them equally balefully. Everywhere was metaphor.

Eventually we were allowed to take them home and plant them in pots/throw them in the bin as levels of parental interest dictated. Mine went in the bin. 'We'd only have to keep looking after it otherwise,' said my mother. My sister and I regarded each other silently and renewed our inner vows never to cross her until we had both attained our majority and secured a shared lease somewhere.

My own gasping search for readerly nourishment at school was soon to be rewarded in full. I was about to be flung into the rich, loamy soil of *Tom's Midnight Garden*. The roots of me are down there still. If you tried to pull them up I would scream like a mandrake. Like *The Phantom Tollbooth*, it is necessary to me.

Miss Dodds had read *The Phantom Tollbooth* to us at the end of morning lessons, before lunch. Mrs Pugh, back from maternity leave and who was otherwise a woman of infinite sense and wisdom, read *Tom's Midnight Garden* to us for the half-hour before home time. Not until the day's work was complete would she begin.

So I spent every day for months in an agony – or was it an ecstasy? – of waiting and most of 1984 wishing a short but painful death on my fellow nine- and ten-year-olds who kept delaying us by mucking about and cutting into the twenty-five minutes (Mrs Pugh also insisted on stopping five minutes before official home time so that we could put our chairs on the desks before we left as school rules commanded) on which my day's happiness had come to depend.

Because the story of Tom Long, who is sent away to stay with relatives while his brother is ill, is exquisite.

Lonely and bored, Tom discovers that when the grandfather clock in the communal hallway – on whose casing is carved the words from Revelation: 'Time no longer' – strikes thirteen, the magnificent garden that once belonged to the house before it was divided up into flats is restored to it – along with the equally lonely Hatty who used to play there as a child and who becomes Tom's night-time companion. Tom gradually realises that he is returning to the nineteenth century, but it takes a visit from his convalescing brother, who accompanies him on one of his nocturnal adventures, to make him realise that time in the garden is moving on and Hatty is growing up. One night, he at last becomes as invisible to her as he has been to everyone else in her world. Soon after that, the garden disappears too and it is almost time for Tom to go home.

There is one last twist, which I am not going to spoil for you, partly because I cannot bring myself to rob you of its power and pleasure by baldly summarising it, and partly because if I had to learn, through Mrs Pugh's meagre apportionments, the painful lesson of deferred gratification, I am most certainly going to force the experience on to others too, wherever I can.

At the time, however, I was so firmly locked in a battle of wills with my teacher that I restrained myself from asking my father to buy the book for me so that I could read on ahead. But as soon as Mrs Pugh had turned the final page, I dragged him down to Dillons so that I could read the whole thing for myself – in one sitting, free from the desire to stab Darren Jones in the heart with his ever-clattering pencil – a process that yielded a better sense of the finely honed shape of the book and its careful, masterly pacing and let me linger over the beauty of the prose and the wealth of possibilities offered by its suggestion that the past and the present could merge into each other if only you knew where to look. And there were no nasty surprises at the shop – not only was the book still in print, it was still Mrs Pugh's edition that was on sale, with its properly glossy green cover, Susan Einzig's beautiful illustrations inside and out.

I see now and delight in the fact that those tortured days of waiting meshed beautifully with the mood of the book. My own hungry anticipation mirrored Tom's impatient wait for his nightly doses of magic perfectly.

More profoundly, I responded to the sense of longing – for companionship, for adventure, for people and places long vanished – that permeates the whole of *Tom's Midnight Garden*. My distance from it – again, being read to is far, far better than nothing but it does not compare to reading to yourself – gave me a heightened sense of how impossible it is to absorb the books we love as fully as we want to. I bet even the Sendak fan who ate the card the writer sent him felt a sense of anticlimax afterwards. We can read, and read, and read them but we can never truly live there. It is an approximation so close that it borders on the miraculous, for sure, and – unless perhaps you are an actor, and a good actor at that – there is nothing else that even comes near it, which is what keeps the bookworm going. But still – you are not in Narnia. You are not actually beneath the floorboards with the Clocks. You are not roaming the prairies with Laura, Mary, Ma and Pa. And yet . . . and yet . . . *Tom's Midnight Garden* is suffused with the pain and the pleasure of yearning. Even as he's playing contentedly in the garden with Hattie before his brother arrives, its nightly appearance and morning disappearance already points to its evanescence. There is always a suggestion that everything is in flux, that nothing can last. The best we can hope for is to live there for a while. And accept that if yew hedges and towering trees cannot endure, happiness too is best understood as fleeting.

C. S. Lewis once discussed the concept of *Sehnsucht* – German for what we would call 'yearning'* – and reckoned this 'unconsolable longing' in the human heart for 'we know not what' was an intimation of the divine. 'If I discover within myself a desire which no experience in this world will satisfy,' he says in *Mere Christianity*, 'the most probable explanation is that I was made for another world.'

But perhaps we're more often just made for reading. Each book was to me another world, and none more so than *Tom's Midnight Garden*, then or now. Because I have reread it countless times since Mrs Pugh closed the covers for the final time, and within three pages, I am my ten-year-old self again. Within six, I am with Tom in his 1950s world and after that we are both in the Victorian garden again with Hatty and the yew trees and hedges that preceded and will outlast them all. I still believe, deep in my heart, that if I wake up at the right moment

* Though as you might expect with such a porous, abstract concept it has slightly different connotations from our word – theirs means something more like 'life longings', particularly for a home, or homelike place that you have not necessarily experienced, or for something unnameable and indefinable.

one night, I, too, will be able to step out of this world and all its inconsolable longings and run wild forever in the gardens of the past. But the best I can do is live there again for a while. Which is, almost, enough. After all, if you are as close to something as you were in childhood, then you have your childhood back again, don't you? Time no longer.

Goodnight Mister Tom

Shortly after Tom's covers closed, I turned ten and received as one of my presents (and thank you, always, everyone who responded to my annual plea that they all be books, or book tokens – I don't know how I would have managed without you) my first ever hardback. 'To Lucy,' it had written inside it by the givers, because this apparently is a thing you do with hardbacks, 'With lots of love for a happy birthday from Mummy, Daddy and Emily'. It was *Goodnight Mister Tom* by Michelle Magorian. As well as being impressive – so thick! So weighty! So altogether grown up! – it was beautiful. The impressionistic cover in lovely muted tones (I go very maiden-aunt these days when I see how LOUD and GARISH children's covers have become – I do not admire this side of myself) showed a little boy walking down a country lane, looking back over his shoulder at an avuncular white-haired man with an eager dog at his side, under a canopy of autumnal leaves. Another gently bucolic tale of Life Way Back When ('Two days before the declaration of war in 1939,' began the blurb on the inside flap. How exciting! I'd never had an inside flap before!), I thought. Just right for someone whose heart had recently been shredded in a midnight garden. And I dived delightedly in.

You might know now, of course, what I found instead. In the thirty-plus years that have elapsed since then, *Goodnight Mister Tom* has become revered as a modern classic, embraced as a staple of the English syllabus in school and made famous by the television adaptation starring John Thaw as the not-quite-as-avuncular-as-an-autumnal-watercolour-cover-would-have-you-believe Mr Tom. The story of William Beech, who is evacuated during the Second World War and comes to live with the reclusive Tom Oakley, long mired in grief for the wife and child he lost as a young man ('He watched helplessly as the old, familiar colour of scarletina spread across both their faces' is a line that will never leave me), is no gently nostalgic tale. It is a dense, potent, perfectly paced and endlessly compelling exploration of what damage life and other people can do to us, and of the healing too.

I felt that I was reading a different order of book as I watched William's relationship with his reluctant host shift and grow and the boy gradually stand revealed as an unloved and – at the hands of his mentaly ill mother – abused child. And it did feel like I was watching, so vivid were the pictures in my mind's eye that Magorian – an actor specialising in mime before she turned to writing and poured all the words she had saved up into her perfect debut novel – conjured.

William and Tom's fear and wariness gradually fall away and a fragile trust is established between them which deepens slowly – so slowly, so painfully and truthfully that to this day I don't know how I stood it – into love. Fellow evacuee Zacharias Wrench ('My parents had a cruel sense of humour') inducts William into the joys of boyhood friendship and gives him a taste of the unfettered childhood he has missed.

There are some harrowing scenes – Zach is killed in an air raid, and later William is forced to return briefly to his mother, who locks him under the stairs with no food or drink and her new baby, who dies of starvation – and I wonder sometimes whether, if my parents had read the book when they bought it they would have hesitated before giving it to me. There would have been no need. It was never melodramatic, voyeuristic or depressing. It never bewildered or upset me in that truly distressing way that comes only with feeling unmoored in a sea of new facts or feelings. Magorian held my hand all the way. She stretched and tugged at my heart and soul, for sure – but she pulled them into a better shape. It is one of the few books I can honestly point to and say – I was different by the end. More than that, I was better. I understood more and it pulled me along the road to empathy. In its delicate portraits of friendship, its careful delineation of the effects of past experiences, good and bad, on the present, *Goodnight Mister Tom* asks in a way children can understand whether it is better to have loved and lost or never to have loved at all, suggests that we can hope to deal with grief and cultivates the first glimmerings of appreciation of what a strangely robust yet infinitely fragile thing the human spirit is. Optimism and compassion power the book. They give it truth and beauty and never steer it – or you – wrong.

I loved it so much that it became the first book I ever pressed upon someone else – Miss Powell, who had taught me a few years lower down and several times commented how interesting the book looked when she saw me reading it in the playground. She was young, kind, pretty and had sorted out the difference between 'q' and 'p' for me, so I lent it to her when I had finished. It was like handing over an organ. She thanked me and then kept it on her desk for weeks. I couldn't believe it. I used to find excuses to pass her classroom door at least three times a day and gaze at my treasure mournfully through the window. How could she resist reading it at once? How could you get a new book and not read it straight away? Hadn't she heard what I'd said about how wonderful it was and how much it meant to me? What was wrong with people? I pestered her every day to see if she had read any of it while I hadn't been looking. Eventually she read it. She liked it. She said it was indeed very good. She gave it back to me. We never spoke of it again. She looked slightly less pretty to me after that. I shouldn't have let it get to me. I certainly shouldn't let it get to me still.

However. Times do change and we, however exhaustive our efforts, change slightly with them and three decades on, the memory of Miss Powell pains me a little less than the thought that *Goodnight Mister Tom* is now part of the school curriculum. Because imagine – imagine reading this impeccably worked, subtle tale under duress, with the dread hand of coursework or examination on your shoulder. Imagine having to sit down and dissect Magorian's 'use of language' instead of immersing yourself in a story in which a small, abused and loveless boy and an old, bereaved and bitter man gradually start to heal each other. It's like asking someone to gas a butterfly and pin it to the card before they have even seen it fly.

I occasionally try and comfort myself with the thought that at least this way the book is brought before many hundreds of thousands of children who would otherwise never see it at all. And I do have faith that even in fragmented form its power is such that some greater sense of it will lodge in some forced-readers' minds and they will later seek it out in order to piece it back together for themselves and enjoy it as God and Magorian intended. But as someone who still cannot fully enjoy *Pride and Prejudice* for the ghosts of annotated underlinings that still appear before my GCSE-affrighted eyes more than twenty years on, I fervently hope that I am able to slide Magorian's masterpiece in front of Alexander before his teachers deem it time, and let him feel the joy and the agony of a full heart unconstrained by the bonds of pedagogy. With lots of love for a happy life, from Mummy.

Private – Keep Out!

'I suppose,' said my mother whenever she spotted me crawling up the stairs or leaning against the wall too weakened by laughter to have full control over my gross motor functions, 'it's that book again?'

It always was. My dad had recently come home with *Private – Keep Out!* by Gwen Grant. It was the third strut that would, with *Tom's Midnight Garden* and *The Phantom Tollbooth*, prop up my personality for years to come.

The heroine and narrator of Gwen Grant's masterpiece has no name but is the youngest of six children growing up in the Hall family, in a Nottinghamshire colliery town just after the Second World War. She is beset on all sides by siblings ('If I didn't know my own brothers personally, I wouldn't believe such a horrible bunch could exist and they make me sick'), Les Dawsonish matriarchs, grudge-bearing neighbourhood children, pitiless dance teachers ('She keeps wanting me to bend one of those bits of my legs that don't bend. I said to her, "They don't bend," and she said, "They will by the time I've finished with them"') and the general illogicality of life. It has bred within her a blend of determination, fatalism and misanthropy that warmed my heart like nothing else.

And clearly it was the funniest children's book ever written. I cleave even more firmly to this view three decades on. I reread it at least once every year and still have to have the emergency services on standby for the bit where her mam and dance teacher Fancy Nancy have to hold her down to get her into her costume for the town concert. The elastic in her knickers is too tight: '"I can't breathe," I said. And she said, "What do you want to breathe for? If them knickers fall down again, you'd be better off not breathing anyway, so just keep quiet and let me finish them."'

My parents became used to me sitting on the beanbag with tears of laughter rolling down my face as I tried to read the choicest bits out to them without choking to death. 'Listen – listen – her brother's just caught the girl who tried to burn her at the stake: "'Come on then,' he says, 'you give her a good hiding' and so I bash her as well and I think, 'I hope she doesn't live round here because when she's untied, she's going to come after me', but I don't let that stop me bashing her there and then. I think perhaps it might be the last chance I get." '

Private – Keep Out! should rank alongside *Just William* as an indispensable part of the children's canon. Alas, and for no better reason that I can discern than the vagaries of chance and/or the misalignment of planets on publication, it has so far failed to find its rightful place.* So let me state for the record: the public has been

* I must here make my marketing stand for another book, starring another lively, distinctively-voiced heroine, almost as beloved and now as long out of print as *Private* ever was: *Life with Lisa*, by Sybil Burr. It was one of the many Dad brought home with him one evening simply because it had caught his eye in the bookshop. Maybe he just read the blurb, or maybe he read the first page or two and was as instantly beguiled as I was.

'When you look at yourself in the glass and your face is a Disappointment to you because you can see you are not going to turn out Beautiful, you know you have got to think of some other way of Making a Success of Yourself. I am very anxious to Make a Success, so Miss Brownrigg will be Sunk.'

Thus begins *Life with Lisa*, the diary of twelve-year-old Lisa Longland who, after coming across Pepys in the library, has decided to record her daily trials at home with her widowed mother and their lodger in a drab, post-war seaside town, and at school with the sarcastic Miss Brownrigg. 'If persons are still wanting to read about your wife's hat after 100s of years,' Lisa reasons, 'they might want to hear about another Ordinary Person (me) because my Life is very interesting in parts.'

Alas, life in Bladsole-on-Sea did not prepare Lisa for the vagaries of life and publishing any more than Nottinghamshire did Gwen Grant's nameless heroine. Burr's book was first published in 1958 but, despite being a deft, funny (especially once you get a bit older and deprived of one (three, with the sequels, which have not yet, alas, been brought back into print) of the funniest children's books ever written. I give it to every child and adult I care about and want to see laughing for the next twenty years.

But it was more than just funny. In the episodic

---

understand all the Pepys jokes) and vividly rendered account of a year in the life of a natural Optimist if not Beauty, it has failed to endure in the collective consciousness. I have met few others who have read it, and I have found no mention of it in any history of children's books. The copy my dad brought home is a 1979 reprint by the ever astute Puffin. There was also a Radio 4 adaptation of it in the early 2000s, which I missed but which captivated a Japanese friend of mine. I adduce this last as testimony both to my impeccable taste in friends and the power of Lisa's liveliness to charm others, even across the oceans.

But she has been out of print again for thirty years and more, although there are always a handful of (unfortunately relatively pricey) second-hand copies to be found on the Internet.

Perhaps if she had gone on to be a naval administrator and MP things would have been different, but that's a tough one for a secondary-modern schoolgirl to pull off, especially when the lodger keeps making Cutting Remarks and sending her out for peppermints, her friend Bert ('a Good Enemy') commands attention, and any spare time must be spent finding ways to amass the frills and furbelows needed to attend her first proper party. 'Mother is always in a Flap about money and she would say: It is waste when you only have a party once in a Blue Moon and you cannot wear white net for Best or Church.' Lisa is a wonderful, beguiling creation – a clear Success to anyone who reads her, but deserving of a wider audience. So do go out and look for her. And if you like her, as you surely will, do spread the word. As our heroine says, 'it is not much good when you want to be famous right now, but Better than Nothing'.

adventures of the Hall family was embedded something I had not known was missing from my other books – the very essence of my family's way of life. I had for the first time a sense of sensibility. The Halls, too, lived by the creed that love and affection are best expressed through sarcasm ('"Get that for me," says our Lucy. "What did your last slave die of?" I says. "A broken neck," she snarls, and I think oh yes, very nice') and brinkmanship ('I pulled a face at our Rose and she hit me on the head with a teaspoon. "I bet you think I'm an egg, don't you?" and she said "If you were, I'd cut your head off with a knife and not just bash it with a spoon"'). The Halls understood what really matters: that when the chips are down, and being ignited at your stake-bound feet, family will come to your rescue, but absent a crisis not one word of warmth, friendliness or gesture of evident regard is ever to pass between you.

C. S. Lewis found his Norse sagas and had his epiphanic vision of 'Northernness'. I found Gwen Grant and had mine. At last I could see myself and my family from the outside in. At least part of our oddness – my oddness at school, their oddness every other bloody place – was explained. Born and bred in London I might have been but, for all of us – and my parents had been down south for ten years before I was born – London never truly 'took'. We were still in some fundamental ways outsiders.

Private – Keep Out!, then, was the book that, in addition to keeping me laughing until what I suspect will be the end of time, awakened me to the idea that discomforts in life might not be (just) down to me – they might sometimes in fact be down to Them. It did what books are supposed to do and broadened my horizons, almost literally. I wasn't just a person moored in a family. That family was moored somewhere and that somewhere didn't necessarily suit us best. But there were other places. The place my parents came from, to which we might one day return. There could even – and I had to brace myself as this thought rushed towards me – be other places that might suit me personally even better.

I think of *Private – Keep Out!* whenever arguments about diversity and representation in books (or any other media) break out, as they periodically do. If I fell on that book (and its sequels) with such hunger and delight . . . imagine, I reason, if I'd been something 'other' in some more significant way than merely 'ethnically northern in a southern world'. How much more would I have longed for and needed to see myself in my books if I'd been disabled, gay, black, non-Christian or something else outside the mainstream message?

By this time – the mid-1980s – writers' and publishers' consciousnesses of matters of sex, race and representation had started to be raised. The first wave of concern had come in the 1960s and 70s, mainly – or perhaps just most successfully – over the matter of heroines. There were some. But not many. And certainly not enough of the right – feisty, non-domestic, un-Meg Marchish – sort. Efforts needed to be made to overcome the teeny imbalance caused by 300 years of unreflecting patriarchal history.

It's this memory that convinces me of the importance of role models and the rightness of including (or as critics of the practice call it, 'crowbarring in') a wide variety of characters with different backgrounds, orientations and everything else into children's books. If it seems – hell, even if it IS – slightly effortful at times, I suspect that the benefits (even though by their very nature as explosions of inward delight, wordless recognition, relief, succour, sustenance, those benefits are largely hidden) vastly outweigh the alleged cons. And I'm never quite sure what the cons are supposed to be anyway. Criticisms usually boil down to some variant of 'I am used to A! B makes me uncomfortable! O, take the nasty B away!' Which really isn't good enough.

William – Melendy – Frisby

I was getting pocket money by this stage. It basically functioned as a sequels stipend; the library, Dad or other benevolent figure would furnish me with a book, I would (generally) love it and disburse my savings to secure whatever else was in the series or other books the author had written. My first task was to build up a complete collection of Richmal Crompton's books about William Brown, with whom I had fallen in love the very first time we met at the paperback carousel in Torridon Library.

In the first chapter of the first of the thirty-nine books of the series (yes, thirty-nine. My finances would be put under severe strain, but a completist learns to live with it), William receives an entire shilling from a generous aunt and swaggers into his local sweetshop to buy an unprecedented sixpenn'orth of Gooseberry Eyes from the surprised owner. And then it reads ' "Gotter bit of money this mornin'," explained William carelessly, with the air of a Rothschild,' whereupon I lost my heart to Crompton's hero for ever. Oh, the exuberant confidence of it – the splendour! The magnificent insouciance!

I did not know then, of course, that Crompton's creation – based on her nephew Thomas – had been famed for his cavalier attitude to life and those who would seek to circumscribe his enjoyment of it ever since he first started appearing in *Home* and *Happy* magazines in 1919 (*Just William*, the first collection of these stories, was published in 1922). As previously noted, I did not know quite what a Rothschild was, but I deduced (and had confirmed later by my father) that it must be the name of a famously rich family, and it was actually this – this oblique promise of induction into a world of fluent and evocative expression – more than William's notoriously lawless spirit, that drew me in.

I realised, I think, even at that early age that opportunities for imitative anarchical exploits were going to be severely limited by my misfortune of having been born a particularly weedy girl in early 1980s suburbia instead of a sturdy village boy sixty years earlier. I didn't have a gang of outlaws or a dog, there wasn't a barn within a day's hike and if I'd ever tried to dig up one of my mother's flower beds she would have beaten me into a coma, not given a weary sigh of resignation and returned to her pile of mending. Why set myself up for failure? Serious injury, and failure?

But the new possibilities for self-expression – well, they were something else. The books I had read so far had all stayed carefully within the semantic and grammatical comfort zone of their readers. But the magazines for which Crompton had first written her stories had been for adults, and she had chosen her language (and honed her satiric edge) accordingly. Now I saw that an author's vocabulary should exceed her audience's grasp – else what's the bloody book for? That they were funny too was the icing on the cake. They sent me into paroxysms of delight and back again and again to the library for more sustaining doses of descriptions like that of the Brown family's profoundly boring and unwelcome house guest, Mr Falkner, whose 'accounts of his varied exploits of dauntless bravery and dazzling cleverness seemed to induce in William's family a certain apathy of hopelessness, which William thought a very proper attitude on the part of a family. No one told him to go and wash his hands and brush his hair again . . . They simply had not the spirit. In fact such is the humanising effect of a common misfortune, they almost felt drawn to him.' Richmal Crompton is the juvenile's Wodehouse.*

* There are lots of things posh people keep from us. Land. Money. Cabinet positions. But I don't really mind about those. We have learned to rub along quite happily – and in many cases, perhaps even more contentedly than we might otherwise – without them. It wasn't until I got to university, however, that I realised They had been keeping something far better, something far more rewarding and uplifting than rolling acres or political power from Us. Every time I went to visit the study of any floppy-haired, privately educated posh boy, there would always be a row of P. G. Wodehouse books somewhere on the shelves, usually bright little Penguin editions from a kindly uncle when the boy hit thirteen or so, always thoroughly thumbed and broken-spined. Intrigued, I asked to borrow one of them from Aloysius (not his real name, but his real name was even worse. That is the price you pay for inheriting

I was on a great polysyllabic spree, a grand tour round the glories of the subordinate clause. William was my guide, my inspiration and the gatekeeper to a new and better world. The suburbs suddenly expanded to infinity.

Unlike Enid Blyton, you can reread Crompton's William books at any age and still not only enjoy them

---

castles). 'It's pronounced Woodhouse,' he said kindly, as he loaded me up with *Jeeves in the Offing*, *The Mating Season* and four or five others. 'Although he's often nicknamed Plum. And you'll need more than one. Start with *The Code of the Woosters*. It's Plum's plummiest plum.'

How right he was, on all counts. I gobbled the books down, and what plums they were – yes, especially *The C of the W* – indeed. Who could fail to warm to congenital idiot Bertie Wooster and his valet/sage/salvation Jeeves, Aunt Agatha, 'the nephew-crusher' who chews broken bottles and kills rats with her teeth? Who cannot feel the agony of being Gussie Fink-Nottle ('Many an experienced undertaker would have been deceived by his appearance and started embalming on sight') or the almost equal pain of being engaged to Madeline Bassett, who thinks the stars are God's daisy chain and that every time a fairy blows its wee nose, a baby is born.

But above all, who cannot fall instantly and irrevocably in love with sentences such as 'I could see that she was looking for something to break as a relief to her feelings and courteously drew her attention to a terracotta figure of the Infant Samuel at Prayer. She thanked me briefly and hurled it against the opposite wall.' Or 'If a girl thinks you're in love with her and says she will marry you, you can't very well voice a preference for being dead in a ditch.' It was joyful, fluting music in paperback form.

There are those who would say that it was bad luck rather than upper-class conspiracy that kept us apart all those years, but I know what I believe. I'm letting others in on both secrets here. Pass them on.

but marvel at the craft and the gift of grandiloquent expression she had. It's saddening to think that, although she was never bitter about the two outputs' relative successes, she always felt her adult fiction (she wrote forty-one novels and nine collections of short stories) was her 'real' work and regarded the William books as 'potboilers'. Perhaps, like Streatfeild and her *Ballet Shoes*, she did not find him difficult to write and distrusted what came so easily. Or perhaps comedy is never taken as seriously or appreciated as much as it should be even by those who create it. Those of us who love the boy and his books can only be grateful that, whatever her frustrations, she continued with both to the end of her life – and even a little beyond. The last volume of William stories – *William the Lawless* – was published in 1970, a year after she died. It includes 'William's Foggy Morning', which was completed from her notes by her niece and literary executor Richmal Ashbee.

Alas, long before I reached William's last, foggy morning, I had to rejig my fiscal policy. I had the first dozen or so volumes, but the project was simply leaving no slack in the system. So I sent out (to myself, you understand) the edict that from now on birthday and Christmas money/tokens would be allocated to William. Pocket money would be for other procurements. It was a necessary adjustment. I had Melendy books to buy.

Dad had brought home one Friday *The Saturdays*, the first in a series of four volumes written and set in the 1940s by Elizabeth Enright about the Melendy children. There is the embryonic actor Mona, dry-witted piano-playing Rush, exuberant Miranda (Randy) and the youngest, Oliver, the calmest, most meditative Melendy.

Cooped up in their family brownstone in New York (I did say this was the 1940s. Even non-Vanderbilts could do that kind of thing then) on a rainy weekend, the children form the Independent Saturday Afternoon Adventure Club and for the next month pool their allowances to allow each of them in turn to take him or herself off into New York to do, for $1.60 or less, whatever suits the club member best.

There is no plot to speak of – the chapters describe each child's solo trip and the characters they meet on the way – but the episodic structure allows each child a chance to shine. In between times, the rough and tumble, the fun and the frustrations of family life are brilliantly drawn and instantly recognisable.

The following two books – *The Four-Story Mistake*, in which the Melendys move to an architecturally challenged pile in the country, and *Then There Were Five*, when the Melendys absorb into the family a neglected boy living nearby – are more substantial stories even better told. The final part of the quartet, *Spiderweb for Two*, I could not find. It was *The Phantom Tollbooth* all over again. Out of print and nobody had any idea when or if it would be published again. This saddened me greatly. And then inspiration struck and I took myself off to the library to look for it. I hardly dared hope for success. I would surely have noticed it before now if it was there. But I was wrong. Just as you don't see a word until you come to know a word and then you can't stop seeing the word everywhere, so you don't see titles until you know you want them. There was *Spiderweb for Two*, in the Es, in crinkly-covered hardback. I stood there, disbelieving. As I recall it, a light shines from the book and a choir of angels sings, but this may be a trick of memory. I pulled it down, got it stamped and renewed it every three weeks for a year. Aptly, it was about a treasure hunt – designed by Mona, Rush and Mark to keep Randy and Oliver occupied after the three older siblings go away to school. Truth be told, it wasn't quite as good as the preceding three – nothing that splits a favourite cast up ever is, though the remaining pair were as real and funny and vivid as ever – but even a sub-par Melendy book was better than just about anything else I could think of, and I would have loved it even without the attendant thrill of discovery and completion.

I handed over another 75p to the Greenwich Book Boat and bought Enright's most famous book, *Thimble Summer*, for which she won the 1939 Newbery Medal. This is the tale of Garnet Linden who finds a silver thimble that brings her luck all summer long on her Depression-era Wisconsin farm. It didn't knock the Melendys off their perch but it did contain something that fascinated me. On the farm during the harvest, Garnet would drop an occasional watermelon on purpose so that it would burst open 'rosy red and cold as a glacier' and she could use it to slake her thirst. At home, watermelon was a fabulously expensive, exotic thing you saw sold in single, carefully wrapped slices in the supermarket. The idea that somewhere they were so common, so plentiful that they could be treated quite differently woke in me some tiny flicker of appreciation that the way of the world I knew might not be the way of the world all over. Different places, different people, different contexts, different circumstances could all work on each other and produce different results, different values from the small batch familiar to me. This glimmer of insight seemed quite a good return on my 75p investment.

Another library find shortly afterwards yielded a similar epiphany. *Mrs Frisby and the Rats of NIMH* was a relatively insubstantial if gripping tale of a field-mouse family that helps a colony of super-intelligent former lab rats to move to a new home where they can live independently instead of simply tapping nearby humans' electricity and food supplies. But one line burst onto my consciousness like a watermelon dropped from on high. When wise old rat Nicodemus is talking to Mrs Frisby about how they live compared to humans, he says: 'A rat civilisation would probably never have built skyscrapers, since rats prefer to live underground. But think of the endless subways-below-subways-below-subways they would have had.'

I read that huddled in the story corner of Mrs Pugh's class, and it felt like fireworks going off in my head. It wasn't just watermelons but the whole world that could be different. It wasn't preordained, or immutable or, indeed, even anything special. Just ours. Built and organised for us, by us, developed to serve our needs. I closed the book gently, almost reverently, almost as awed by its power to provide me with such new, previously unthinkable thoughts as I was by the thought itself. I was just about catatonic with the shock of these revelations, but fortunately one of the eighteen Darrens in our class picked that moment to start throwing Lego at my head, so mental crisis was averted.

Nicodemus, his subways and his skyscrapers are the

reason this is still the book I hold up during the periodic rows that break out among adults of a certain stripe about the worthlessness of certain children's books (and I write this in the full knowledge that I will be coming out, and coming out hard, against *Gossip Girl* and Stephenie Meyer, but, believe me, I would be going a lot further were it not for Mrs Frisby's gently restraining paw on my psyche) and assure them that you simply never know what a child is going to find in a book (or a graphic novel, or a comic, or whatever) – what tiny, throwaway line might be the spark that lights the fuse that sets off an explosion in understanding whose force echoes down years. And it enables me to keep, at bottom, the faith that children should be allowed to read anything at any time. They will take out of it whatever they are ready for. And just occasionally, it will ready them for something else.

School Stories

I was getting ready for something else now. Secondary school was looming. I had, though it seems risible now, high hopes. I had, after all, done much research about it in the library. Just as the pony story, I felt, had left me well prepared for any equine emergency or sudden relocation to the countryside, so must the school story for – well, school. And again, Torridon's shelves were for some reason heaving with them, despite the fact that their popularity – although their heyday outshone and outlasted pony books' – had undoubtedly been similarly on the wane for years.

I am referring specifically, I should say at this point, to the girls' school story. The genre began, because the schools themselves did, with boys. *Tom Brown's Schooldays*, published in 1857 and based on the author Thomas Hughes' years at Rugby School in the 1830s, is generally lauded as the first of its kind. Though there had been other stories set in boarding schools, this was the one that really made the school aspect a central feature rather than simply a setting against which traditional literary adventures and moral lessons played out. Although it didn't stray far from its roots as a moral lecture (in the preface to the sixth edition, Hughes states with the certainty that blessed the age that although many people had said to him that they hoped he would preach less in the next one, 'this I most distinctly decline to do. Why, my whole object in writing at all was to get the chance of preaching! When a man comes to my time of life and has his bread to make, and very little time to spare, is it likely that he will spend almost the whole of his yearly vacation in writing a story just to amuse people? I think not') it – and its portrayal of 'muscular Christianity' – was massively popular and established the school story as a definite genre.

It was followed in 1858 by *Eric, or Little by Little* by Frederic W. Farrar, which was even more muscularly Christian and even less fun. It tells the story of Eric Williams' gradual corruption by the vices and follies available to him once he has been sent off to school. It begins with a desire to keep in with his schoolmates which prevents him from 'expressing a manly disapproval of the general cheating' that goes on in his form and soon he has gone totally to the dogs. There is drinking. In a pub. In vain do his pious best friend and brother expend their dying breaths exhorting him to change his ways and seek salvation, but alas, Eric attempts to escape his disgrace by running away to sea. He gets ill and comes home to die, repenting at last. And in case you were in any doubt about what you were supposed to take from it, Farrar's preface reads: 'The story of "Eric" was written with but one single object—the vivid inculcation of inward purity and moral purpose, by the history of a boy who, in spite of the inherent nobility of his disposition, falls into all folly and wickedness, until he has learnt to seek help from above. I am deeply thankful to know—from testimony public and private, anonymous and acknowledged—that this object has, by God's blessing, been fulfilled.'

You will be deeply thankful to know that things relaxed somewhat thereafter. By the time Talbot Baines Reed's *Fifth Form at St Dominic's* was published in 1881, which was the most popular of the many school stories he published, it had become the thing we think of now when we think of school stories – japes, mischief, comic and villainous staff, cosy studies, enduring friendships, sporting prowess and bravely borne accidents and injuries playing out over a term.

Meanwhile, back in real life, (middle-class) girls were starting to be publicly educated too! They were moving out from under governesses' skirts, into day schools and – come the early 1900s – boarding schools too. The stories duly followed, beginning with L. T. Meade in the 1890s, and on through the likes of May Baldwin, Dorothea Moore and Mrs George de Horne Vaizey, all of them Pulleinishly prolific but all dogged by a rather confused public attitude to their work: on the one hand, people (which is to say reviewers and opinion-makers, which is to say men) approved of their girls' school stories because the authors never deemed a heroine worthy of the name until she was fully conversant with the art of denial, self-sacrifice and other feminine necessities – the distaff equivalent of the noble, manly, empire-building skills advocated in the boys' books – but on the other hand . . . well, they were books written by women, about girls, and about just girls. Girls supporting each other, being busy, happy, productive and competent and altogether managing just fine without boys or men to make their lives meaningful. Their authority figures were female teachers and headmistresses (God and empire taking very much a back-seat role) who would dispense comfort, wisdom and discipline in roughly equal proportions from their book- and flower-filled studies, with occasional trips outside in inclement weather to rescue foolhardy charges blown over cliffs at midnight and catch lung infections, the better to bring home to them the consequences of thoughtless behaviour. (Though we must in all fairness note that none of them beat the headmaster of Kipling's *Stalky & Co.*, who attends the sickbed of day-pupil Stetson and sucks out through a tube the thick diphtheria mucus that is about to choke Stetson to death, knowing that he will probably contract the fatal disease himself as a result. If he doesn't, he will almost certainly die of a surfeit of honour instead.)

A world of happy, self-sufficient females was terrifically unsettling, what? Girls should be encouraged to read, but only the least challenging, least potentially corrupting stuff. Where did these school stories fall? Nobody knew.

Because of this, and because it was so popular and popularity is always suspect, because it was by and for women, because anyone could – and it sometimes seemed, did – try their hand at it, the genre quickly became perceived as inferior and, as lesser writers copied tropes from abler ones and made them both simpler and more commonplace, also became slightly moribund.

Then in 1906, like a wayward lacrosse ball into a swimming pool, Angela Brazil's *The Fortunes of Philippa*, landed with a splash in the stagnant genre and started its revival. She wrote firmly from the schoolgirls' point of view, happily incorporating their slang, wholly on their side. She was swiftly followed by Elsie J. Oxenham with *Rosaly's New School* in 1913 and in 1920 by Dorita Fairlie Bruce with *The Senior Prefect* (later renamed *Dimsie Goes to School*). Fairlie Bruce was the first to write a series of school books about the same characters – Dimsie, the lively new girl with a spirit as irrepressible as her fine head of brown curls and her friends Erica (stern), Rosamund (soft), Jean (poet) and Pam (sporty) – and I found them all waiting for me on the shelves of Torridon Library.

I had loved already Enid Blyton's Malory Towers and St Clare's series but the Dimsie books were an even more detailed and intriguing window onto a bygone scholastic and social era – when a sunny day meant teachers could spontaneously decide on a nature ramble without consulting the national curriculum, something called the honour of the school could be at stake and adolescence could be free of sex and full of sorority.

They were a great solace to me. At ten, school, sex and sorority were giving me no end of trouble. As we all entered double figures, the split that had started three or four years earlier was complete. Where once boys and girls had played together happily, now they . . . didn't. The girls had hived themselves off and stopped running around and getting sweaty. They played with each other's hair and compared frilly ankle socks and fancy pencil cases instead. If a boy spoke to you now, you had to giggle instead of answer. The boys were baffled. I was baffled. I tried giggling once, but it was not to be. And now no one was allowed to read. If you were a girl it was because it was unfeminine and left you less time for comparing sock notes, and if you were a boy it was because it was unmanly and left you less time for football. I felt this was at the very least illogical but I couldn't find anyone who cared, much less agreed with me, when I tried to point it out. I withdrew from the fray. Literally – I could read undisturbed, I discovered, in the outside loos. Cold in winter, smelly in summer, no one ever went as far as the last cubicle in the row or lingered in the outhouse longer than they had to. If I'd had the wit, I'd have taken a few cushions down there and decorated the place like Dimsie and her pals did their sixth-form studies in later books. Or added some wine and candles and called it a salon. A shiterary salon. Could've been nice.

For Dimsie, by contrast, all was broad sunny uplands of both the real and metaphorical kind at the Jane Willard Foundation. Reading and learning of all sorts were encouraged. So were sports, but I was willing to overlook that. I couldn't work out if it was because they were free of boys, modernity, or both, but the girls seemed able to be themselves. Yes, impractical daydreamer Jean (poet, remember) was frequently told to buck up, but that was fair enough. She did keep accidentally starting fires in potting sheds, after all. And Dimsie did form the Anti-Soppist League to curb Rosamund's penchant for crushing on unsuitable seniors but this only gladdened my heart. Anti-soppism was exactly the movement I needed. It stood for everything I couldn't put into words. It was anti-convention, it was anti-self-indulgence, it was, above all, anti-mindless-femininity. It gave those of us who couldn't master the conventions a means of rejecting them and another banner to gather under. I say 'us'. I mean 'me'. I wouldn't find another five like-minded souls in real life until I went to university, but thanks to Fairlie Bruce and her creations, I didn't really need them.

Of course, though I and innumerable other readers who through the vagaries of time, class, space and fortune had not managed to go to the Malory Willard St Winifred's Chalet Foundation took these tales as virtual reportage, the schools, these enclaves of spirited yet honourable girls and dedicated teachers, were always idealisations. If reading were purely about providing us with accurate renderings of social history, this would be a problem. But of course it's not, and it wasn't. However buffed and polished the setting and the selection of characters, the deeper truths remained. Theirs was a world that pointed towards a different way of organising things, a different set of priorities (some of them deliciously intangible – it wasn't until I had read my way several times through the series that this nebulous concept of 'honour', for instance, be it individual or 'of the school' began to resolve into some kind of comprehensible shape) and beyond that, to the idea that nothing is immutable. *Ars longa*, even when shaped by genre constraints. *Vita* remains remarkably *brevis*.

It wasn't until many years later – when I actually was at university, in fact, haunting the Haunted Bookshop in St Edward's Passage in Cambridge and gradually piecing together a collection of Dimsie editions from the 1920s and 30s, of which the owner always kept a plentiful stock – that I realised that the colourful hardbacks in the library had been modernised editions. They had still seemed wonderfully old-fashioned to me, but the real things had a much more distinctive tang. However carefully you update a book, and especially one from a genre like the girls' school story which is so redolent of a particular time and place, you are interpolating something between the reader and the writing and creating detachment. When you read original Dimsies (or Brazils or Oxenhams), whatever their flaws, they speak untrammelled early twentieth century to you. They speak without irony, without muddied waters, without self-consciousness, without fear of parody. They feel as young, bold and innocent as their heroines themselves. A different time, living on between buckram covers for as long as there are people willing to open them.

Just how long that will be, I don't know. Their popularity began to lessen in the late 1950s as private boarding and day schools became, with the advent of free secondary education after the Second World War, a thing of the past. Now, the better part of a century on from when most of them first appeared, they are ancient relics. To come across them at all at the right age requires the tomes either to have been passed down through at least four generations of readers and still to be lingering on accessible family bookshelves, awaiting discovery, or for a ten-year-old to have a particularly early affinity with second-hand bookshops and the wherewithal to fund what can now be a fairly expensive habit. In my day, Elinor Brent-Dyer's Chalet School books, recounting the adventures of Joey Bettany, Mary-Lou Trelawney and Len Maynard at school in Austria/Guernsey/the Welsh borders/Switzerland* were still on sale in shops (albeit updated versions again, for Fontana – like the recent bowdlerised Blytons they did not, apparently, sell well) and they were still a potent enough cultural presence to make plays such as *Daisy Pulls it Off* a success. Now they and the world they dwelled in and which dwelled in them have slipped beyond the immediate reach of folk memory and I suspect there is little chance of their popularity returning.

There are clay tablets dating from around 2000 BC recounting anecdotes set in schools for the entertainment of ancient Sumerian child readers, and similar texts – the *colloquia scholastica* – were common in medieval England, and included all the banter, bullying, laziness and cheeking of teachers that has apparently been the mainstay of the educational experience since it began. There have always been and always will be plenty of stories set in school, for at least as long as children go to school. But they are not the school stories of

* Brent-Dyer had to relocate during the war years so that her fictional charges didn't end up in occupied territory.

yore. Yore's gone, and with it its stories. Rosamund would no doubt weep. The rest of us must just stop being so madly maudlin and simply buck up.

But I am getting ahead of myself. Let us return to my new hopes for my new school.

I reckoned that the fact that it would be all girls, plus the maturity we would all gain over the summer – we would be eleven by the time we started the term! Eleven! I wondered if I should start saving for a pension* – meant that I was almost certain to find myself in Catford's answer to the Jane Willard, or – at a pinch – St Clare's. The details would be different – skirts instead of tunics, tarmacked playground instead of lacrosse pitches, a bus down the high street every day instead of termly drop-offs from a steam train – but beneath that? SAME.

* I didn't. But only because I didn't know about them. I was already saving for a house. No, really. Remember, we're into the second half of the 1980s now. The only thing in the news and the only thing adults talked about was house prices, which were skyrocketing. My parents were appalled and anxious. As nature abhors a vacuum, into the void left by my mother's quietening of my nuclear-war fears rushed that of future homelessness. How would I ever be able to buy somewhere to live? Thus I became consumed at a very early age with the need to own – not rent, I knew I would never be able to relax if I was renting, because a landlord could kick you out at any time – a home. Didn't have to be big. Didn't have to be fancy. But it had to be mine. As it turned out, this was one of the more sensible anxieties to have, and that if you save hard from pre-adolescence onwards, you can actually amass enough for a small deposit. You have to spend it all on anti-anxiety therapy in the end, but still. You were close.

Thus it was that I discovered that as well as expanding your mind, your consciousness, your empathetic facilities, your vocabulary, your sense of awe and wonder at the multitudinous possibilities offered by the world, books could also lie through their teeth.

9

Darkness Rising

Secondary School and, Not Unrelatedly, Dystopia

Oh, look, it wasn't too bad. So people wouldn't leave you alone to read and hated you if you tried. So there were no outdoor loos to escape to. So life became an even greater welter of unspoken and fast-changing rules about everything from acceptable skirt length (labia-skimming) and first bra (Tammy Girl, padded) to schoolbags (Chelsea Girl only or you might as well not even bother, yeah?) to bands (I don't know – I got lost after Bros) to smoking (Consulate, upstairs in McDonald's, like a lady, not Burger King). These things are sent to try us.

At least secondary school had a better library. A full classroom of wooden shelves, all round the walls and extra ones sticking out into the room. It was proper. It even had a few little carrels here and there – high-sided nooks where you could work or read almost unseen. Sit there and it was like having your own personal section of a Womble burrow.

I needed the security, for two reasons. First, because I had just discovered dystopian fiction. This was new to me, and fairly new to the world of children's books as a whole. Although the world of fables and fairy tales and the golden age of railway children and secret gardens had been smashed to pieces by the cosh of two world wars, the growing realism of children's fiction that replaced it took a while to shake off fully the impulse to protect young readers and embrace presenting them with Possible Worse Fates instead. You need time to recover from real-life catastrophes before you can bear to face and posit new ones to come. Authors like John Christopher – maybe more safely distanced by the double remove of writing not just fiction but science fiction – got there first, in the late 1960s, with books such as his Tripods trilogy (later quartet), wherein the human race is enslaved by their 'cappings' by an alien race, to be followed by the likes of Peter Dickinson's The Changes series ('science fiction without the science' he called his story of the human race turning against machinery and regressing to a feudal state).

My introduction to the genre was through the two that perhaps best symbolised and distilled the nuclear anxiety of the 1970s and 80s: Robert Swindells' *Brother in the Land* and Robert C. O'Brien's *Z for Zachariah*, two tales of post-nuclear-war survival so harrowing that I couldn't keep them in the house. Lucy Donovan's cousin Sophie had lent me the former and I kept having to return it to her and re-borrow it the next day, so that I could read and try and process once more the unsparing story of Danny and his attempts to look after his younger brother Ben as their fellow survivors become increasingly desperate and those in charge steadily more tyrannical. Anyone disabled, injured or shocked beyond help ('spacers', they're called) is poisoned or shot. A concentration camp is established, prompting the formation of a rebel movement that – for a brief and shining moment, until it becomes clear that the irradiated, barren land will make it impossible for anyone to survive for long – seems set to carry the day. The story's careful detail (the hair falling out in clumps, the 'trillions of deadly radioactive particles . . . settling like an invisible snow on the devastated earth') and psychological truth (the survivors grow ruthless by degrees as resources and hope diminish) made it compelling and almost unbearable at the same time. Forced to confront unspeakable horrors and follow them through with Danny to the quietly shattering end I closed the covers each time with a sigh of relief and some disbelief that I had survived.

Z for Zachariah belonged to the school library and I read it there when I could* and then put it firmly back on the shelf until the next time.† Back then I found the

* There was one drawback to the school library, which was that you weren't allowed to use it. You would have English lessons in there occasionally, which would sometimes finish early and allow you half an hour's browsing time, but you weren't allowed in there at lunch or playtime. I suppose this was probably due to a lack of money and staff, plus an underlying belief in the value of getting some fresh lead poisoning in your lungs before afternoon lessons began, but still it seems a bit of a shame.

† I am actually sitting here now trying to decide if I could buy it and keep it in my house now. I think not. Maybe in Kindle form? No, because pixels of it could leak out and pollute the place like those trillions of deadly particles 'drifting on the wind, landing unseen on clothing, skin and hair . . .' OH, GOD.

story of Ann, a lone survivor on a remote farm, and her relationship with a radiation-poisoned man, John Loomis, whom she nurses back to some kind of health after he stumbles across her home a year after the war, slightly less traumatic than *Brother in the Land* (at least once I had got over the shock that the same mind that had given me lovely Mrs Frisby was also capable of creating this). But now, the multiple threats posed by the controlling and manipulative Loomis strike me the hardest. He is emblematic, in a way I didn't appreciate then, of a kind of man that is if anything more threatening, through the sheer weight of his numbers, before an apocalypse than after, when there are only a few lives left to ruin.

By the end of those two, I felt I'd come a very long way from Milly-Molly-Mandy.

Rereading them now still harrows my inner twelve-year-old but it gives the rest of me a twisted hankering after a simpler time. From this distance – *O tempora! O mores!* O Brexit! O Trump! – we seem to have had it easy. One major worry, one simple solution: read the cautionary tales and don't set off The Bomb. Job done!

All in all, it's a mad, mad, mad, mad world out there. Perhaps the best and only real remedy there is is to grab a good book-cum-survival manual, hunker down and pray for daylight. Meet me in the bunker – but if you come with *Brother in the Land*, please, please, please, keep it to yourself.

Just as I was getting to grips with these page-bound horrors, real life dropped something of a bomb on us all too. My dad – very quietly – went and got cancer. The world was quite dystopian altogether.

He had been – very quietly – under the weather for ages. He had what seemed like flu for so long that it eventually became obvious that it wasn't flu at all and the GP started sending him for tests. My parents tried to keep it from us, but they were relatively unpractised in the secretive arts and we knew something was up. At one point, when doctors were still cycling through possible diagnoses, we overheard my mother on the phone to Grandma, saying something about 'Legionnaire's disease'. In a moment that demonstrates as neatly as any moment ever could the fundamental difference between my sister and mud-turtle me, my sister headed straight for the dictionary to work it out and I waited to be told. Unfortunately, it didn't have the actual phrase, so her research only ended in further confusion. We understood that having little members of the French Foreign Legion walking about inside you would make you feel unwell, but not how they would get there. I thought maybe he had caught it when we watched the TV series *Beau Geste* a few years earlier and the soldiers had lain dormant in his blood before . . . I don't know, going to war over his lymph glands? We had heard that phrase being whispered too. No, the whole thing was implausible. We knew we must have missed a step somewhere along the way.

So, it turned out, had the doctors. While they retraced their paths, Dad sat – quietly – on the sofa, getting thinner. And quieter. Mum got busier. And noisier. Grandma came down more often and played more 'Bobby Shaftoe' for us.

Eventually the doctors found what they had missed, and it turned out to be Hodgkin's disease, or cancer of – ta dah! – the lymph glands. 'You're very lucky!' said his doctor, still flushed with the thrill of discovery. 'It's a young man's disease, but if you'd got it then, you'd be dead! Things are much better now.'

And they were, in the very important sense that Dad didn't die. But it was a gruelling year of treatment for him, and for my mother, as he sat on the sofa, getting thinner still, and quieter, and colder – we used to heap more and more blankets on him as each cycle of treatment progressed, and then peel them off as each one ended – and balder and bluer, as the dye telling all the scanner and radiation whatnots where to go worked its way through his system.

My sister used to sit behind him and stroke what remained of what she called his 'rabbit hair'. I want to say that I retreated into my books, but I'm not sure that's true. Partly because I was already reading as much as was humanly possible – I couldn't have retreated further into my books without coming out the back and meeting myself round the front again – and partly because again, my sister and I were protected from the worst of it. We never really knew that he might die and, not really having any understanding of what chemotherapy felt like, that was all that mattered to us. Except for one awful evening, when he started to cry (and Emily and I, thinking he was pretending, started to laugh) over the supper we were all eating on our knees – his heavily blanketed – in front of the television, we thought that everything was basically okay.

But I think perhaps my books did become more important to me than they might otherwise have done. Maybe I wasn't retreating in the sense of reading more, but perhaps I escaped more fully into them now that there was something to escape from.

At a more practical level, his illness threw me back on already-accumulated resources. I reread more, and books I hadn't quite fancied when Dad had first brought them home took on a new attractiveness now that my main supply had been cut off at source.

One day, up in my room (the rules about reading only in communal areas having been temporarily suspended), I reluctantly picked up a paperback that seemed to have been hanging around for ages. It looked awful. Its cover was so drab – even for me, a child with an abnormally high drab tolerance – that it almost made me cross. The whole thing was in tones of brown – a picture of a wood-panelled corridor and a big wooden noticeboard, relieved only by the (dark, almost brownish) blonde hair of the twin girls standing in front of it and the dark blue of their tunics. One had her hands covering her face in sorrow and the other was gingerly trying to comfort her.

The set-up was not inviting. Also, it was a school story; *End of Term*, by Antonia Forest. At twelve, I felt a bit too sophisticated now for school stories. A bit played out in the whole jolly-hockey-sticks field, y'know?

But, needs must. And so I lay on my bed and opened those uninviting covers. By the time I closed them, several hours later, a towering, passionate and enduring love had been born in me, for the Marlow twins, their friends and above all for their creator, who had given me a new world to live in, and a new level of writing – and reading – to get to grips with.

Richard Adams said of *Watership Down* that he had set out to write a grown-up book for children.* Forest did not set out with any such conscious intention (in fact, her first book about the Marlow family, *Autumn Term*, was conceived as simply the most likely way to get a publishing contract at the time – 1948), but nevertheless, that is exactly what she did too.

End of Term (and *Autumn Term*, *The Cricket Term* and *Attic Term*, which I would discover in due course) are technically school stories. They are set at Kingscote boarding school and the events the twins (Lawrie and Nicola) and their sisters take part in there include many of the standards: being unfairly left out of teams, getting (and not getting) parts in the school play, negotiating friendships, shifting loyalties and small treacheries. But there are no high dramas – no gorse-anchored clifftop rescues, no hidden heirlooms, no near-drownings, no mysterious figures who turn out to be long-lost uncles or overzealous guardians. Boarding-school-story conventions are in fact often lightly mocked. At one point, for example, Tim (real name Thalia – 'A muse or something. Mother would have it, though Father did his best') likens Nicola to a character being 'very, very competent and awfully, awfully keen'. Kingscote is not an idyll. Its

* This crossover mindset years before the concept was (marketably) understood was perhaps one of the reasons it was rejected by seven publishers before finally finding a home with Rex Collings in 1972. It has not been out of print since.

pupils are not perfect and neither – more shockingly – are its teachers, whom the pupils see at all times with clear rather than ennobling/idolising eyes. Rowan, one of Lawrie and Nicola's older sisters, describes her relationship with headmistress Miss Keith as 'delicately balanced on a razor-edge of mutual toleration'. A wonderful phrase that I took instantly to my heart and have used many times in life since, and it encapsulated what I was most drawn to about the characters and the writer – the cool command they shared, the slight sense of detachment from life in order to keep perspective on it. It was like a bracing plunge bath after the close, sweaty sauna of more traditional school stories. You emerged from a Forest novel – and I instinctively reach for that word rather than book or story because everything was as finely and accurately drawn as in any fiction for adults – as braced as you had been entertained. My mind felt keener and sharper after every reading. Maybe it even was.

Forest's characters – especially Nicola, who is at the heart of all but one of the Marlow books – grew and developed in the course of the book and the series in a way I had not come across before. Everything about them was so precisely drawn that it made me whimper with pleasure. At the beginning of *End of Term*, for instance, Nicola befriends through force of circumstance a new girl, Esther. They get on well enough, but don't really have much in common. By the end of the book, Nicola regards her new acquaintance thus: 'She still thought Esther awfully pretty – beautiful, she amended shyly – but she wouldn't really mind if she ended up in another form.' The first time I read that,

I genuinely wriggled with delight. That the forthright, rigorously honest Nicola would amend her thought is perfectly judged. That her undemonstrative nature would also cause her to amend it, even within the confines of her own mind, shyly, ensured that the readerly cup of satisfaction runneth over. And the overlapping layers of consciousness involved in moments like Patrick's interest in Nicola's tale of woe at being lied about by the treacherous older girl Lois Sanger (again, not drawn as a simple villain but a messy tranche of human flaws and weaknesses, none decisively contemptible in themselves but together amounting to something much worse than the sum of their parts). 'How queer,' he says. 'I wonder how she thinks about it? . . . Well – what does she tell herself? I mean – how does she make it alright for herself? Or doesn't she? Does she think she's a heel too?' Which in turn makes Nicola a bit cross. 'She would rather have a bit of sympathy, she decided, than all this speculation about Lois Sanger.' But Patrick has been out of school too long – and, maybe, is simply too much a boy – to quite understand. As a portrait of how we interpret ourselves, each other, ourselves to each other, each other to each other and how little ever goes unmediated in life, it is quite brilliant.

Patrick, incidentally, was also Catholic (like the author, who converted from Judaism at a young age) – the first I'd met in a book, and it pleased me very much. He displaced Dickon in my pantheon of childhood literary crushes. I recognised his various struggles with his conscience in me, and his stubbornness and frustration with his faith in the members of my wider family, and he felt, immediately, deeply, like a friend.

Again, it makes me wonder as *Private – Keep Out!* made me wonder – if that tiny thing meant so much to me, how much more does seeing yourself mean when you diverge more fully from the expected narrative?

The hits just kept on coming in *End of Term*. There was the moment the singing director for the school Christmas service, Dr Herrick, coaches Nicola in the singing of her opening solo. 'Try to sing it with regret,' he urges. '*Once* in Royal David's City. Not *now*, you see. Now we have only been pretending. But once, long ago, if we'd only had the luck to be there, just once this thing really happened.' Have you ever come across anything that better captures the evanescent magic of a carol service? A better evocation of the mass of love and memories, past and present, yearning, joy and sadness all knotted up together that for most of us comprises Christmas? Under Forest's and Dr Herrick's tutelage I could hear the deep music in a glorious song of old.

And then (and then, and then, and then – I could go on forever about this single book of Forest's but I will limit myself to just one more scene) there was the truly revelatory moment that came after Lawrie, who has recently lost out on the coveted part of Shepherd Boy in the school play to Nicola, crawls into bed with a secretly injured leg (another standard trope which again in Forest's hands becomes so much more than a simple plot device) to consider whether she should suggest that Nicola – who has similarly been left out of the netball team for unknown reasons – pretend to be her and play in the match instead. She runs through the different possibilities. First, 'the easy one' – what fun it would be for Nicola to play and how nice of Lawrie to let her.

Second – 'less disinterested'– that if she does let her, *someone* will *somehow* arrange things so that she can have a crack at playing Shepherd Boy. And finally, 'the underneath part, the bit she didn't like' thinks that if Nicola does play netball and gets found out, she will be chucked out of the play and then even though Lawrie won't be playing Shepherd Boy either, she won't feel so bad about it.

It was the most comprehensive, delicate anatomising of someone's inner life I had yet met, and I raced on. As the Marlow series progresses, Nicola, her friends and her siblings discover that life in and outside school is hard to negotiate, full of compromises and moral equivocations and that the adult world is no promised land. Forest provides agonisingly exact portraits of the psychological bullying in which girls – then, now and for ever – specialise, and there is a quiet, heart-stopping moment in *End of Term* when Nicola realises that the friend they made in the first book, *Autumn Term*, Tim, is no longer her friend as she is Lawrie's. 'She sat very still. Even her legs stopped swinging. Because it was nearly always like that, she took it for granted that people liked her better than Lawrie. Only Tim didn't. Tim liked Lawrie best.' I could feel that simple, bald final line dropping like a cold pebble into my soul as it must have Nicola's. In *Cricket Term*, death intrudes, followed by a subtle and yet brutally realistic and unsentimental scene in which the girls try to navigate not just their first experience of death but the death of someone they didn't like very much.

The school-set books are interspersed with others about the Marlows at home in the holidays. They weren't available to buy by the time I was looking – urgently – for them but still hanging on, just, in libraries. I eventually tracked down *Falconer's Lure* (a pony book in which the pony is replaced by a falcon), *The Marlows and the Traitor* and *Runaway Home* (adventure stories), all of whose traditional ingredients and constraints are as transformed and transcended by Forest as the school stories are in the others, and *Peter's Room* whose story of the Marlows imitating the Brontës' Angria- and Gondal-weaving antics I worshipped beyond all the others – until I discovered what I think is Forest's masterpiece, *The Ready-Made Family*.

Karen, the oldest sister, returns from Oxford with the news that she is marrying Edwin, an older, widowed-while-separated don who already has two children. After the wedding, they all come and stay at the Marlow family pile, Trennels. The rest of the book has a perfunctory plot while the meat of it explores the tensions created by the sudden advent of Edwin – a difficult man to like at the best of times – and his children, and their rarely articulated burden of sorrow, into the family's life. In the final chapters, one of the children, Rose, runs away. Nicola realises she has probably gone back to her mother's house in Oxford and rescues her from the near-clutches of a man who is pretending to be her uncle. A lesser writer would make the return of Rose to her new family and a new start the happy ending of the book. Instead, Forest lingers on Rose's train ride back to Trennels with her father and Nicola, and delivers a delicate, almost unbearably moving portrait of and meditation on grief.

Edwin asks Rosie why she ran off and she says she just wanted to go home.

'But you knew there'd be no one there.'

'I thought p'raps—' there was a long pause. Then Rose turned her face against Edwin's coat and said 'I do miss Mummy so.'

Almost absently Edwin put his arm around her. Presently, in a voice as low as her own, he said 'So do I, Rosie. So do I.'

There are times, as Nicola discovered at that moment, when it is more tactful to stay put than go discreetly away . . .

She clenches her fists, trying to prevent floods of tears 'for Rose, for Edwin – most of all, perhaps, for Karen. At the time she could have found no words to describe this engulfing melancholy; but a year later, when her friend Miranda was called on during a Latin lesson to translate the time-smoothed phrase *sunt lacrimae rerum*, which she did doubtfully as "there are tears of things" only to be asked by Miss Cartwright what that was supposed to mean, Nicola, though she could have offered no better translation, thought of that train journey and knew exactly what it meant.'

Nothing is simple in Forest's world, because people are not simple and she is an (elegant but) uncompromising realist. Hers are complicated books, but among the most fulfilling I ever read as a child and remain so for me today. Rose's ageless grief, known to Virgil and before recorded time, is captured forever in her pages. The Marlow books (and Forest's one non-Marlow volume, *The Thursday Kidnapping*) are an intimation of the deeper joys than narrative excitement that fiction can yield. It is for the psychological acuity – and the beauty and clarity with which it is expressed. It was all of this that prompted the author Victor Watson, who has written widely about children's literature, to describe Forest as Jane Austen for the young. But unlike Austen, Forest has never received her due. She fell out of fashion – she was thought to be too dense, too complex and just too full of Latin tags for the hip young things of the 1970s onwards – and spent a long time out of print. In the 1980s, only the school stories were reprinted and seemed weirdly disjointed without the intervening books to explain references to earlier adventures and the appearances and disappearances of multiple characters. Forest would probably never have been an author with a mass audience, but this dicking about with the books must surely have contributed to her work's relative anonymity throughout her life. It is an inequity that made me rage violently when I first discovered it, but the edge of my tide of fury was turned when a tiny independent publisher called Girls Gone By started republishing them all a few years ago. Antonia Forest fans remain a small group compared to those of Elinor Brent-Dyer and others, but we are mighty and evangelical. We will, together, spread the word and hopefully ensure a flourishing Forest for years to come. Consider this a couple of acres' worth, and a tiny dent in the debt I owe her.

I also had a lot to get through elsewhere. The school library turned out to be pretty fertile ground. As well as harrowing dystopias it also had old favourites like *Tom Sawyer* in the classics section, new meaty stuff like Alan Sillitoe's *The Loneliness of the Long-Distance Runner*, and lighter fare like *Sugar Mouse* – the story of a girl coming to terms with her diabetes – and, glory of glories, *The Lily Pickle Band Book*. I looked up at the top of the cabinet one day, where a few hardbacks were standing on display and there it was, cartoonish figures on a white background, shining down at me while a celestial choir started singing in the background – another book by my beloved Gwen Grant. I reached up reverently and took it in my humble hand. It was true. She had written another book for me. Not about the same girl, but as near as dammit. The heroine, Lily Pickle, is a reincarnation of the nameless heroine of *Private – Keep Out!*. She still lives in a Nottinghamshire mining town but this time contemporaneously-ish (the book was written in 1982 – there are council estates and a certain amount of lightly sketched deprivation, but no hint of the Iron Lady and the trouble she was about to cause), and still as gobby, world-weary and altogether magnificent as her ancestor. Lily's dad left when she was six but is reckoned no great loss to the family as he wanted to name her Honolulu Baby after 'this lass wearing nothing but a blade of grass and a smile' he once saw in a film. Like *Private*, the book is basically her diary – this time about the putting together of a neighbourhood children's band by indefatigable local troupers, Mr Kendal and Mrs Warren. 'This band though is different from any other band I've ever heard about because you don't have to know how to play anything at all to be in it. All you have to do to join is nod.' Lily, Mavis Jarvis ('about twelve feet tall, twelve feet wide and a hundred feet thick in the head. You could spit rivets at her head and she wouldn't even notice them going in') and assorted other juvenile flotsam and jetsam from the surrounding flats nod, and various chaotic escapades ensue. It wasn't quite as good – nothing will ever be quite as good – as the Private trilogy, but it was still a joy, and all the more so for being so wholly unexpected.

In lessons, alas, we were still murdering books aloud, this time on a grander scale. *Lord of the Flies. Nineteen Eighty-Four. Jane Eyre. Wuthering Heights.* Out loud. In their entireties. Page by seemingly infinite page at a time.

On the upside, by the time we finished, the first year of school was over and my dad was better. Weak, thin, still bald and looking almost as battered as our copies of *Wuthering Heights*, but cancer-free, as he has remained ever since. So hurrah, may I say – and, while I've got an audience, a big thank you to modern Western medicine – to that.

10

A Coming of Age

I had also by the end of that first year – hold onto your hats here – made a friend. No, a real-life friend, made out of flesh and blood and everything. Although not much flesh, now I think about it.

Sally was – and is – a gangling wreck of a human being. She was tall, thin, had giant goggly eyes in a tiny face and was mostly out to enjoy herself. This usually took the form of pulling faces and periodically making a reverberating 'Oooourrgh' noise which could express joy, disappointment or interest as the mood took her, but it was usually done just to unsettle people. With only the paltry resource of the written word at my disposal, I can neither reproduce nor do full justice to its jarring effects as it emanated from her fragile frame. She was kind, she was funny, she was ten types of idiot and I insisted that she became my friend. I called her Pinhead because of her tiny head (which was responsible for her tiny face – I don't know what was responsible for the eyes) and she called me Bubblehead because, she pointed out, my skull was not round like normal people's but had a big lump at the back that made it look like it was blowing a bubble.

We commended each other's honesty and accuracy and were inseparable from then on.

She also, it emerged, liked books. Not quite as much as she liked people – this was at first baffling but would become increasingly useful over the years* – but she read them, lots of them, and she liked them. Our tastes overlapped rather than matched. Sally was a romantic rather than sensible person like me. She liked poetry, which only ever made me go hot with embarrassment at all the naked emotion on display.† She even liked *Jane Eyre* and the roiling lunacy that was *Wuthering Heights*.

But we both loved Jill Paton Walsh's *Fireweed*. It was a love story sufficiently full of feeling to engage Sally but short and sparing enough with its emotions not to embarrass me. The tale of Bill, an unhappy evacuee during the Second World War who returns to London

* On 6 June 1822 a fur trapper called Alexis St Martin accidentally shot himself in the stomach. The local doctor William Beaumont saved his life, but St Martin was left with a hole in his stomach through which Beaumont was able, over the years, to view and learn much about the digestive process. I used Sally in much the same way, viewing and learning all sorts of things through her as we made our way through adolescence together without ever having to delve into anything messy myself. She really has been useful.

† This is why there will be almost no talk of poetry in this book. I can't bear it and never could. All that *feeling*. All that true, fully accessed, held up to the light, turned slowly round and examined in all its microscopic, exquisite, agonising detail, owned, digested *feeling*, felt by the writer and then rendered slowly, painfully into the handful of allusive words, the clutch of evocative sentences that will convey it in its purest form to the reader, who will then embark on the same process in reverse. Madness. Who wants to put themselves through that?

to fend for himself until his soldier father comes home, and Julie, a fellow fugitive whom he meets while sheltering in a tube station during an air raid, was the first time since *Goodnight Mister Tom* that a book had caught me off guard.

As the Blitz shatters London around them, Bill's feelings for Julie deepen and flourish like the fireweed that takes root in the bomb sites all over the city. When Julie is eventually injured and hospitalised, her parents find her, and the intrusion of adults and their all-consuming concerns about class and propriety destroy Bill's fragile idyll. They whisk her back home and Bill is left to wander the ruins of London alone, watching the plant take hold everywhere. 'They will build on this again someday,' he says in the final lines. 'But I like it best like this. Grown over. Healed.'

We both clutched our adolescent chests – me metaphorically, Sally literally – as our hearts swelled and threatened to burst with the repressed passion and nobility of it all. It was glorious. All the more so for the feeling being shared. Maybe this was what those *Puffin Post*-ers had been enjoying all those years. Hmm.

I was quietly devastated to discover a few years ago that the author is no longer terribly enamoured of her book. I went to a lecture (about Philippa Pearce) and at a gathering afterwards someone pointed out Jill Paton Walsh to me. I had had just enough white wine to give me the courage to tell her how much I loved *Fireweed*. She listened gravely to whatever idiotic fragments of introduction and explanation made it out of my mouth and then proceeded to tell me briskly (I remembered then that she had been a teacher before turning to writing for a living) that she did not like *Fireweed* at all any more, that the parents' intervention was crass ('They seemed to come from another book') and that although she had considered it all right at the time, she now looked on it more or less as juvenilia.

Suitably chastened, I slunk away. But now (at a safe chronological and geographical distance) I find that my marginally mutinous teenage self is stirring and I wish to say – so what? A book belongs as much to the reader as to the author. I have reread it recently, and although I can see what she means now about the parents' intervention, it didn't matter to me then and I am sure that it won't matter to any young reader who takes it down from the shelf at any point during that happy time when romantic longings are still outpacing critical faculties, and that they will find it as illuminating, moving and satisfying as I did. I hope they have a Sally to share it with too. That really is a good feeling.

As a final flourish at the end of that triumphant year, I won a prize. Nominally for Effort and Achievement, probably in fact for Having a Dad with Cancer. No matter. All winners were allowed to choose any book they wanted, as long as that book was under £2, and one Friday lunch hour they bundled the twenty of us down to the children's section of Catford shopping centre's WHSmith, where we were allotted ten minutes to make our choices.

I scanned the shelves. There was not much there, and what little there was I – fortunate, indulged child that I was – already had. I was about to settle for a treasury of something or other (the completist in me already hated treasuries with a passion that has not abated over the years. Give me a whole book, or give me nothing. Either's fine. But don't give me extracts. Don't tease me) when I saw them. The Macmillan William Brown books. White spines, red lettering, a full set of Richmal Crompton's finest taking up at least half a yard of an upper shelf. My prize money allowed the purchase of two. Did they have the ones I needed to complete my collection – *William and Air Raid Precautions* and *William and the Evacuees*? They did. I floated out of the shop on air.

To my surprise, my parents shook their heads in disappointment at my choice. I should have gone for a hardback, something more classic and uplifting than William Brown, apparently, as a prize. This notion of book-as-object rather than mass-of-content was new to me. I considered it with interest, and rejected it entirely. There was, I reasoned, a finite amount of cash and number of opportunities for acquisition in this world and neither should be wasted on getting a book that was beautiful but that you didn't want to read. Quantity of content over quality of livery has been the philosophy I have clung to ever since, which is why when I die second-hand book dealers (in the unlikely event that they have survived that long) will not be looking over my accumulated library with a covetous eye but advising my surviving relatives on how many skips to hire.

(I was once interviewed by a man from a book-collecting magazine because he refused to believe that I had 10,000 books in my house that were all merely – in the parlance of the trade – 'reading copies'. He came. He saw. He left. He wrote that it looked like I 'had a jumble sale hoisted on my walls'. I was hurt on my books' behalf, but couldn't argue.)

Back home, things were better in the sense that my dad wasn't ill (just convalescing) but worse in the sense that, having failed to get better in the time decreed reasonable by his boss, he had lost his job. And things were the same in that, as my parents were the nonpareils of rainy-day savers, this did not plunge us into penury, although as time wore on we did start taking in foreign students from the TEFL place down the road as lodgers. Which was fine. They used all the hot water and I had a lot of cold showers, but generally they stayed out of my way and I stayed out of theirs. One of them once tried to help me with my Spanish homework but she was Brazilian and it turned out that they spoke an entirely different kind of Spanish from school Spanish so we went back to just nodding and smiling as we passed each other on the landing after another hot/freezing shower.

It would make more sense if at this point I developed a taste for fantasy. But I went the other way instead and discovered Bernard Ashley's 1974 novel *The Trouble with Donovan Croft*.

Donovan Croft is what was then called 'the product of a broken home' – his mother has had to return to Jamaica and his father cannot work sufficient hours at his low-paid job and still look after his son, so he is put into foster care. His trouble, by the time he arrives to be looked after by thirteen-year-old Keith's family, is that he doesn't speak. That, at least, is the trouble with Donovan Croft for everyone else. A number of them also consider the fact that he is black to be equally bothersome, but for everyone who has his welfare at heart – his despairing father, his stymied foster family, his frustrated head teacher and social workers – it is the retreat into silence that matters.

Bernard Ashley's story was part of a movement that started in the 1970s towards providing children with stories about modern protagonists facing contemporary difficulties (or old difficulties with a contemporary spin). A lot of these so-called 'problem novels' dealt with single issues (divorce, bullying, sexism, racism) in fairly basic, one-note ways. Perhaps aided by his years of experience as a teacher (his first stories were written for the children in his special-needs class; they were seen by an educational publisher visiting his school and published in 1966 – *Croft* was his first novel) as well as his natural talent, Ashley's wasn't one of them. His book is the story of what happens when the normal patterns of life are disrupted, about the effects of insecurity and unhappiness on children, particularly, and on those around them, compounded in Croft's case by racism.

All this is woven in and out of a pitch-perfect evocation of the wordlessly growing friendship between Donovan and the Chapmans' son, Keith (despite Keith's own frustration with his mute foster brother, and his own ostracism that follows from his association with the weird new kid in the playground) and of Donovan's profound sense of being an afterthought in a grown-up world (familiar to all children, though usually to a lesser extent). I remember the strange feeling of having privileged access to his inner monologues and the urge, which grew to almost unbearable proportions as the book continued to refuse to yield easy answers to a boy's despair, for him to speak, speak, to Keith, to his father, to anyone about a misery lying too deep for either tears or words.

It was further proof, to add to *End of Term*'s, that people contained multitudes. But more than that, *The Trouble with Donovan Croft* made it clear that people's perceptions of each other were rarely pure and never simple. When Donovan's authoritarian form teacher reacts with violent hostility to what he (aided by a degree of racism) perceives as his new pupil's 'dumb insolence', it started to become clear to me for the first (conscious) time that we might all be looking at each other through the distorting prisms of our own limited understanding and various prejudices. This was both interesting and infuriating. Life, it seemed, could turn out to be a lot more complex, and frankly exhausting, than I had originally thought.

I then went on a little 1970s-gritty-realism spree. I polished off a few more Ashleys, including *Break in the Sun* and *Running Scared*. *Break in the Sun* (which was on television at the time though I refused to watch it as I refuse to watch all book adaptations on the grounds that nobody should be encouraged to mess with perfection) almost broke me. That a child could be driven to running away from home for real – by, in this case, a violent stepfather – rather than Catherine-Storr's-Lucy-style seemed to me about the most awful thing imaginable. *Running Scared*, a novelisation of the 1986 TV drama he wrote for the BBC which didn't suffer the drop in quality most novelisations do and was shortlisted for the Carnegie Medal, was less harrowing. I writhed in delicious agony throughout this tense thriller that posed endless questions about divided loyalties and matters of conscience that rereading now I find the intervening thirty years have done nothing to simplify.) Then came Sylvia Sherry's *A Pair of Jesus Boots* and its sequel, *A Pair of Desert Wellies*, whose (anti?) hero Rocky O'Rourke, growing up in a poor part of Liverpool, gradually comes to realise that the wayward big brother he idolises is not as worthy of his adoration as he thought and that he must choose whether to follow the family's or his own path.

Sally and I both read Katherine Paterson's *Bridge to Terabithia*, a beautifully written story of a friendship that grows between two school outsiders Jesse and Leslie who establish their own private kingdom – Terabithia – by a stream in the woods. While Jesse is away, Leslie goes there alone, falls and drowns. Sally was shattered. I was not. Upon questioning, it turned out that I had not understood what had happened. The denial Jesse moves into had confused me; I didn't understand what he was doing and thought therefore that everyone else must have got it wrong and Leslie was indeed, as Jesse insisted, still alive. Sally, both a better reader and more emotionally literate than I was, instructed me to re-read the end and this time, with Paterson pulling me gently on and Sally pushing valiantly from behind, I got it. I was shattered in my turn, and Sally was satisfied. I began to see how maybe, just occasionally, books and people could work in harmony. Maybe it wasn't always necessary to reject the one in order to embrace the other. It would be many years before I acted on this thought, but still, I was glad to have it.

The library yielded Cynthia Voigt's *Dicey's Song* and I slogged through it. It was the first time I ever found myself unable to suspend my disbelief. The idea of four children, abandoned by their mentally-ill mother in a Connecticut car park making it all the way to their aunt's and then grandmother's house umpty-billion miles away without getting kidnapped, killed or at least picked up by the police and sent straight to the foster homes they are desperate to avoid seemed to me, in such an otherwise acutely realistic book, impossible. Somehow, though you would think my incredulity would have inoculated against it, it was nevertheless harrowing. They reach their destination and are eventually taken in by their grandmother, but their mother remains in a catatonic state in a Boston hospital. It seemed to me that without your mother – in a functional state – there could not, should not even be an attempt at a happy ending. With the great continent slowly flooding, how would you be able to do anything but try and beat back the rising tides of anxiety, fear and misery? No, Cynthia – your American optimism was not for me. It was all deeply unsettling.

I took a brief break in the light-hearted world of *Hangin' Out With Ceci* – about a rebellious teen who travels back in time and ends up becoming friends with her own, now also teenage, mother – by Francine Pascal (whose Sweet Valley High series I was – O happy California summer's day! – very soon to meet). Then I returned, slightly gingerly, to the fray with some Betsy Byars from the paperback carousels in Torridon and the school libraries. *The Pinballs, The Cybil War, The Eighteenth Emergency, The Cartoonist* – the last was my particular favourite, though less for its lightly, but beautifully and accurately sketched depiction of the family dysfunction caused by an immature mother and her preference for one son over the rest of her children, than for the protagonist Alfie's attic. A room of your own (soon under threat from the return of the prodigal son, Bubba, who their fond mama insists needs the attic to live in) was my dream and I lusted over Alfie's as I had Jo March's a few years before. Alfie drew cartoons and pinned them up all round him. I planned to write and keep everything hidden, but other than that we were soulmates.

I have a room of my own now, incidentally, and it is every bit as good as I thought it would be.

SVH

Hey, d'you know what? I'm getting a bit of a rush of blood to the head and wanting to go crazy for a moment. Let's take our own break from these tales of misery, maternal favouritism and child roadside abandonment and turn our faces to the bright, glorious, gloriously stupid sunshine of Sweet Valley High right now. I don't know what's happening – the wild, carefree spirit of Jessica Wakefield seems to be moving through me – but let's do it!

This was the first book craze ever to hit school. Suddenly, everyone was reading. Pink, yellow and lilac paperbacks blossomed like flowers across the playground. Everyone loved them. I loved them. It was a heady time. Nobody could get enough of them. Especially me, as I wasn't allowed to buy them.

Well, that's not quite true. My parents never forbade me to buy any book. But they made their feelings known. And somehow, when my mother made her feelings known, I never really felt like butting up against them any more than I have ever felt like butting up against an electric fence or bundle of razor wire.

Also they were, compared to other books, fantastically expensive. £1.75 a throw in 1986 was serious money. I presume now that this was a result of the fact that the books were not books in the traditional sense, written by A Writer and published by a normal firm in the normal manner but part of a sprawling industry creating merchandise rather than Art. Brighter sparks in the playground might have realised that producing a dozen books a year was beyond the scope of even the most prolific authors, but I did not. Astute observers might have noted that the covers read 'Created by' rather than 'Written by' Francine Pascal, but I did not. It was only in recent years that I realised they were composed by conglomerate.

I always like to imagine Pascal sometime in the early 1980s suddenly sitting bolt upright in the middle of the night and a satin-sheeted bed and crying 'Twins! The same! Yet so different! And lavaliers!' before falling fast back to sleep again, the better to birth her creation, refreshed, in the morning. I am delighted to tell you now that that is basically what happened.

Pascal had previously worked with her husband as a TV writer. In 1982 in the middle of a sticky patch while writing her latest book for teenagers (*Love & Betrayal & Hold the Mayo*), she remembered an idea she had had for a soap opera about teenagers. An editor friend of hers suggested that it might be better as a series of books. Possibly this was an artistic consideration, but equally possibly it was a commercial one, to capitalise on the fact that by now, teenagers controlled a decent amount of money of their own and were buying books for themselves rather than relying on parents and librarians to choose and hand them down from on high. Either way, Pascal went to her typewriter and banged out this: 'They are the most perfect twins in the world, Elizabeth and Jessica Wakefield. One is good, one is bad. Cliffhanger endings. Continuing characters. The action is always carried by the kids. They run their world, which is very appealing.'

Yes, Francine – YES!

She is named as author of the first two of what would become a 143-strong core series plus innumerable spin-offs. The rest were entirely produced by a host of freelance ghostwriters. Their job was to create, as far as possible, uniform products for a company dedicated to the Pascal–Wakefield enterprise, 17th Street Productions. They used a 'bible' (notes on themes, characters, settings and so on, compiled by Pascal) to ensure consistency, and worked to outlines she provided. They were a band of typing postgrad monkeys stretching from sea to shining sea, producing for a fixed fee 140 pages every six to eight weeks. They blended blue jeans, good-hearted hunks, glowering bad boys, motorcycle accidents, Fiat Spiders, southern Californian ocean views, split-level housing, Spanish-tiled kitchens, rich bitches, occasional comas and bouts of hysterical paralysis in perfect proportions. For which sterling efforts I – and, judging by the response my Twitter feed gets whenever I mention your output, the rest of my generation – remain eternally grateful.

I hunted down what scraps I could of this perfect escapist fluff (Torridon only stocked a few of the 12 million copies that were in print by 1986, while the school library eschewed them entirely) and their idealised world and formulaic nature was a joy. They were the Enid Blytons of early teendom, except that (as long as I shut down critical faculties for the duration and ignore the preponderance of rapey boyfriends*) I can still read them now with delight. You could settle down with *Taking Sides*, *Perfect Shot* or *Wrong Kind of Girl* and know that you were in safe hands. Elizabeth and Jessica would always be blonde, size 6 twins with sparkling blue-green eyes and those golden lavaliers (what were they? No idea! So glamorous!†) round their necks and feeding each side of your warring adolescent psyche in turn. Elizabeth was ego – sensible, responsible, good at English and impulse control. Jessica was untrammelled id, a slender sociopath you couldn't help but love. Unless you were Todd, who hated her. Until he didn't. But let us not dwell on sororal treachery now.

The lean SVH years came to a sudden end with the most remarkable stroke of good luck. Sally went to a local jumble sale one Saturday and found – just lying

* Yes, YES Bruce Patman I'm looking at you.

† They are pendant necklaces. Which apparently repel nuance, characterisation and feminism, and thank goodness for that.

there on the book stall as if they were ordinary paperbacks instead of manna from the teen romance committee gods! – a twenty-strong run of SVHs. She gathered them in trembling arms and in a quavering voice asked how much they were. 'Ten pence each,' came the unbelievable reply. Sally, whose mouth usually got her into more trouble than it ever talked her out of, had the sense this once to keep schtum. She piled them into a box, handed over her dues and got the hell out of Dodge. Her face still lights up at the memory now. For barely more than the price of one new volume, we gorged for days on the adventures of SoCal's finest. Jessica pretended to be Elizabeth for bad reasons. Elizabeth pretended to be Jessica for good reasons. Todd did various Toddish things Toddishly. Enid arrived (she was the one who got the hysterical paralysis B-plot, like Fallon in *Dynasty* which I was – not coincidentally – consuming with almost as much avidity at the time). Jessica crushed people's dreams, manipulated her family as naturally as she breathed, stole innumerable boyfriends from innumerable lesser, nicer females, drove the vulnerable to attempt suicide and everyone continued to find her rising sociopathy vaguely charming (just as they did with Alexis Carrington. And Elizabeth is Krystle! Cultural synergy!). People pretended to be rich, other people pretended to be poor. Bit-parters died of leukaemia and of trying drugs once (just say no, kids!). Elizabeth, after discovering that even getting kidnapped by a hospital orderly (just say no to candy-striping too, kids) doesn't make her interesting, rebelled against her good-girl image and – uh – went surfing. Steven came and went from college, tripping a few plot switches along the way. Unhappy rich girls shoplifted, chubby people lost weight, and I daresay a few ghostwriters lost their minds. The *New York Times* must certainly have had to pop a restorative pill or two when *Perfect Summer* became the first young-adult novel ever to make its paperback bestseller list, as it did in 1985 – alongside books by Norman Mailer, Leon Uris and John Updike.

No matter. We loved it all. Yes, we were being indoctrinated with constricting and toxic messages about sexuality, femininity, wealth and assorted other aspects of humanity and society you would prefer people kept as free and open a mind about as possible, but on the other hand – Robin got slim and won the school-sponsored beauty pageant (school-sponsored beauty pageant! WTactualF was going on in 1980s SoCal?) and got made a Phi Beta Bumcrack AND became co-head of the cheerleading squad, guys! It was *awesome*!

BLUME

Sally and I found much else in biblio-common. We were moving into the lighter end of adult fare, for some reason via the biographies of the more or less picturesquely poverty stricken – Christine Marion Fraser's *Blue Above the Chimneys* and Helen Forrester's *Twopence to Cross the Mersey* figured large. But our greatest bond was Anne Digby's Trebizon. This was another boarding-school series but – get this – *set in the modern world*. It was disconcerting. All the standard fixtures and fittings were there – a new girl (Rebecca Mason) who, after temporarily falling for the blandishments of what was not, even in that modern setting, quite known as a bitch, realises the error of her ways and becomes firm friends with an established gang of school stalwarts with one defining physical characteristic and talent apiece: in this case, Tish (good at games, unnaturally thick legs*), Sue (good at music, wore glasses), Mara (Greek, good at supplying office equipment for the new Juniper house magazine), and Sally 'Elf' Elphinstone (fat, good at making up a quintet) in time to solve the mystery of who has stolen Rebecca's poem and passed it off as her own.

Rebecca, in case you were wondering, was tall and blonde and good at tennis and writing poetry. She got double helpings of everything because she was the Main Character, you see.

The Trebizon series also had – brace yourselves, please – BOYS in it. The fourth book in the series is actually called *Boy Trouble at Trebizon*. Rebecca starts going out with Tish's brother Robbie. I know! Martha – bring me my digitalis . . . In real life – these are the twelve-to-fourteen years – my classmates were discovering real boys. I thought I was doing quite well to have discovered them in books. Had I looked like one of the Wakefield twins, I might perhaps have followed Sally's lead and got interested in dating, but the mirror and my

* 'She had been surprised to notice that Tish had very thick, muscular legs when the rest of her was quite slim and graceful.' To this day I don't quite know what Anne Digby was thinking here. Sure, she says it to minor villain Debbie, which gives her a chance to stick the knife in later, but still. Thick legs. It's just a bit . . . weird.

family and friend's ongoing refusal to palter with the truth militated against this. The very vocal consensus was that, while I might end up passable eventually, between the braces, the glasses, the grease, the blackheads and a seven-stone frame that made me look more like a drowned chick than anything human, let alone nubile, I should for the foreseeable future keep very much to my books. I look back on the few photographs that were taken during this period and think – yep, fair enough.

You will probably not be surprised to learn that I didn't really have a proper teenage rebellion. I looked around at everyone else's – the goths, the slags, the booze, fag 'n' drug experimenters, the tantrum-throwers, the weepers – and it seemed like a lot of work. So I remained outwardly composed and compliant. But inwardly, I like to think, I was as miserable as the best of them. I kept my unhappiness about never fitting in, about not having more than one friend, excellent though she was, and about looking like someone's discarded parasitic twin, to myself. Being apparently unbothered by everything only made me more of an outcast, but I just didn't know how to join in. As the clamour and frenzy of others' angst gathered ever more thickly and cacophonously round me, I felt like Ernest Thesiger, the Edwardian actor who when asked about his experiences at the front during the First World War cried 'My dear – the noise! The people!'

Then – a break in the clouds. We all, overnight – or so it seemed – discovered Judy Blume. I don't know how it happened – maybe Mrs Heathfield got a memo from the Department of Health saying 'It Is Time' and unlocked a secret cupboardful of her works and our hormones drew us towards them in a kind of reverse Bisto-sniff – but suddenly she was everywhere. Judy Blume was the second and last book craze ever to hit school, the last author to unite bookworms and normals in common reading purpose. In her books was everything that SVH left out – reality, mess, humanity and wit.* To have another shared passion was brilliant. It gave us all – even me, especially me – something to talk about, to enthuse about and the break from self-imposed cynicism and relentless manufacture of scorn was in itself a joy. But the sensation of gaining a friend and mentor in Blume herself, someone older and wiser and yet still so completely understanding, with such perfect recollection of the grotesque, tumultuous time of adolescence, of its bravura and its awful vulnerabilities was so, so much better.

It's hard to remember which one of Judy Blume's books I read first – they were all consumed so quickly and have been part of me for so long. But I think – and the publication dates of my battered collection suggest – that it was *Are You There God? It's Me, Margaret.*

* In an interview in 2012, promoting what turned out to be the abysmal sequel to the SVH books *Sweet Valley Confidential*, which picked up Jessica's and Elizabeth's story ten years after high school, Pascal talked about some of the sacrifices she had had to make in order to turn a 100,000 audience for her books into a 100 million strong army – 'Humour is one of the things I gave up. It is a very sophisticated tool and it didn't work in these books.' Rereading them now, however, is A Right Laugh.

All together now! 'We must, we must, we must increase our bust!'

I don't know whether to curse la Blume for giving me false hope or gratefully acknowledge the fact that, false or not, it was frequently only the faintly flickering hope that a bosom and assorted other physical accoutrements might one day arrive that kept me hacking on through the fetid swamp of adolescence.

'We must . . .' was the rallying cry of Margaret, Nancy and the rest of the teenage coterie with whom Margaret becomes involved when she moves house, and encapsulated the fervent desire of every pubescent reader to be able to do something, anything to hurry along the dreaded and longed-for day when the long-promised 'changes' would start to arrive. Menstruation, first bras, masturbation, self-regard, self-loathing, hormonal mood swings, slut-shaming (there wasn't a name for it yet, but the practice itself was alive, well and here aimed at poor, overdeveloped Laura Danker in her swollen sweaters) and all the hideous, fabulous rest of it are here in Blume's first foray into a part of the children's literary landscape she would make her own during the 1970s and 80s. Her insistence on writing about these things has made her a controversial figure for much of her career, especially in her native America where she was the subject of an organised book-banning campaign in the 1980s after Reagan's election and remains one of the country's most frequently challenged authors of the twenty-first century. Truly, the world is frightened of those who would speak truth unto teenage girls.

Though it's maybe broader than that. Maybe it's anyone who wants to speak truth to children. Katherine

Paterson's *Bridge to Terabithia*, for example, is still number 28 on the list of 100 Most Frequently Challenged Books published every decade by the American Library Association, presumably because it deals with the subject of death and so prompts adults to consider the perennial question of how much reality children can bear. When the answer is felt to be 'not very much', a book tends to become Officially Controversial and make it onto lists like this.

But the question is really – how much reality can we bear to let our children bear? On the one hand, children are inadvertently quite good at protecting themselves. By and large when reading, the things they aren't ready for simply go over their heads or flit lightly across their minds, leaving a faint impression that can be deepened and shaded later by experience or exposure to other books (or films, or TV, or Internet . . .) as the years go on. On the other, this is a hard thing for a parent to trust in, running as it does counter to every primitive instinct in us that wants to keep our children safe from all possible harm. Lead-lined bunkers instead of Roald Dahl, remember? But of course we can and we must, otherwise – well, you only have to look at the rest of the ALA's list to see what madness can unfold. *In the Night Kitchen* is there at number 24. Naked bottoms in crazy dreamscapes are apparently worse than child mortality. Eric Carle's *Draw Me a Star* is at number 61. Did atheist parents object to the picture book's parallels with the Bible's creation story, or did a cross-denominational group balk at the human figures having no clothes on? It is truly impossible to imagine what objections were lodged to bring Iona and Peter Opie's *I Saw Esau* – a book of traditional children's rhymes – in at number 98. Is 'Donkey walks on four legs / And I walk on two / The last one I saw / Was very like you' enough to give anyone the vapours? The last edition published did have illustrations by Sendak. So maybe that's enough?

But back to Blume. I raced through everything else she had written for my age group – *Deenie*, *Blubber*, *Tiger Eyes* (I only managed that once – the death of a parent was something I was not willing to contemplate for too long. I'm still not), *Then Again Maybe I Won't* (a kind of *Are You There God?* from a boy's point of view), *Starring Sally J. Freedman as Herself* (which I somehow forgot to take on holiday with me to Preston when it had me most firmly in its grip. I spent the fortnight in a fever of yearning to get back to its ten-year-old vivacious heroine, her aunt's borscht and Sally's equally vivid imaginings about being Esther Williams and of unmasking Hitler, who she suspects is one of her neighbours, hiding in plain sight after the war). And – oh gosh, there's one other, what WAS the name of that again? Oh yes – *Forever . . .*

Certain books had done the rounds over the previous year or so with their rude bits marked for quick perusal – various Jilly Coopers, Shirley Conran's *Lace*, Judith Krantz's *Scruples* and so on – but the rudest of them all was *Forever . . .*, and this time we all read every word. The story of Katherine, Michael and Ralph is engraved on every adolescent heart that has beaten since it was first published in . . . well, guess. You won't believe this – I didn't, because we all think we were the first to discover it, just as every generation thinks it's the first to discover sex, and that she therefore must have written it three months max before we found it – but *Forever . . .* was first published in 1975. Blume wrote it after her daughter Randy bemoaned the fact that she couldn't find a book about two kids having sex in which the girl didn't have to be punished (with an unwanted child, an abortion, or by being sent away from the boy to stay with relatives in one of the less fun states, or death) afterwards, and its depiction of mutually desired, ugly-consequence-free sex remains, over forty years on, still surprisingly rare. It's the book I always want to press into the hands of any teenage girl I see engrossed in the *Twilight* saga.

For the uninitiated, *Twilight* is the first in a series of four books by Stephenie Meyer about seventeen-year-old Bella Swan who falls in love with Edward Cullen, who turns out to be a vampire. He has renounced the drinking of human blood but the hunger remains. Thus they can never have sex, because WHO KNOWS what urges might be released in the throes of passion and he fears that he might end up killing Bella instead of making sweet, sweet love to her. Over the course of the book(s) Bella becomes more and more passive, training herself not to respond to his kisses (when she does respond, he draws away and berates her for endangering herself), gradually isolating herself from her friends and family in order to protect his secret, and generally learning to subordinate her every impulse and desire to the need not to upset Edward and his instincts. You don't have to squint too hard to see dubious parallels between this and the real-life dynamic of abusive relationships. Meyer is a practising Mormon who generally argues that her books are about learning to master your nature, and fans defend her take on romance as the erotics of abstinence. To me, the whole thing reads badly (in every sense – Meyer is no great stylist) and feels toxic, anti-feminist and regressive and should be staked through its black, black heart. In love with a hundred-year-old vampire Bella may be, but Buffy, she ain't. Nor is she Katherine, who in *Forever* . . . not only has and enjoys sex without regrets, but also doesn't marry Michael. By the end, she has even survived the sadness of breaking up and has moved on.

And Edward? You may have a sparkly face and great abs, but you are no Michael. Or, indeed, Ralph. Ralph was the name Michael gave to his penis and Ralph really was entirely positive about people responding to his interest. This is how things should be.

A few years ago, I interviewed Judy Blume at an event in Waterstone's Piccadilly. The place was packed with thirtysomething women who listened intently to the tiny, fragile-looking, seventy-six-year-old woman talking about her forty-odd years writing for adolescents, the fights she'd had and continues to have with censors, though nowadays less on her own behalf than on others', and her memories of writing the various books that people had clutched to their chests. By the end of the interview, it was just a roomful of tearful women queuing to have their books signed and trying to find the words to tell Blume just what she'd meant to them for so many years, how it felt to see their stories in print, being depicted with truth and compassion and without condescension.

I didn't manage it myself. I couldn't afford to. The only time we had to chat was before the interview, and I couldn't risk reducing myself to a puddle of gratitude and emotion. But I did ask if I could be cheeky and get her to sign beforehand not one but two books – *Are You There God?* and *Starring Sally J. Freedman as Herself* – because, I explained, they had both at different points meant everything to me. I couldn't choose between them and – yes, I actually said this – I didn't want one to feel left out. She understood completely.

She always understood completely.

When the first bloom of Blume was over for me, I filled the void with Puffin Plus books. If you are slightly older than me and remember the Puffin Peacocks books – well, this is what that series evolved into. Whereas Peacocks had gone quite heavy on the historical fiction,* Puffin Plus was a bit more progressive. A

* Such a lot of historical fiction there used to be (Peacocks was not alone). Barbara Willard, Cynthia Harnett, Geoffrey Trease, Ronald Welch, Hester Burton, Margaret Irwin were all authors of multiple books, often centring on one family's fortunes through the ages. To say nothing of the likes of Leon Garfield, whose books – like *Jack Holborn*, *Smith* and *The Strange Affair of Adelaide Harris* – were set in a hazy, Victorianish past even if they didn't depend on real historical events or pinpoint background detail for their plots or settings. I love and revere them all now but I never came across anything but Joan Aiken's *The Wolves of Willoughby Chase* at the time. They simply weren't in fashion. Maybe this was because history had stopped being taught in the old-fashioned way (comprehensively, linearly) in school. Certainly by the time my generation was in education, it was just scraps and husks. I have no more idea of how this country or the world came to look and function the way it does than I do of how my computer is producing these words on the screen or saving them on its innards. And you need a certain amount of knowledge of the past before you can enjoy – or, perhaps more importantly, even want to

bit cooler. But, like Blume, they were precursors to what is today known as YA (young adult) fiction, and as nearly young-adult persons Sally and I lapped them up.

---

pull down from the shelf – a book about the past. Of course it can/will/should supplement your knowledge once you do, but as with anything there is a *de minimis* requirement before it will all hang together, before you can get enough out of it for its pursuit to be worth your while. I could barely follow, let alone enjoy, *The Children of the New Forest* (despite doing so at an age so advanced that I am not even going to admit what it was here) because I'd never heard of the English Civil War – and wouldn't until after I left university. So I had to do so much work just keeping Cavaliers, Roundheads and the hastily researched basics about Puritanism and King Charles II in my brain that I had no mental energy left to enjoy the story properly. (Though I must urge anyone who feels that they would be similarly afflicted to give it a go anyway. The Civil War stuff basically brackets the long section in which the children shuck off their aristocratic clothes and habits and learn the ways of the foresters, and this is all that even anyone properly educated remembers. The Beverley kids beat down acorns for pigs, trap hares, learn the minutiae of caring for hens, building cow-houses and stalking, shooting and skinning stags. By the end of it I was at least able to recompense Dad for some small fraction of the information he had imparted to me over the years with the news that a stag was a brocket until three years old, a staggart at four, a warrantable stag at five and a hart royal – there is still no more splendidly evocative phrase – after that. However scanty your historico-factual knowledge may be, you can always feel the primeval pull of the forest and want to run your hands over the texture of that life, as rough as bark and as delightful in its detail. But I still wish I had been taught some stuff. I would have got a lot more *Blackadder* jokes for a start.) Multiply that mindset by however many children there are per reading generation and you can see the market for historical fiction falling away pretty rapidly.

Some, like *The Best Little Girl in the World* (about a girl with an eating disorder, written by an American psychologist who specialised in treating – but not, I must sadly note on rereading, in writing terribly well about – eating disorders) were 'issue' books, to be read with interest but rarely good enough to be loved. Some were passed around, like the Jilly Coopers had been, for their rude bits (one had a blow job scene but – in recognition of how little interested we were in the Not Rude bits of Rude Books, I cannot remember the title. It may have been *I'm Kissing As Fast As I Can*. It rings a bell and sounds plausible), and one – just one – was funny.

That one was June Oldham's comic teen romance novel *Grow Up, Cupid*. It was easily the funniest book I had read since *Private – Keep Out!*. We are introduced to the lead character, seventeen-year-old Margaret Dermot (Mog to her friends) thus: 'Ever since the day Margaret had been observed in the Infants' playground lifting her dress and showing her knickers to a circle of uninterested boys, Mrs Dermot had feared for her daughter's morals. The subsequent twelve years spent in tremulous vigilance had done nothing to relieve her anxiety.' I laughed till I cried.

Mog, when we meet her a few pages later, has (to the only cautious relief of her mother) dumped her boyfriend Keith for spending too much time writing poems to her, and sworn off men. Instead, she throws herself into a variety of more rewarding pursuits, including recruiting students for a writer's after-hours class and gently terrorising the college head ('old enough to have lost, as hostages to the years, much of his cerebral hair and an athletic figure. That is how he referred to what others called bald and fat') into organising a crèche. She also starts writing a Mills & Boon novel to earn some cash.

One cannot write a book requiring a convincing representation of the Perfect Man without at least a modicum of research, of course, and so Mog does a spot of fieldwork with one of the fathers from the crèche, Denis from the writing class, a quick but ultimately unsatisfactory re-try with Keith, before finally taking a run at punk-haired fellow student Bysshe (his mother had a crush on Shelley) who, though a Mills & Boon heroine might faint at the very sight of him, proves to be the perfect man for Mog.

At fourteen I loved the book for being funny. Now, although there is still something to make me laugh on every page I love it even more for having such a bright, inquiring, active, charming heroine, full of life, anarchy and sarcasm – a perfect rendition of the true teenage spirit. The capturing of that spirit – and of teenage humour, without which we would surely none of us have made it past fifteen – is still rare, at least for the upper age range of YA readers at which Mog and Puffin Plus were aimed. Slightly younger readers have, these days, the likes of the late, great Louise Rennison, whose heroines are full to the brim with a zest for life and one-liners. And whenever I am feeling down, I reach for any of Holly Smale's Geek Girl series about oddball Harriet Manners, fact-collector-and-regurgitator extraordinaire who nonplusses everyone around her, especially when she manages to fall backwards – almost literally – into a modelling career. All six books are miracles of perfectly pitched and maintained tone – Harriet is so idiosyncratic and naïve that she could easily become frustrating and unreal, but the whole is so funny and engaging she never falls off the tightrope – and leave me with a daft smile on my face for hours afterwards. But comic fare for older teens seems thin on the ground still.

Summer of My German Soldier

I was buying most of my books for myself now. It wasn't like I had a social life making any demands on my purse, and Dad had to start saving for a pension at some point. But he would still occasionally bring me a surprise present. One of them was *Summer of My German Soldier*, by Bette Greene. This dense, beautiful, astonishing, intricate portrayal of love, friendship, hatred, prejudice and sacrifice packs so much pain, beauty and wisdom into its compass that when I reread it now, I have to put it down every few pages and walk around for a bit to let it all bed down before I am ready for the next chapter. There is a whole cadre of books, especially from the 1970s, that attempted to show the inhumanity of war from all sides and show the grey areas within it, rather than deal simply in Goodies and Baddies, but never was it better done than in Greene's debut novel about Patty Bergen, a twelve-year-old Jewish girl living in the Deep South of America. Her family is barely tolerated by their neighbours and she is barely tolerated by her family. Her mother finds her constantly wanting – in femininity, in social graces and all the other things that would make her worthy of the role of daughter, especially when set against her younger, prettier and more biddable sister

Sharon. Her father – in some of the most expertly, vividly, unsensationally rendered scenes of violence you'll read this side of the boy Cromwell being battered in the opening of Hilary Mantel's *Wolf Hall* – frequently beats her senseless, and senselessly. Her grandparents and the family housekeeper Ruth do what they can to protect and to love her, but it is not enough.

Patty's intense need and vulnerability lead her to help hide a German soldier, Anton Reiker, after he escapes from a nearby POW camp. He is a conscript into the army, the son of a historian who spoke out against Hitler until it became too dangerous ('He chose acquiescence and life rather than resistance and death. Not a very admirable choice, but a very human one') and his mother was a gardener from England. Anton teases Patty, teaches her and appreciates her. Everything that brings her hostility and bruises at home – her intellect, her curiosity, her unbiddability, her 'unfemininity' – brings her happiness and growing friendship in the soldier's hideout. She learns that she, just as she stands, just as she is, is worth something.

It ends brutally. But the book – originally rejected by eighteen publishers, who presumably took fright at the thought of how inflammatory a depiction of a non-evil Nazi befriending a Jewish girl could be – was another landmark one for me. It was my first exposure to the idea that even something as irredeemable as Nazism could contain nuance and complexity (at the very simplest level, I hadn't even known about conscription before – were you as culpable if you'd been forced to join up as those who did so voluntarily? This alone caused my brain to stutter) and my first step along the road to answering the simple question that arises in every child's mind when they first start learning about Hitler and the Holocaust: how did it, how did he, happen? Anton's explanation to Patty of how Hitler succeeded is still my go-to reference as I'm reading the headlines about the rise of whichever new (or ancient) evil is dominating the news cycle that day. 'His first layer is an undeniable truth, such as: the German worker is poor. The second layer is divided equally between flattery and truth: the German worker deserves to be prosperous. The third layer is total fabrication: the Jews and the Communists have stolen what is rightfully yours.' Evil builds in increments. Your understanding of this basic truth may grow in sophistication and detail over the years, but the earlier and harder you grasp the simple, unchanging bastard fundamental, the better off you'll be.

*

It is impossible, of course, to say exactly when childhood reading stops and adult reading begins. I was coming up to sixteen and my intake was already fairly evenly split between both groups. I was still rereading old favourites like *The Family from One End Street* and *Tom's Midnight Garden*, especially when tired, under stress or on holiday. But I was also turning increasingly (and as gleefully and as indiscriminately as I had with all my other reading) to John Irving, Maeve Binchy, Stella Gibbons, Margaret Atwood, Margaret Mitchell, Thackeray (I still haven't touched Dickens), J. G. Ballard, Daniel Defoe, Julian Barnes, Jonathan Swift, Philip Roth, David Lodge,

Josephine Tey and Peter Tinniswood. In a year or so's time, I would discover Jane Austen and a whole new level of adoration. *Summer of My German Soldier* was, I think, one of the last children's books I read for the first time as a child. After that, I would continue to reread old favourites, but my new acquisitions would tend to come from the adult shelves of bookshops and the library.

Adult reading – by which I mean reading adult books at a roughly adult age – is different from reading children's books as a child. It is still my favourite thing to do, it is still absolutely necessary to me, I still become fractious and impatient if I do not get my daily 'fix' – but the quality of the experience is different. I do not get absorbed as easily or as fully. I am more pernickety. Where once any book would have done, I now frequently have to try a few to find one that suits. The joy, once guaranteed simply by opening a cover, is now more elusive. As an adult, your tastes (and/or prejudices) are more developed and particular, your time is more precious and your critical faculties are harder to switch off. As an adult, worries are greater and it takes a more powerful page to be able to banish them for the duration. Perhaps you appreciate it all the more when it comes, but I miss the days of effortless immersion, and the glorious certainty of pleasure.

Even today, my greatest chance of recapturing those heady days comes with sitting down with a children's – or YA – book. The ones that were around when I was young but which I somehow missed, like Dodie Smith's *I Capture the Castle* or the books that followed on from

Joan Aiken's *The Wolves of Willoughby Chase** have all recreated those early joys despite my late discovery. And of the books written long after I reached my majority – well. The piledriving power of Suzanne Collins' The Hunger Games trilogy or Michael Grant's Gone series will keep you up all night at any age. The delicate tracery of a Frances Hardinge story will make you hold your breath until the end, lest you disturb the perfect balance of it all. You cannot help but start pressing copies of Patrick Ness' thrilling, heartbreaking, altogether extraordinary Chaos Walking trilogy on everyone you know as soon as you've finished it. Meg Rosoff makes you wish she had been writing for the last forty years instead of just fourteen. Everything Melvin Burgess writes crackles with genius. And I spend long

* This was the story of two cousins, Bonnie and Sylvia, who are turned out of Bonnie's home by the wicked Aunt Slighcarp and sent to a viciously cruel orphanage, from which they eventually escape with the aid of a loyal servant and the forest-dwelling Simon, travel to London to find the family lawyer and ensure that justice is done. I never realised then that this book is just the first in the Wolves Chronicles, Aiken's series of books set in an alternative version of England, during the reign of King James III. Most of the rest, which I discovered and devoured in virtually a single sitting about ten years ago, centre round a vivid, sprightly girl called Dido Twite. The dozen volumes are full of tiny, wondrous details, highly coloured characters and a sense of imagination perpetually fomenting, dark and joyous by turns. Taken individually and together they are fine-grained and sweeping epics, almost overwhelming to the senses but not quite – the perfect preparation, in fact, for Dickens. I blame my ongoing inability to tackle him on the absence of Dido in the formative stages of my biblio-life.

hours wondering whether I wish J. K. Rowling had been around when I was young or whether I'm more grateful to have her now, so that Harry Potter can catapult me back and let me read, in that headlong, careless rush once more whenever I am most in need.

When I look back, I come out in a cold sweat of relief at all the lucky breaks being a bookworm gives you. Beyond the pure and simple joy it brings, a love of reading grants you an easy life at school. It pleases teachers, who also assume you are clever (I was not) and hard-working (I was, but only because giving into my natural laziness would have earned me a solid beating at home). It gives you a facility with language which means all essay-based exams halve in complexity (and later makes covering letters and job applications a great deal more persuasive than they should be) and altogether eases your passage through life far more than any lucky break should.

Once you're out of the education system, things even up a bit. The genuinely clever people get the promotions and the money, which is as it should be (and sometimes they will buy you a bottle of nice wine if you help them with their applications and covering letters). We bookworms don't mind, because we only need enough money for books, and promotion would mean longer working hours and less time to read.

As I have got older, I have occasionally questioned whether it is possible to take the bookworm thing too far. 'People say that life's the thing but I prefer reading.' Yes, I have thought in my weaker moments, but you really do need to live some life, don't you?

But then I come back to myself and think – no. No, I

don't. I have lived so many lives through books, gone to so many places, so many eras, looked through so many different eyes, considered so many different points of view. The fact that I haven't had time to do much myself seems but a small price to pay. I live my life quite as fully as I want, thank you. Books have not isolated me – they have connected me. What non-bookworms get by meeting actual people, we get from reading.

C. S. Lewis believed in reading as spiritual consolation – or at least the best substitute for it – and whatever depredations time, the outside world and adulthood have wrought (the cruellest of these being that the Little House on the Prairie books now read like prepper manuals for the coming apocalypse instead of charming, nostalgic tales of days gone by), it is still mine. Books remain what they have been to me since that first awful awareness dawned that I was an individual, separate from everyone else and, until and unless you come to know better, alone: they have been an endless comfort. Books connect you to others. It sounds trite but it is true. You are kept company by characters, by a story and by the consciousness – held literally in the hand, seemingly entire – that wrote the book. They all speak to you now across time and space, a commonality of minds, a sharing of experience, a proffering of thoughts and philosophies effortlessly spanning dimensions that would otherwise defeat all such efforts. They are insurmountable proof that the bundle of flaws, fancies, idiocies, instincts, anxieties and aptitudes that is you is neither unique nor alone. A man in Brooklyn can think up a story about a boy riding through a purple tollbooth – a purple tollbooth, for heaven's sake! – and twenty, thirty, forty, fifty years later (and counting) it can delight and boggle the mind of an eight-year-old in Catford, a ten-year-old in Canberra or anyone at any point in between. You can share the adventures of a large family in Otwell or a tiny one under the floorboards just by knowing how twenty-six letters variously combine and which way up to hold a book. A boy and a garden that exist only on the page can intimate as long as that page endures that all of humanity yearns for the past, needs to know where it comes from in order to know where it's going. If that doesn't strike you as a near-divine miracle, nothing will.

I do have – in case you were wondering, or worrying – some real, flesh-and-blood friends too. We don't meet very often and when we do we talk mainly about books we have read or are thinking of reading, but that is exactly how we like it.

If you're a parent of a bookworm without being one yourself – first of all, may I say: better that than the other way round. I have serried ranks of books waiting for my son, untold joys patiently biding their time on the bookshelves all round the house, but he is nearly six at the time of writing and is showing no signs of following in the footsteps of his two bookworm parents. I literally don't know what to do with him. By this age, I didn't need parenting, just feeding and rotating every few hours on the sofa to prevent pressure sores. I am entirely adrift. Please send help.

Second of all – I can see that bookworm offspring can be a bit of worry. We are rare and we are weird and no parent wants that; we want our children to have the safety of the crowd. But – and let this FREE you – there is nothing you can do to change us, any more than I can force my son to be like me. Really – don't try. We are so, so happy, in our own way. Just be glad we are not into something actively harmful, like smoking, or noisy, like almost everything else a child cares to do. Be glad of all the benefits it will bring, rather than lamenting the fresh air avoided, the friendships not made, the parties not attended, the exercise not taken, the body of rewarding and potentially lucrative activities, hobbies and skills not developed. Leave us be. We're fine. More than fine. Reading's our thing.

Lucy's Bookshelf

1. The Very Hungry Reader

The Very Hungry Caterpillar
A Week with Willi the Worm
Sugarpink Rose
The Tiger Who Came to Tea
When Hitler Stole Pink Rabbit
Mog the Forgetful Cat
Janet and John
Mog's Christmas
Mog in the Garden
Goodbye Mog

Nursery And Clinic

What-a-Mess series
Babar the Elephant
Babar's Travels
Dogger
Meg and Mog series
Mr Men series

The Birth of Illustrated Children's Books

Der Struwwelpeter (Shockheaded Peter)
Orbis Sensualium Pictus

A New Lottery Book of Birds and Beasts for children to learn their letters by
A History of British Birds
Songs of Innocence
This is the House that Jack Built
Sing a Song of Sixpence
Beauty and the Beast
The Baby's Opera
The Baby's Bouquet: A Fresh Bunch of Old Rhymes and Tunes
The Diverting History of John Gilpin
Under the Window
Mother Goose
The Pied Piper of Hamelin
International Companion Encyclopaedia of Children's Literature

Sendak

Where the Wild Things Are
Church Mice series
A Hole is to Dig
Kenny's Window
Very Far Away
The Sign on Rosie's Door
Nutshell Library
Higglety-Pigglety Pop
In the Night Kitchen
Outside Over There
Spot the Dog

2. To The Library

Dr Seuss

There's Going to Be a Baby
The New Small Person
King Baby
Topsy and Tim's New Brother
Understanding Dogs
Lake Wobegon Days
The Cat in the Hat
Why Johnny Can't Read
Dick and Jane series
Peter and Jane series
Did I Ever Tell You How Lucky You Are?

Blake – Burningham – Scarry – Briggs

The Enormous Crocodile
Patrick
A Drink of Water
Mouse Trouble
The Telling Line
Borka: The Adventures of a Goose with No Feathers
Come Away From the Water, Shirley
Time to Get Out of the Bath, Shirley
Would You Rather . . .

School

Confessions of a Failed Southern Lady
Father Christmas
Fungus the Bogeyman
When the Wind Blows

3. Now I am Six

Plop

My Naughty Little Sister series
The Owl Who Was Afraid of the Dark
Les Livres, Les Enfants et Les Hommes
The Gruffalo

Teddy Robinson and Mildred Hubble

Teddy Robinson Goes to the Fair
The Worst Witch
Ginnie
Lucy
Lucy Runs Away
Tottie: The Story of a Doll's House

Tottie And Milly

The Doll's House
Milly-Molly-Mandy series
The Wombles
Adventures of Purl and Plain

The School Carousel

Happy Families series, including:
Master Bun the Bakers' Boy
Mrs Wobble the Waitress
Mr Tick the Teacher
Mr Cosmo the Conjuror
Adventuring with Brindle
Maggie Gumption
Flat Stanley

Henry and Ribsy
A Girl from Yamhill
Beezus and Ramona
Ramona's World
Ramona and Her Mother

Ladybirds

Napoleon Bonaparte
John Wesley
Book of Printing Processes
The Computer: How it Works
Gulliver's Travels
The Swiss Family Robinson
Stone Soup!
Our Land in the Making
The Ladybird Book of the Hipster
The Gingerbread Man

Dahl

The Magic Finger
Fantastic Mr Fox
James and the Giant Peach
George's Marvellous Medicine
The Twits
Charlie and the Chocolate Factory
Danny the Champion of the World
The Witches
The BFG
Matilda
The Bears' Bazaar
A Giant Book of Fantastic Facts
It's Not the End of the World, Danny

4. The Blyton Interregnum

Five on a Secret Trail
Five Run Away Together
Come to the Circus!
Six Cousins at Mistletoe Farm
Children of Willow Farm
The Sea of Adventure
The Little Black Doll
Autumn Term

5. Through a Wardrobe

The London Child
The Family from One End Street
The Hobbit
Further Adventures of the Family from One End Street
Holiday at the Dew Drop Inn
The Borrowers
Lord of the Rings

Narnia

The Lion, the Witch and the Wardrobe
The Last Battle
Surprised by Joy
The Magician's Nephew
Prince Caspian
The Voyage of the Dawn Treader
The Silver Chair
The Horse and His Boy

A Tale of *The Tale of Troy*

The Tale of Troy
King Arthur and his Knights of the Round Table
Sir Gawain and the Green Knight
Pearl in the Myddes
The Saga of Asgard

Streatfeild

Ballet Shoes
Curtain Up
White Boots
Jackie Gets a Pony
Jackie and the Pony Thieves
A Pony for Jean
Jill's Gymkhana
Jill Has Two Ponies
Out With Romany
The Phoenix and the Carpet
The Horse in Sickness and in Health

6. Grandmothers & Little Women

Sam Silvan's Sacrifice: The Story of Two Fatherless Boys
A Book for Boys and Girls/ Divine Emblems; or Temporal Things Spiritualised
A Token for Children: being an Exact Account of the Conversion, Holy and Exemplary Lives, and Joyful Deaths, of Several Young Children
Divine and Moral Songs for Children
A Little Pretty Pocket Book
The Governess

Fabulous Histories (later *History of the Robins*)
The History of the Fairchild Family: The Child's Manual, being a collection of stories calculated to show the importance and effects of a religious education
The King of the Golden River
Tales from Shakespeare
Holiday House
Anne of Green Gables

Classics

Winnie the Pooh

7. Wonderlands

Alice's Adventures in Wonderland

Frances Hodgson Burnett

The Secret Garden
Little Lord Fauntleroy
That Lass o' Lowrie's
A Little Princess

E. Nesbit

The Treasure Seekers
The Railway Children

Twain – Coolidge – Montgomery

The Adventures of Tom Sawyer
What Katy Did
What Katy Did Next
School

8. Happy Golden Years

Puffin

Stig of the Dump
Charlotte's Web
Stuart Little
Trumpet of the Swan

Tollbooths And Gardens

The Starlight Barking
The Hundred and One Dalmatians
The Phantom Tollbooth
Tom's Midnight Garden

Goodnight Mister Tom

Goodnight Mister Tom

Private – Keep Out!

Private – Keep Out!

William – Melendy – Frisby

Just William
William the Lawless
The Saturdays
The Four-Story Mistake
Then There Were Five
Spiderweb for Two
Thimble Summer
Mrs Frisby and the Rats of NIMH

School Stories

Tom Brown's Schooldays
Eric, or Little by Little
Fifth Form at St Dominic's
Stalky & Co.
The Fortunes of Philippa
Rosaly's New School
*The Senior Prefect (*later *Dimsie Goes to School)*
Chalet School series

9. Darkness Rising

Secondary School and, Not Unrelatedly, Dystopia

Tripods series
The Changes series
Brother in Land
Z for Zachariah
End of Term
Watership Down
Autumn Term
The Cricket Term
Attic Term
Falconer's Lure
The Marlows and the Traitor
Runaway Home
Peter's Room
The Ready-Made Family

The Library

Sugar Mouse
The Lily Pickle Band Book

10. A Coming of Age

Fireweed
The Trouble with Donovan Croft
Break in the Sun
Running Scared
A Pair of Jesus Boots
A Pair of Desert Wellies
Bridge to Terabithia
Dicey's Song
Hangin' Out With Ceci
The Pinballs
The Cybil War
The Eighteenth Emergency
The Cartoonist

SVH

Sweet Valley High series
Taking Sides
Perfect Shot
Wrong Kind of Girl
Perfect Summer

BLUME

Blue Above the Chimneys
Twopence to Cross the Mersey
Boy Trouble at Trebizon
Are You There God? It's Me, Margaret
Draw Me a Star
I Saw Esau
Deenie, Blubber, Tiger Eyes

Then Again Maybe I Won't
Starring Sally J. Freedman as Herself
Forever . . .
Twilight series
The Best Little Girl in the World
I'm Kissing As Fast As I Can
Grow Up, Cupid
Geek Girl series

Summer of My German Soldier

Summer of My German Soldier
I Capture the Castle
The Wolves of Willoughby Chase

Acknowledgements

Thank you to everyone at Square Peg, especially Rowan Yapp, Susannah Otter, Harriet Dobson, Lucie Cuthbertson-Twiggs and the whole design team. You are all as patient, kind and perceptive as any writer could want. Thank you to my wonderful agents, Juliet Pickering and Louise Lamont, for your knowledge, your fortitude and in particular your ability to interpret half-sentences sobbed down the phone and consequently sort vast portions of my working life out with a few brief, beautifully worded emails.

Thank you to my godmother Anne Precious. To my friends Emily Church, Sian Evans, Claire Harrington, Theresa and Al Lyons, Sali Hughes, Michael Hogan, Mark Forsyth, Jason Hazeley, Jenny Colgan, Katy Cooper, Tom Rippin, Pete and Ange Harris, William Carslake, Jenny Milligan, Esther Schutzer-Weissmann, Maya Lester and Judy Byrne and to many more for the moral support and for the memories of your favourite children's books that did so much to restore mine.

Obviously I owe more than I can say to my family – my parents, my sister and my virtual sister Lucy Donovan – and my oldest, gangliest, dearest friend Sally Wright who all make appearances in these pages, though I have done none of them justice. I owe slightly less to my husband Christopher and son Alexander because I haven't known them as long. On the other hand, I couldn't write anything without their love, support and willingness to play Battleships quietly while I type on and neglect them utterly. Thank you all so much. I love you.